A DEEPER, DARKER TRUTH

A DEEPER, DARKER TRUTH

Tom Wilson's Journey into the Assassination of John F. Kennedy

---

Donald T. Phillips

DTP/Companion Books

Illinois, U.S.A.

A DEEPER, DARKER TRUTH. Copyright © 2009 by Donald T. Phillips. All rights reserved. Except as permitted under the U.S. Copyright Act of 1976, no part of this publication may be reproduced, distributed, or transmitted in any form or by any means, or stored in a database or retrieval system, without the prior written permission of the publisher.

DTP/Companion Books
Illinois, U.S.A

ISBN: 978-0-615-30099-3
1. United States – Nonfiction
A DEEPER, DARKER TRUTH: TOM WILSON'S JOURNEY INTO THE ASSASSINATION OF JOHN F. KENNEDY

First Printed Edition: Fall 2009

Visit our Website at www.DonaldTPhillips.com

CONTENTS

Prologue	1
1 / Metal Badge	10
2 / The Zapruder Film	21
3 / Somebody Has to do Something	35
4 / Five Autopsy Photographs	54
5 / On the Ground in Dallas	76
6 / Suspicious Images in Dealey Plaza	89
7 / The Oswald Backyard Photographs	111
8 / X-Rays and More	124
9 / The Fatal Headshot	137
10 / Autopsy X-Rays in the National Archives	148
11 / Autopsy Photographs in the National Archives	181
Epilogue: The Darker Truth	198
Author's Note	240
Reference Notes & Credits	242

Prologue

"There is trouble in the motorcade. I repeat, there is trouble in the motorcade. Parkland has been notified to stand by."

> Sam Pate, KBOX Radio
> November 22, 1963
> 12:30 PM CST

"We interrupt this program to bring you this special report from ABC Radio. Here is a special bulletin from Dallas, Texas. Three shots were fired at President Kennedy's motorcade today in downtown Dallas, Texas. This is ABC Radio. . . . We're going to stand by for more details on the incident in Dallas. Stay tuned to your ABC station for further details. Now we return you to your regular program."

> Don Gardner, ABC Radio
> November 22, 1963
> 12:36 CST

CBS NEWS BULLETIN [Interrupting television program *As The World Turns*]: *"Here is a bulletin from CBS News. In Dallas, Texas, three shots were fired at President Kennedy's motorcade in downtown Dallas. The first reports say that President Kennedy has been seriously wounded by this shooting."*

> Walter Cronkite, CBS News
> November 22, 1963
> 12:40 CST

At 12:30 PM CST on Friday November 22, 1963, John F. Kennedy, 35th President of the United States, was assassinated in Dallas, Texas. He had been on a two-day trip to the state, having stopped the day before in San Antonio and Fort Worth. After speaking at a Fort Worth breakfast gathering in the morning, Kennedy boarded Air Force One for a short flight to Love Field in Dallas where he was scheduled to attend a luncheon at the Trade

Mart. Afterwards, the itinerary called for him to fly to Austin for a Democratic Party fundraiser. First, however, he would ride in an open limousine during a 10-mile motorcade through downtown. It would be the last sixty minutes of his life.

President and Mrs. Kennedy's arrival at Dallas Love Field.

The presidential limo, second in the procession, was driven by Secret Service Agent William Greer with Agent Roy Kellerman sitting on the passenger side of the front seat. Texas Governor John Connally and his wife, Nellie, sat in the middle seat, while the President and Jacqueline Kennedy rode in the back seat. Riding in the lead car just in front of the President were Dallas Police Chief Jesse Curry (driver), Dallas County Sheriff Bill Decker, and Secret Service Agents Winston G. Lawson and Forrest Sorrels. Behind Kennedy was his "follow-up" car, which carried the President's security guard. In the motorcade's fourth car were Vice President and Mrs. Lyndon Johnson and Texas Senator Ralph Yarborough. Secret Service Agent Rufus Youngblood rode in the front seat next to driver Hurchel Jacks, a Texas State Trooper. The rest of the procession included the Vice President's "follow-up" vehicle, five cars for local officials, three press cars, and three buses for White House staff and other members of the press. Finally, a number of Dallas Police motorcycle officers, acting as escorts and providing security, were scattered throughout the procession and along the route.

Presidential limousine shortly after leaving Love Field.

The motorcade left Love Field at 11:30 AM CST, took West Mockingbird Drive to Lemmon Avenue, then Cedar Springs Road to North Harwood Street before it turned onto Main Street for the long stretch through downtown Dallas's tallest buildings. At the end of Main Street, the procession turned right onto Houston Street, proceeded north for one block, and then took a 120-degree left turn onto Elm Street for the slow downhill glide into Dealey Plaza. There were three structures on the corner of this intersection: the Dal-Tex building, the Dallas County Records building, and the Texas School Book Depository. Now the motorcade had only one block to go before its planned exit onto Stemmons Freeway and the five-minute drive to the Trade Mart.

In the presidential motorcade route.

Dealey Plaza was a 3-acre, triangle-shaped bowl where three main east-west Dallas arteries (Main, Commerce, and Elm Streets) converged under a railroad bridge called the triple underpass. On the north and south sides of the plaza were two small white pergolas situated on grass knolls. The north side of Elm Street also featured a line of trees and shrubs along a five-foot high wooden picket fence that ran west up to the triple underpass. Behind the fence was a parking lot and, beyond that, the Dallas rail yards.

Dealey Plaza from the air (L). Looking down Elm Street toward the triple underpass (R).

The crowds of onlookers had significantly thinned at this point in the motorcade route. However, there were still several hundred people scattered about as the first few cars in the procession descended into the plaza. Moving slowly, the presidential limousine stayed in the center of three lanes. President Kennedy was waving to his right, Mrs. Kennedy to her left.

Presidential limo turns onto Houston St. (L); on Elm St. (R).

Suddenly, when the limo neared an exit sign for the Stemmons Freeway, one or more shots were fired. Witnesses described the sounds like "a firecracker," "a motorcycle backfiring," or a "burst of gunfire." President Kennedy stiffened and his hands jerked upward to his throat. As the limousine proceeded slowly forward, a man near the sign pumped an umbrella up and down several times. Next to him, a Hispanic-looking man held his right arm up in the air and made a fist. Kennedy began slumping to the left toward his wife. Then, close together, there were two more volleys of gunfire. One bullet ricocheted off a concrete curb. Governor Connally was hit and quickly pulled down into the seat by his wife. A puff of smoke billowed out from the trees along the picket fence. A bullet ripped into the grass on the south side of Elm Street. The president's head exploded and he was propelled backward. Bits of brain, bone, and blood flew into the air. Jacqueline Kennedy instinctively crawled

First shot strikes President Kennedy in neck (L); headshot propels him backward (R).

out onto the trunk of the limousine to retrieve a piece of her husband's skull. Secret Service Agent Clint Hill, who had sprung from the follow-up car immediately after the first shots, now jumped onto the presidential limo and pushed Mrs. Kennedy back into her seat. The President had since slumped downward. Seeing the right rear portion of the President's head missing, Agent Hill slammed his fist onto the trunk several times in anger and anguish. Then he grabbed onto something as the limousine accelerated and sped off through the triple underpass. The entire shooting sequence lasted less than ten seconds.

Clint Hill jumps on limo (L); car heads through triple underpass (C); speeds to Parkland (R).

In the lead car, Dallas Police Chief Jesse Curry issued an order on his radio: "Get a man on top of that triple underpass and see what happened up there," he said. "It looks like the President has been hit. Have Parkland stand by."

County Sheriff Bill Decker issued similar instructions: "Move all available men out of my office into the railroad yard to try to determine what happened in there," he ordered. The presidential limo then sped up the ramp onto Stemmons Freeway and raced toward Parkland Memorial Hospital, only a few miles away.

Back in Dealey Plaza, hundreds of onlookers were stunned. Most froze in their places. Some had fallen to the ground to avoid gunfire. But as reality set in, there was screaming, confusion, and mayhem. Several motorcycle officers leaped off their bikes and drew weapons. Up near the intersection of Elm and Houston Streets, a passerby told one officer that shots came from the Texas School Book Depository. Another bystander farther down Elm Street yelled that shots came from behind the picket fence on the grassy knoll. Dozens of people rushed up the hill toward the picket fence and the triple underpass. Others streamed into the parking lot and rail yards.

Onlookers drop to ground, rush grassy knoll where picket fence and underpass merge.

At Parkland Hospital, President Kennedy was attended by a team of emergency room doctors and nurses who tried unsuccessfully to resuscitate him. At 1:00 PM CST, a half hour after the shots rang out in Dealey Plaza, the President of the United States was pronounced dead. Shortly thereafter, Deputy Press Secretary Malcolm Kilduff announced that Kennedy "died of a gunshot wound in the brain." Pointing to his right temple, Kilduff also stated: "Dr. Burkely [Kennedy's personal physician] told me it was a simple matter of a bullet right through the head. . . . . It is my understanding that [the bullet] entered in the right temple." Early newspaper articles further reported that the President had been hit in the right temple and in the front of the throat.

Kennedy's body was placed in a bronze ceremonial casket, but as it was wheeled out of the emergency room and into the main hall, an argument ensued between Dr. Earl F. Rose, Dallas County Coroner, and Secret Service Agent Roy Kellerman. Dr. Rose stated that Texas law required an autopsy be performed in Dallas so as not to break the chain of evidence. But Kellerman, backed up by other armed agents, stated that the President's body was going to be taken to back to Washington, D.C. It quickly became obvious that Kellerman was going to use force, if necessary, to have his way. Eventually, Dr. Rose stepped aside and the casket was taken to Love Field and loaded onto Air Force One. At 2:38 PM CST, Lyndon Baines Johnson was sworn in as the 36th President of the United States on the airplane, which then took off for the flight back to Washington, DC. After arrival at Andrews Air Force Base (at 6:08 PM EST), the casket was transported by car to Bethesda Naval Center where President Kennedy's autopsy was to be performed.

Parkland Hospital (L); Kilduff points to right temple (C); LBJ on Air Force One (R).

Back in Dallas, only 45 minutes after the assassination (approximately 1:15 PM CST), Dallas Police Officer J. D. Tippit was shot and killed near the intersection of 10th Street and Patton Avenue in the suburb of Oak Park. Half an hour later, 24-year old Lee Harvey Oswald was arrested at the Texas Theater about a mile from the scene of the Tippit shooting. He was brought to Dallas Police Headquarters at approximately 2:00 PM CST, interrogated, and held in isolation. Later that night, Oswald was formally charged with the murders of both Officer Tippit and President Kennedy. While in custody, however, Oswald never confessed to either crime. In fact, he consistently maintained his innocence. "I'm just a patsy!" he professed.

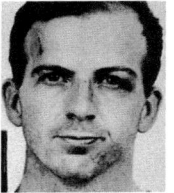

Officer J. D. Tippit (L); Lee Harvey Oswald arrested Texas Theater (C); Oswald mug shot (R).

Two days later (on Sunday, November 24th at 11:21 AM CST), while being transferred to the county jail, Lee Harvey Oswald was shot by Dallas nightclub owner Jack Ruby in the basement of Dallas Police Headquarters. He was pronounced dead an hour and forty-five minutes later at Parkland Memorial Hospital. Over the ensuing months, the international news media portrayed Oswald as the lone assassin of President Kennedy. Of particular note was a February 21, 1964 cover story by *Life* magazine, which published backyard photographs linking him to both alleged murder weapons used in the killing of Kennedy and Officer Tippit.

Jack Ruby shoots Oswald   Feb. 21, 1964 cover of *Life*

On November 29, 1963 (one week after the assassination), President Johnson issued Executive Order 11130, which appointed a Commission to "examine the evidence developed by the FBI and any additional evidence that may come to light" and to "evaluate all the facts and circumstances surrounding" the assassination. Appointed to serve on this Commission were: Senator Richard Russell (D-Georgia), Senator John Sherman Cooper (R-Kentucky), Representative Hale Boggs (D-Louisiana), Representative Gerald R. Ford (R-Michigan), John J. McCloy, former assistant secretary of war during World War II and former US high commissioner in occupied Germany, and Allen Dulles, who had formerly served for nine years as Director of the Central Intelligence Agency. The Chairman would be the sitting United States Supreme Court Chief Justice, Earl A. Warren, which is why the popular name given to the investigative body was the "Warren Commission."

After a ten-month investigation, an 888-page "Warren Report" was released to the American public (on September 27, 1964). Two months later (November 1964), and almost exactly one year after the assassination, the Commission published 26 volumes consisting of more than 16,000 pages of testimony and exhibits to support its findings.

Specifically, the Warren Commission concluded that Lee Harvey Oswald, "using a Mannlicher-Carcano 6.5-millimeter Italian rifle . . . owned by and in [his] possession," fired three shots from the southeast window on the sixth floor of the Texas School Book Depository. One bullet "entered the base of the back of President Kennedy's neck slightly to the right of the spine and exited from the front of the neck." This same bullet, the Commission stated, continued onward and struck Governor Connally in the extreme right side of his back, traveled through his chest, exited, passed through his right wrist, and caused a wound to his left thigh. Another bullet struck President Kennedy in the "rear portion of his head, causing a massive and fatal wound." A third bullet missed the presidential limousine entirely. The Commission further concluded that Lee Harvey Oswald killed Dallas Police Patrolman J. D. Tippit, and that the bullets that killed him were fired from a revolver owned by Oswald and in his possession.

Warren Commission members give final report to President Johnson.

Finally, the Warren Commission stated that it "found no evidence that Lee Harvey Oswald was part of any conspiracy, domestic, or foreign, to assassinate President Kennedy." It concluded that he acted alone and that his motives included a "deep-rooted resentment of all authority," an "inability to enter into meaningful relationships with people," an "urge to try to find a place in history," a "capacity for violence," and an "avowed commitment to Marxism and communism."

Almost immediately, many researchers and experts questioned the government's three-shot, lone assassin theory. And over the years, increased public discontent resulted in several additional government inquiries. The Ramsey Clark Panel (1968) and the Rockefeller Commission (1975) both affirmed the conclusions reached by the Warren Commission, although neither explained the basis of their findings in public hearings. Finally, more than fifteen years after John F. Kennedy's death (in March 1979), the 13-member House Select Committee on Assassinations (HSCA) published a report and twelve accompanying volumes on its three-year investigation into the assassination. The HSCA's conclusions were as follows:

Lee Harvey Oswald fired three shots at President John F. Kennedy from the sixth floor window of the southeast corner of the Texas School Book Depository building.

The second and third shots struck the president. The third shot killed the president.

There is a high probability that two gunmen fired shots at the president [and therefore,] John F. Kennedy was probably assassinated as a result of a conspiracy.

That's what the history books say.

1 / *Metal Badge*

In November 1988, Tom Wilson was at home watching a television program marking the 25th anniversary of the assassination of President John F. Kennedy. As was his habit, he slipped a cassette into his VCR and recorded the program. He saw the news bulletin that interrupted regular programming to broadcast that the president had been shot in Dallas. He heard the formal announcement made that Kennedy was, indeed, dead, and that Texas governor John Connolly had been seriously wounded and was in surgery. And then the famous home movie taken by Abraham Zapruder (often touted as the most compelling evidence of the crime) was shown.

Tom had seen all this before. He was aware of the Warren Commission's conclusion that Lee Harvey Oswald was the lone gunman who had fired three shots from the sixth floor Texas School Book Depository. Like many Americans, Tom never questioned that explanation. He was aware that the new president, Lyndon Johnson, had appointed a panel of seven prominent Americans to investigate the crime, a lot of time and effort had been spent going through the evidence, and the findings had been issued in 26 comprehensive volumes.

Tom had also heard about some of the conspiracy theories. The CIA and the FBI had murdered Kennedy. The mob did it. The Soviet Union engineered it. Castro did it as revenge for the Bay of Pigs invasion. "Ridiculous!" thought Tom. It was much more believable that one man killed Kennedy, just as the government said. No need to debate the issue further. He had better things to do.

However, when the announcer on this particular program began explaining some of the various conspiracy theories, Tom wondered about the government's so-called "single bullet theory." This was the Warren Commission's finding that one bullet fired at Kennedy hit him in the upper back, came out the front of his neck, went through Governor Connolly's torso and wrist, and came to rest in his thigh. When the bullet that was supposed to have done all this damage was shown to be in almost pristine condition, Tom paused for a moment. "Well, that doesn't seem too realistic," he thought.

Later in the program, a photograph taken by Mary Moorman was shown. Ms. Moorman, twenty-one years old at the time, and standing directly across the street from Abraham Zapruder, was taking Polaroid pictures of the president's motorcade and handing them to her friend Jean Hill. Coincidentally, she snapped one at the very moment that the final shot rang out. This was the reported third shot that hit President Kennedy in the head. Mary Moorman was standing approximately ten feet from the presidential limousine at the time she took the picture.

Mary Moorman's Polaroid photograph (from video).

The program next noted that some assassination researchers had zoomed in on the photograph to an area behind the picket fence, and discovered what they believed was a man dressed in a police uniform possibly shooting at the president. The enlarged version shown on the television did, in fact, appear to be a man looking toward the presidential limousine. But Tom wasn't overly impressed with the image. He knew from experience that it could be the result of glare and reflections, and that the brain can play tricks on you. According to researchers, a white spot in front of the man in the image was interpreted to be smoke from a rifle. A smaller white spot located to the lower right of the enlargement appeared to be a policeman's badge.

"A badge?" thought Tom, raising an eyebrow. "A *metal* badge?"

* * * * *

Tom Wilson was fifty-six years old in 1988 and living in the Pittsburgh, Pennsylvania area. He had spent thirty years with US Steel Corporation as a research and development engineer working with automated inspection systems that detected flaws in metal products. Retired for about five years, and now an independent consultant, Tom had designed a state-of-the-art image processing and computer analysis system that could be used for industrial quality control. Now being tested in his home office, the system had been performing perfectly for several weeks, and was in the final testing phase before factory trial runs were to begin.

A couple of days after watching the Kennedy program, Tom was analyzing a steel plate for potential flaws. By simply using a videotape, his image processing system could "see through" the surface layers of the steel to detect imperfections not visible to the human eye. Some of Tom's industrial clients viewed this ability to be almost unbelievable, and certainly futuristic in nature. But Tom pointed out that he was simply employing the same technology that the FBI and NASA's Jet Propulsion Laboratory had been using for years. It was all based on photonics, the science and technology of transmission, control, detection, and measurement of light. Light is comprised of particles called photons. Even though the photons are microscopically small, they still occupy space. By using solid-state cameras, computers, and various image processing techniques, the technology is able to extract information that is beyond human visual capabilities. Light reflected from flaws (such as scratches, dents, or holes, etc.) in any object are different than those reflected from unflawed areas. Tom had simply adapted the technology and refined it to be useful in the manufacturing industry.

On this particular evening, Tom had indeed detected a flaw several layers below the surface of the steel plate. The defect (in this case, a dent) can be seen in the upper right hand corner of the third layer photograph below.

Image processing of steel plate. First layer (L), second layer (C), third layer (R) revealing defect in upper right corner.

Tom was pleased after completing the test. He had accomplished what he had set out to do that evening and the system was working well. In considering what else might still need to be perfected, Tom thought about the fact that he had programmed the computer to provide a visual sparkle (flash of brightness) when metal was detected in any image under observation. It was still early in the evening, he thought. Maybe he should work on that.

Tom tapped his fingers on his desk and glanced over at the television. He saw the JFK videotape on top of the VCR. Remembering the supposed policeman's badge behind the picket fence on the grassy knoll, Tom figured that if there really was a badge there, his system might pick it up. So he removed the metals tape and inserted the JFK tape.

Images could be presented to Tom's processing system in many forms: live camera, videotape, photographs, specimens on slides –

you name it, it really didn't matter. But the overall primary function was to extract all available information in an unbiased manner based solely on the physics of light. No information was thrown away. Because Tom's system bombarded the subject image with light, the extracted information came back in the form of reflected light energy bouncing off the image. That energy, in turn, was quantified by the system in terms of standard light measurements (wavelength and frequency). And because light reflects differently off metal than other objects, once Tom gauged that particular measurement, he was easily able to program his computer to "flash" when metal was detected.

As the Kennedy videotape played, Tom found himself fascinated by all the processed images emanating from the various scenes. After all, this was somewhat new to him. He had never before run an entertainment program through his system. And, sure enough, the moment the Mary Moorman photograph appeared, the president's limousine glowed from all the metal it contained. But there was also a very prominent visual sparkle coming from the area where the badge was supposed to be – behind the picket fence on the grassy knoll. Also noticeable were a couple of smaller, less intense flashes in the same general vicinity.

Now Tom felt he had something of a dilemma. His state-of-the-art image processing and computer analysis system was about to be factory-tested. It had to work. If it didn't, he could not, in all good conscience, market it as reliable. In his mind, there was only one of two possibilities. Either years of image-processing development was flawed, or there was a metallic object behind the fence. He simply had to check it out to determine what was back there.

Tom put his other industrial projects on the back burner, obtained a hard copy of the Mary Moorman photograph from a book, and began analyzing the image. He taped the photo up on his lightboard where he could bombard it with strobes and a high intensity light source. A solid-state camera hooked into his computer would then capture the data and process it.

Tom Wilson in his home office with his image-processing setup.

The Mary Moorman Polaroid photograph on Tom's lightboard.

Tom began by zooming in on the area behind the picket fence until he could see the purported policeman and the supposed badge.

Moorman Photograph   Enlargement #1   Enlargement #2

Enlargement #3   Enlargement #4   Apparent man and badge

From this point, Tom let his sensing equipment go to work. Information entered the system through an optical "eye" – a solid-state camera containing a metal oxide semiconductor chip, which performed mathematically complex calculations on the light energy passing through. Behind the camera was another lens – a light valve optical device that filtered the reflected light into categories based on shades of gray. The resulting data was then passed to the computer for presentation in pictorial images on the monitor. Essentially, the computer analyzed all the spatial information contained in any image and displayed it in a manner that went far beyond what could be seen by the naked eye.

The first thing Tom did was to have the computer assign density values to the reflected energy in the image of the purported policeman and his badge. Then he performed several enlargements of the resulting image (presented in shades of gray) to focus specifically on the badge.

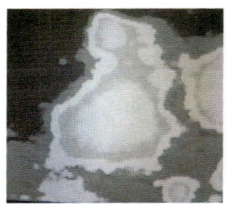  

Density values   Badge enlargement # 1   Badge enlargement #2

Tom's next step was to have the computer tag each shade of gray with a separate color. This technique, known as "false color images" or "pseudocolor," highlights variations in the overall image and helps the human brain identify content. To further expose the image, Tom presented the spatial information in three axes (horizontal, vertical, and depth), making it possible to create varied 3-D versions of the image.

  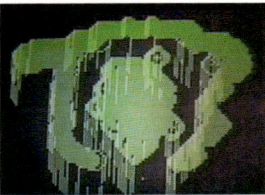

Badge; pseudocolor   3-D with pseudocolor   High 3-D

When Tom saw these images appear on his computer monitor, he had no doubt that his system had, indeed, detected metal behind the picket fence and that it was, in fact, the badge of either a police officer or a security guard. But now he wanted to know more. In an effort to determine some details of the badge, he removed the pseudocolor and 3D images and had the computer present the data only in black and white. Similar to what he did with the steel plate, he then began to filter away several layers of gray and enlarge the resulting image.

To Tom's trained eye, there appeared to be some sort of design near the top of the badge. When he enlarged the detailed image, he became convinced that there was a left-facing eagle's head with wings just above it. "Makes sense," he murmured. "Most law enforcement badges have some version of an eagle on them."

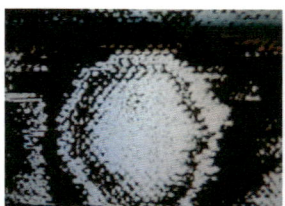 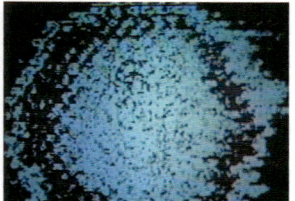 

Badge; black & white   Second layer, enlarged   Detail; eagle's head

Tom next took a closer look at the image of the man wearing the badge. Since the removal of gray layers had yielded some detail on the badge, he decided to do the same thing to the entire image. The original enlargement appeared to show a man's forehead at the top, dark hair merging into the background, and possible smoke from a weapon covering the lower portions of the face. At least that was what some researchers had concluded.

No sooner had Tom stripped away a few shades of gray than he noticed the forehead and hair start to fade away. Also dissipating were the outer layers of the apparent smoke. At the same time, however, the center of the smoke became brighter. Tom believed this phenomenon was due to the fact that the smoke was originating from another piece of metal (perhaps a rifle), which was being highlighted by the computer's programmed visual sparkle. (The badge was also much brighter in this image). The smoke, itself, was doing exactly what it would be expected to do. It was similar to the headlights on a car – denser at the source, and more dispersed farther away. Therefore, early layer removal peeled away the outer edges of the smoke and got closer to the hidden metal object the system was detecting.

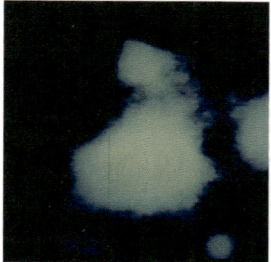 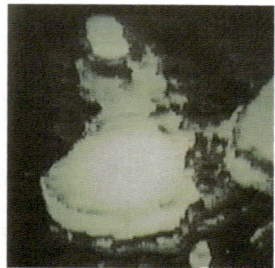

Original enlargement.   Several layers removed.

Also hidden behind the smoke was an image of what appeared to be the left side of a man's head. It was smaller than what the original image had shown as a forehead and hair. But then again, earlier image processing had revealed that the badge was significantly smaller than the original image seemed to indicate. In some way, Tom believed, the reflections of light as indicated in the original photograph had magnified and distorted the subjects behind the picket fence. But by carefully stripping away the layers of gray, Tom's system was eliminating any atmospheric distortions and revealing true sizes.

Zooming in on the face behind the smoke, Tom's first enlargement delineated coarse dark hair parted on the left side, and the man's left ear and eye. In a second enlargement, the eye became more distinct, revealing the iris and even the pupil. There also seemed to be a mole or pox mark on his upper left cheek, just below the eye.

Enlargement #1; flash of light, smoke, eye, ear, and hair visible.

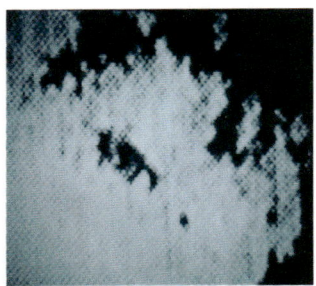
Enlargement #2; iris and pupil of eye detail; pox mark.

When Tom saw the details of the eye, he was certain that he was looking at the left side of a man's face. This image processing system worked only with real data. It did not lie. In all probability, Tom felt he had detected a man peering down the telescopic sight of a rifle aimed at President Kennedy. Remember, Mary Moorman had snapped this photograph at the very moment of the fatal headshot.

All excited now, Tom jumped out of his chair and called for his wife, Marcie. "Look at this! Look at this!" he exclaimed when she got to the computer screen. "I peeled away the layers of smoke – and there's a guy there firing a rifle. He's dressed in a policeman's or security guard's uniform. I can see the badge. And look at the face, here. There's something on his cheek below the eye – maybe a mole."

"It's a little difficult to see," replied Marcie. "Can you enhance it?"

"No, no, no," said Tom. "Never enhance. 'Enhance' is not the word. That implies that I've done something to the image that makes it different than what it really is."

"Well, can you blow it up?" asked Marcie.

"Yes, I can do that real quick. Look! There it is. Can you see the eye – the pupil and the iris?"

"Yes! I see it. There's a man there. But it's still a little fuzzy to me."

"I might be able to make it more clear if I had a better copy of the original photograph, a more pristine copy," said Tom. "This one was from a magazine and its clarity is not the best."

"Are you going to try to do get a better copy?"

"Well, I need to do something, that's for sure. This is new evidence, and people need to know. There *was* a person behind the picket fence. There *was* more than one gunman shooting at the president. It's bone-chilling! And if there's information in *this* photograph, then there's probably more somewhere else. I can't leave it at this. Not now."

* * * * *

Tom spent the next several weeks verifying his findings. In order for any new information to be considered credible evidence, Tom knew that it would have to pass two stringent tests. First, the process had to be repeatable no matter how many times the information was extracted from the image. And second, neither the original image nor the processed information could be altered in any way. Keeping these two principles in mind, Tom went back and repeated the process for every stripped layer, every tagged pseudocolor, and every 3-D image he produced. He also checked the mathematical data and verified that everything was accurate. In the end, his system never had a problem. It passed with flying colors.

Tom's next step was to go to the public library and do some research on specifics of the Kennedy assassination. He checked out copies of the Warren Report, *The Death of A President* by William Manchester, and reviewed a number old newspaper articles. He also purchased several books that were contrary to the government's one-lone-gunman conclusion. These included *On the Trail of the Assassins* by Jim Garrison, *Contract on America* by David Scheim, and *Best Evidence* by David S. Lifton.

Tom then started thinking about the badge he had detected in the Mary Moorman photograph. "Just what kind of badge was it, anyway?" he wondered. "Did it belong to the Dallas Police Department or the Dallas County Sheriff's office? In an effort to find out, Tom started researching different types of law enforcement badges, including state, local, and federal government agencies. He was looking for a design that had a left-facing eagle's head near the top with wings just above it. After sifting through hundreds of pictures, Tom narrowed in on two designs. One was listed as "Deputy Sheriff, Atchinson County (Kansas)." The other was "Detective, Paris Police (Texas)." The Paris, Texas badge was closer in design, Tom thought, but neither was an exact match – at least, from the information he could discern at this point. But the exact badge had to be out there somewhere, he believed. Perhaps if he could someday obtain more detail, he'd be able to make an exact match.

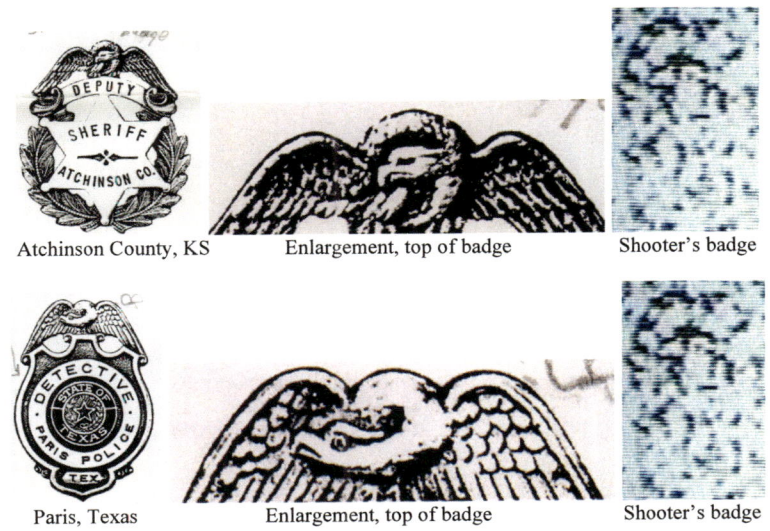

Atchinson County, KS   Enlargement, top of badge   Shooter's badge

Paris, Texas   Enlargement, top of badge   Shooter's badge

Looking for the badge of the shooter behind the picket fence was just the beginning of Tom Wilson's search for the truth in the assassination of President John F. Kennedy. Quite by accident, his image processing had revealed what he believed to be hard evidence that the Warren Report was wrong. There was, in fact, a shooter, wearing a law enforcement badge, positioned behind the picket fence on the grassy knoll in front of and to the right of the approaching presidential motorcade. He had seen it with his own eyes on a machine that did not distort the truth.

Tom Wilson was an average American with a strong sense of right and wrong. He was also a trained professional who believed that the best way to answer problems was through an engineering- and science-based search for the truth. And the more he thought about what he had uncovered, the more concerned he became. There had to be more unrevealed evidence contained in other photographs and motion pictures taken on November 22, 1963 in Dealey Plaza. There just had to be.

From this point on, Tom decided to abandon nearly all of his consulting projects. He was going to travel back in time and examine available images of the JFK assassination. And he would begin with the famous home movie taken by Abraham Zapruder.

2 / *<u>The Zapruder Film</u>*

The story of Abraham Zapruder and his home movie of the Kennedy assassination, as reported in the national news media shortly after the assassination, is well known. A fifty-eight-year-old Dallas dress manufacturer, Zapruder left his fifth-floor Dal-Tex Building office overlooking Dealey Plaza shortly before the presidential motorcade arrived. Intent on finding a good vantage point to take a home movie with his new Bell & Howell camera, he settled on a four-foot-high pedestal on the grassy knoll just north of Elm Street. According to Zapruder, because he suffered from vertigo, he asked his receptionist, Marilyn Sitzman, to stand behind him on the concrete pergola while he filmed the presidential motorcade.

Abraham Zapruder

Zapruder posing with his camera.

Zapruder's position can be seen in a full, uncropped version of the Mary Moorman photograph. It is at the very far right of the picture.

Uncropped Moorman photo.

Enlargement #1; Zapruder at far right.

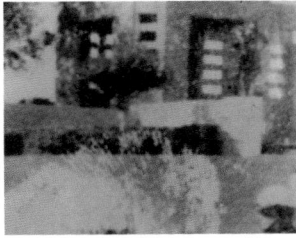
Moorman enlargement #2

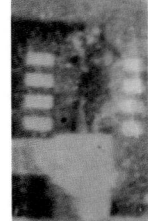
Moorman enlargement #3

Conversely, the Zapruder film (frame #303) shows Mary Moorman standing next to her friend, Jean Hill. She is seen moments before taking her famous photograph, wearing a blue raincoat and holding her Polaroid camera up to her face.

Zapruder Film Frame #303.
Mary Moorman in blue raincoat, camera to face; Jean Hill in red.

The 26-second Zapruder film recorded the entire assassination sequence – from the moment it turned from Houston Street west bound onto Elm Street until it eventually passed out of view under the triple underpass. It was a crucial piece of evidence used by the Warren Commission to establish its finding that Lee Harvey Oswald was the lone gunman who killed the president. (Below are sixteen representative frames out of the total 486).

| 343 | 368 | 388 | 419 |

* * * * *

In late 1988, Tom went to the Pennsylvania Public Library Film Center in Pittsburgh and obtained several videotape copies of the Zapruder film. He then spent the next several months examining the home movie on his image processing and computer analysis system. As he did so, Tom developed new and varied methods to extract as much information as possible. He figured the best place to start was with the headshot. After all, it was the exact instant Mary Moorman snapped her famous photograph. So Tom would begin at that moment in time, and then proceed backward or forward as his findings dictated.

Zapruder's position was approximately sixty-five feet away when the final shot was recorded in frame #313. The front right side of Kennedy's forehead appears to explode in an orange-reddish blob, which obscures both the president and first lady's faces. Also appearing over Kennedy's head is what has been described as a "halo" effect. According to the Warren Commission, this third bullet entered at the back of the president's head and exited the right front side (causing the orange-reddish blob), blowing blood, brain, and skull material into the air.

Zapruder frame #313.

Frame #313 enlargement.

After running one of the Zapruder film videotapes through his system, Tom isolated and enlarged frame #313, and then converted it to a black and white image. Light was then bounced off the picture, and the machine's optical eye captured the reflected energy. This light valve, designed to mimic an eye of a fly, contained 250,000 sensors, each of which worked independently and simultaneously. Although humans can distinguish only 30 shades of gray, the optical eye could detect 256 shades of gray.

Frame #313 enlargement.   Frame #313; Enlargement; B&W.

Because light travels in waves, each shade of gray has its own wavelength, which can be measured by the optical eye. By filtering out various wavelengths, Tom's computer was able to strip away shades of gray near the surface of the image. As the layers of Zapruder frame #313 were removed, Tom equated it to peeling an onion. Each time a layer was removed, it revealed what remained beneath. Part of the image would disappear, but the rest would remain. If he peeled down far enough, and carefully enough, he knew that any information hidden to the naked eye would be revealed. Tom often said it was like looking at a photograph of a man standing in a darkened door leading into a long hallway. The naked eye cannot see what is in the doorway, which appears only as a black shadow. At the end of the processing, however, the man's face will be visible.

As Tom peeled away the first and second layers of frame #313, the orange-reddish blob and halo at the front of Kennedy's head was prominent and appeared as a white cloud. By the third layer, however, it had completely disappeared. Left behind at the back of Kennedy's head was a somewhat roundish black feature.

 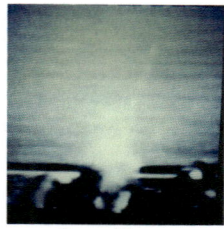 

Frame #313, first layer   Second layer   Third layer

Wondering what it might be, Tom decided to tag the entire image with pseudocolor and then remove another layer. Seeing rings of color in the round feature at the back of Kennedy's head, he decided to enlarge the image.

 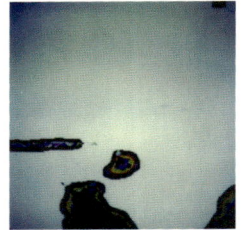

Third layer with pseudocolor.   Fourth layer (pseudocolor; enlarged) round feature at back of head.

Looking at the feature more closely, Tom realized it had to be some sort of dome or hole. That's the only way the shades of gray (highlighted by tagged pseudocolor) would show up in a ringed fashion. But before he zoomed in on the feature any further, Tom wanted to know exactly where it was in the original photograph. So, for comparison purposes, he took the color image of Zapruder frame #313 and fit it to the same scale as his fourth layer pseudocolor enlargement.

 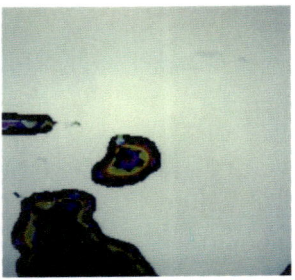

Zapruder frame #313 (enlarged).   Fourth layer (pseudocolor; enlarged).

Comparing the two images, Tom determined that the feature was located at the upper back portion of Kennedy's head. Now he wanted to see more detail. As he focused in on the circular feature, he filtered out one more layer and enlarged the resulting image. Then he removed the pseudocolor and produced a 3-D version. When Tom saw that 3-D image, he was stunned. It was *definitely* a hole. And a *huge* hole, at that. Looking into the wound, Tom perceived that he was observing three separate features – first, at the outer edges was the scalp, then the bone, then at the center was the brain, which seemed to have an even smaller hole in it. "What in the world is going on here?" Tom wondered.

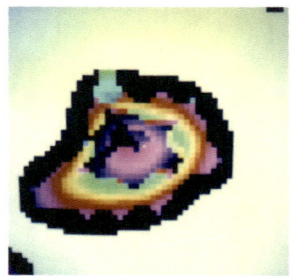 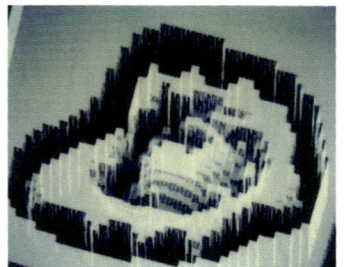

Fifth layer (pseudocolor; enlarged); hole in back of head.

Fifth layer (gray; 3-D; enlarged); scalp, skull, and brain visible.

After a few moments of wondering what this finding might mean, Tom decided to approach the hole just the way he would if he had discovered it in a piece of steel. He would document it with several different images, he would verify it by repeating the process, and then he would measure it. The approximate dimensions of the inner hole were 3.0 inches by 3.0 inches (7.6 by 7.6 centimeters); and the outer hole measured approximately 5.0 inches by 4.0 inches (12.7 by 10.2 centimeters).

Tom was aware that the Warren Commission had concluded that the third and final shot had struck President Kennedy in the back of the head and had exited in the right front and side. However, it was clear to Tom that the hole he was looking at was far to large to be an entrance hole. It had to be an exit hole. Therefore, the bullet had to have entered from the front. Could the shooter behind the picket fence have inflicted this wound?

Tom decided to save all these images in a computer file so he could come back to them for a more detailed analysis. He was eventually going to find out where that bullet entered President Kennedy's head. But for now, he wanted to try tagging with pseudocolor an original image of frame #313, and then stripping away the layers. That technique had yielded some interesting results when he'd tried it on the badge, and Tom wanted to see if it might show a different effect on the Zapruder film.

Applying the same meticulous procedure, Tom began with one of the other versions of the Zapruder film he had obtained from the Pennsylvania Public Library Film Center. He loaded the videotape into his system, isolated and enlarged frame #313, and then converted it to a black and white image. In the black and white image, the orange-reddish blob and the halo over President Kennedy's head merged into a single whitish cloud.

Frame #313 (L); halo merging into single white cloud with processing to B & W image (R).

After tagging all the shades of gray with pseudocolor and stripping away the first layer of gray, Tom was surprised to see how pronounced the whitish cloud had become. It stood out so much, in fact, that it looked like it had been painted on – at least that was his first impression. But it was the second processed layer that shocked Tom almost beyond belief. That image showed the presence of all kinds of material in the air, which Tom believed had to be scalp, bone, and brain particles blasted out of the hole in Kennedy's head. The whitish cloud was smaller in size, but still quite pronounced. "What in the world is that white thing?" he wondered.

Zapruder #313; (pseudocolor) 1st layer.   2nd layer; skull, scalp, and brain material blasted into air.

Tom had his answer when he filtered away the next layer of gray and enlarged the image. While there was still plenty of airborne material, the whitish cloud (which represented the orange-reddish blob and halo) had now completely disappeared. Obviously, it had been painted on the film to both obscure the airborne material and give the impression that the bullet had exited the front of the president's head. Furthermore, when Tom stripped away one more layer of gray and performed another enlargement, he was convinced that the larger particles were part of President Kennedy's skull.

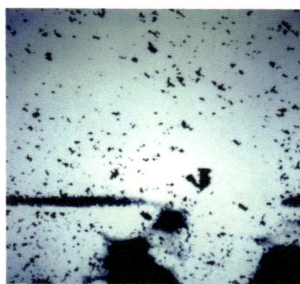 

Pseudocolor; 3rd layer; enlarged.   4th layer; enlarged; skull fragments.

At this moment, Tom became very upset. He ran into the kitchen and grabbed Marcie. "Come look a this. Come look at this," he insisted When they got to the computer screen, Tom was almost frantic.

"Look, do you see all these head parts in the air?" he asked. "They're parts of Kennedy's brain and skull. They were blown in all directions by a gunshot – backward, upward, forward. Can you see it? Can you see it?"

"Oh, yes," Marcie replied. "I see it."

"And look here," said Tom as he grabbed his mouse and pulled up the three-dimensional image of the hole in Kennedy's head. "There's a big exit wound in the back of the president's head. I found it after peeling away four or five layers. You can look down into it and see his brain. I think it was caused by a bullet from the front."

"From the shooter with the badge?" asked Marcie. "Behind the fence?"

"Maybe. I'm not sure, yet," replied Tom. "But you know what this means, don't you? It means the government has lied to us all these years."

"Are you sure about this?"

"Yes, I'm positive," exclaimed Tom. "This machine tells the truth."

There was a long pause as Tom and Marcie stared at the screen.

"I can't believe it," said Tom, finally. "I just can't believe that, in the United States of America, the government would lie to the people – especially about something as important as the president's assassination."

"Well, just how do you know they lied?" Marcie asked.

"Because the Zapruder film has been intentionally altered," he replied. Tom then pulled up the image of frame #313 and showed Marcie the orange-reddish blob and halo.

"Do you see that?" he asked. "It's been artificially added. And the back of his head has been darkened to hide the exit hole. I peeled off the top several layers, just like I would a piece of steel to reveal a flaw. The artificial coverings disappeared, the real wound was there, and the head debris appeared. That must have been pretty close to what it looked like before they covered it up."

"I don't understand," said Marcie. "How could they do that to a movie?"

Tom paused.

"Well, I don't know," he said, at last. "I guess I'm going to have to find out."

Tom was not a professional photographer. And he knew next to nothing about how such alterations could be made, especially to films. But after researching the subject at the public library, he came to the conclusion that, in 1963, there were most likely two techniques that could have been used to alter the Zapruder film. Both involved the use of composite photography.

The first, and simplest method was called the halftone process, in which an image was re-photographed through a screen so that variations of light and dark are merged into one to give the appearance of continuity. This can be done frame by frame in a film, and would have been the simplest method to cover up the exit wound in the back of President Kennedy's head.

The second, and more complicated process, was known as insert matte photography, which involved the use of sophisticated equipment similar to that used for special effects in the motion picture industry. An optical printer was first used to create a copy by re-photographing the original film, one frame at a time. A matte artist could then paint a new picture on top of the existing image. Other types of optical equipment (such as a process camera and a step printer) were then used to change additional frames of the film. The entire duplicate was then run back through the optical printer to produce a new "original." Tom reasoned that this process must have been how the orange-reddish blob and halo effect had been added to the Zapruder film.

Both the halftone and insert matte processes were considered state-of-the-art in 1963. However, by the time Tom Wilson began looking at the Zapruder film (1988-1989), digital enhanced photography was in its infancy. And of course, it was that same new digital technology that allowed the creation of Tom's image processing system.

Realizing that he was now finding new unreported information in old Kennedy assassination evidence, Tom became obsessed to know more. He began spending ten to twelve hours a day at the computer, often losing track of time. He would stop to eat when he got hungry, and sleep when he got tired. But often, he would work into the wee morning hours. Those were the nights when Marcie read.

* * * * *

Shortly after finishing his research on types of photographic film alteration, Tom decided to take a look at the Zapruder frames on either side of the headshot. He was curious if they, too had been altered. So he began by isolating frame #312, enlarging it, converting it to black and white, and then tagging it with pseudocolor.

Zapruder frame #312.

Frame #312 enlargement.

Frame #312 enlarged.

Frame #312; B & W.

#312 pseudocolor.

Tom then began to strip away the layers and enlarge the images as he went along. The head area in this frame did not appear to be changed and, certainly, Tom did not detect the gaping hole in the back of Kennedy's head (because the head shot had not yet been fired). However, parts of the president's right arm and chest, and Jackie's left arm, had obviously been altered. They showed up as white, but Tom was unsure if it was done by halftone or matte insertion. Clearly, though, there were alterations.

But why? What was in the area of the president's chest that needed to be concealed?

Pseudocolor; 1st layer.   2nd layer; enlarged.   3rd layer; enlarged.

Having no answers as to why such alterations were made before the headshot, Tom took a look at several of the frames after #313. It was obvious that, *after* the head shot, the hole in the back of Kennedy's head would have to be masked, the blob and halo would have to continue, and the airborne head parts would have to be covered.

Just as he did with #312, Tom isolated frame #316, enlarged it, converted it to black and white, and then tagged it with pseudocolor.

Zapruder frame #316.   Frame #316 enlarged.   Frame #316; B&W.

When Tom stripped away the first layer, he immediately recognized several alterations, including the blob at the front of Kennedy's face, his right hand, the back portion of his neck and, of course the back of his head. Also obvious were alterations to Jackie Kennedy's left hand and portions of the grassy area just south of the limousine. After stripping away another layer and creating a 3-D image, the alterations became more obvious – showing up in one dimension compared to the rest of the three-dimensional image. Tom's image of the third stripped layer revealed an even larger portion of the grass that had been altered.

32 A DEEPER, DARKER TRUTH

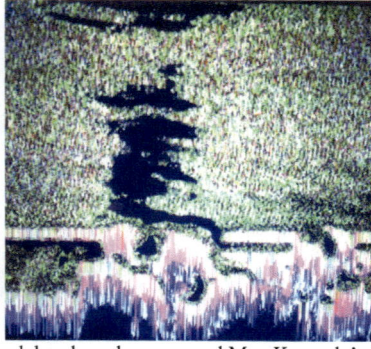

Progressive layering of #316 – alterations to head, hand, neck, grass, and Mrs. Kennedy's left hand. 1st Layer, pseudocolor (L); 2nd layer, pseudocolor (C); 3rd layer, pseudocolor, 3-D (R).

    By the time Tom stripped away the fourth layer, all the alterations had disappeared, and what remained beneath was revealed. At this point, it was perfectly clear to Tom that the alterations had been made on the surface of the film by either insert matte or halftone processes, possibly both.

    Tom verified these findings by processing other frames after the head shot (in the same film) – and other versions of the Zapruder film in the same corresponding frames. A good example is frame #335 (shown below) where Tom enlarged the image, converted it to black & white, tagged it with pseudocolor, and removed an additional layer. Tom's findings showed the grass portion above the limousine to have been photographically altered to remove the image of the actual grass. In addition, the so-called head flap, the top of Jackie Kennedy's head, and a portion under the head flap *are not* reflections. Rather, they are portions of the film that had been altered at the same time as the grass area. Clearly, they are not part of the original film. In fact, Tom concluded that all copies of the Zapruder film he viewed were made from the same altered original.

Zapruder frame #335.   Frame #335 enlarged.

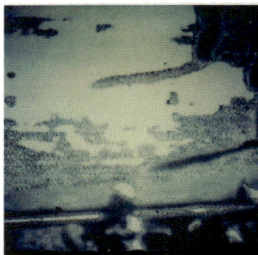 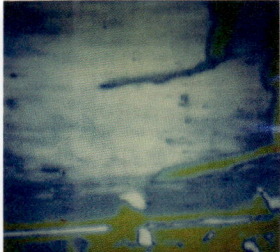 

Progressive layering of #335 – alterations to head, hand, neck, grass, and Mrs. Kennedy's left hand. 1st Layer, pseudocolor (L); 2nd layer, pseudocolor (C); 3rd layer, pseudocolor (R).

Now interested in what the president's head wound might look like below the alterations, Tom took the frame #316 black & white image, tagged it with pseudocolor, stripped it down to a fourth layer, and then enlarged the image. The massive wound in the back of Kennedy's head did indeed show up. But Tom was surprised to also see what appeared to be several smaller holes just below.

 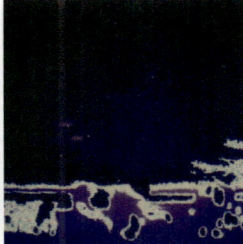 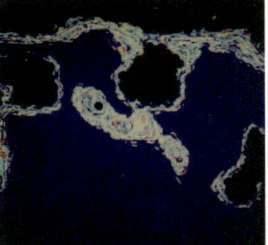

Image processing of Zapruder frame #316 reveals hole in back of head and several smaller holes below. B&W (L); 4th layer, pseudocolor (C); 4th layer, pseudocolor, enlarged (R).

Curious to learn what these smaller holes might be, Tom backed up one frame and took a look at Zapruder frame #315. He performed the same processing techniques he'd done with frame #316, including conversion to black and white, pseudocolor tagging, and stripping down to the fourth layer.

Zapruder frame #315.   Frame #315 B&W, 4th layer.

This time, though, when Tom got down to the fourth layer, he created a three-dimensional image. Not only did the massive hole in the back of Kennedy's head show up, but so did the other two holes. The more visible wound appeared to be located in the back of the president's neck, while the less clear one was in his back near the upper right shoulder. After stripping away one more layer and digitally expanding the 3-D image, both holes showed up clearly.

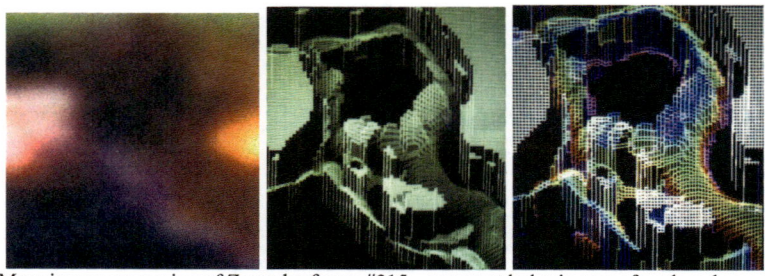

More image processing of Zapruder frame #315 – apparent holes in rear of neck and upper back near right shoulder. #315, enlarged (L); 4th layer, 3-D (C); 5th layer, 3-D, expanded (R).

"Wow! What's going on here?" Tom blurted out loud. "How can this be?"

Tom called for Marcie, again.

"This is never-ending," he told her. "Everything I look at has something new and shocking! Everything!"

"What did you see this time?" asked Marcie.

"Two more bullet holes – one in the back of the neck, one in the back shoulder."

Marcie could see that Tom was very upset. "Why don't we go out to dinner?" she suggested.

"Good idea," he replied. "Let's go down to Dick's Diner and get some meatloaf. I can't look at any more right now. I need to take a break."

3 / *Somebody Has To Do Something*

When Tom finally sat back down in front of his computer screen after seeing the shocking images he'd pulled from the Zapruder film, he was more composed, more curious, and more determined than ever to continue his investigation. So far, he was fairly certain that the final shot fired at President Kennedy inflicted the massive head wound that killed him. But what about the wounds in his back and neck? When were they inflicted? And were they entrance or exit holes? The Warren Commission only reported one bullet wound in the lower neck region. Is that what he was seeing, in part? Had he discovered an additional bullet hole they had missed? What was going on here? Nothing was adding up.

"Okay, what did the Warren Commission say again?" Tom asked himself. According to the single bullet theory, the missile hit Kennedy in the back of his neck, emerged out the front (nicking the top of his necktie knot), and then entered Governor Connolly's back. "All right," thought Tom, "I'll just back up to the point on the Zapruder film where that first shot struck the president and see what there is to see."

After doing some research and then extensively reviewing the earlier portions of the movie, Tom began to focus on the sequence of frames from #224 to #227. Here, as the presidential limousine emerges from behind the Stemmons Freeway sign, President Kennedy raises his hands to his throat in apparent reaction to being shot. This obviously is the shot that the Warren Commission concluded came from the sixth floor of the Texas School Book Depository, above, behind, and to the right of the limousine.

Frames 224-226 as presidential limousine emerges from behind the Stemmons Freeway sign.

The first full image of the president emerging from behind the sign is in frame #225. Because Kennedy's hands were not yet fully up to his throat, Tom decided to focus on this image to see if he could see a bullet hole. As before, he enlarged the frame and converted it to a black and white image.

Zapruder frame #225 enlarged.   Frame #225 enlarged; B&W.

Tom next cropped the image to focus in only on Kennedy. He enlarged it, tagged it with pseudocolor, and started peeling away the layers of the onion. After processing the third layer, Tom saw a hole in the front of the neck, just at the top of the necktie knot. He then enlarged the image, tagged the hole red, and took some measurements. The hole was small, very small. Much smaller than the hole in the back of the neck.

Image processing of Zapruder frame #225 reveals small bullet hole in base of President Kennedy's throat (tagged red). B&W, enlarged (L); 3rd layer, pseudocolor (C); 3rd layer, pseudocolor, enlarged (R).

Tom's initial reaction was that the hole at the front of the neck was an entrance wound, and the hole at the back of the neck was where the bullet had exited. He used his computer to correct for the president's slumped position in frame #315, and drew a straight line between the two neck holes. The path was on the horizontal – definitely not anywhere near the high angle necessary to conclude that the shot had originated from the sixth floor of the Texas School Book Depository. What's more, extending the straight-line path of the bullet forward led right back to the picket fence on the grassy knoll – to the right front of the presidential limousine.

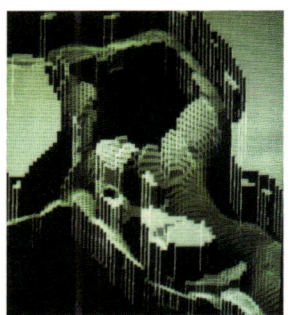

Zapruder frame #315, 4th layer, enlarged, 3-D, showing neck exit wound and hole in upper back.

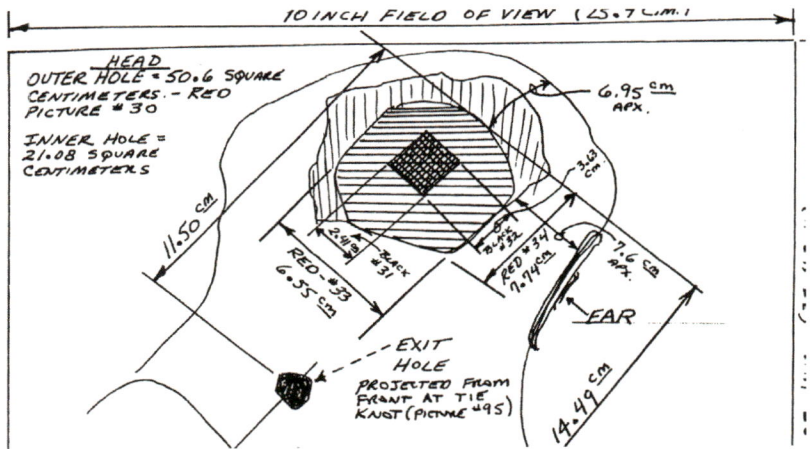

Tom Wilson's sketch of head and neck exit wounds.

So now Tom had evidence for *two* shots fired from the front right. One hit the front of the president's neck and exited the back of his neck. The other hit him from the front and blew out the back top of his head. At this point, Tom decided he had better return to his previous work and take a closer look at the shooter behind the picket fence.

A quick review of his first saved file reminded Tom that, after peeling away several layers of gray, a partial face had been revealed behind the gun smoke. This man was dressed as a policeman and peering down the telescopic scope of a rifle. He had coarse hair and a mole (or pox mark) on his cheek just below the left eye. The right side of his face remained obscured behind the rifle smoke. The metal badge he was wearing appeared to have a left-facing eagle's head on it, rather than the star that appeared on the badge of the Dallas Police Department.

As Tom took another look at that badge, he noticed some sort of extension at the upper left. After enlarging the image, he determined that it was probably a metal button on a pocket flap.

Pseudocolor image of badge.

Enlargement showing metal button.

That meant that the position of the badge was on the shooter's left chest adjacent to the shirt pocket. A small detail, Tom thought, but he hadn't noticed it before. "Hmmm," mused Tom. "What other details did I miss."

Looking for additional information he might have overlooked, Tom pulled up his close-ups of the shooter's face. He looked carefully at the hair, the eye, the mole, and the skin, but saw nothing unusual. Then he gazed over at the ear and thought something appeared odd. "Looks like an object is attached," Tom thought to himself. "But I can't tell exactly what it is."

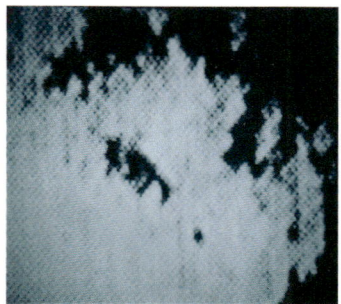
Face of shooter behind picket fence.

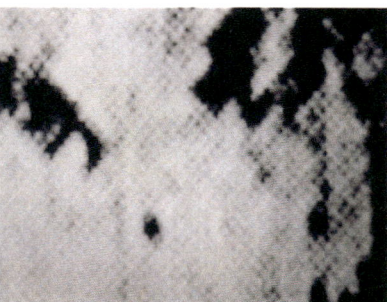
Electronic device in left ear.

After thinking about it for a while, Tom reasoned that, since this man was an assassin it was probably wearing an electronic earpiece, perhaps a radio receiver. He attempted to focus in and strip some more layers away, but the quality of the original image was insufficient to gain further details.

Looking straight into the eye of the shooter, Tom got an idea. "I wonder if I can determine what color his eyes are?" he asked himself. Over the next several days, Tom studied the gray scale images of both brown and blue eyes and compared them to the iris in the image. His finding was conclusive. The shooter had brown eyes. It was an exact match.

Tom then paused and took a look at the rest of the shooter's face. He couldn't see the nose or mouth, because both were obscured by gun smoke. But he could draw a sketch of what was visible – complete with measurements so that somebody in the future might be able to search for the shooter. So that's what Tom did. He prepared a sketch documenting the thick coarse hair, the eye, the ear, and the mole (or pox mark). And then, believing the mole might be a key to the identity of the shooter, Tom measured its exact location in relation to the left eye. He determined that it was 1.76 centimeters down from the centerline of the iris and 1.62 centimeters to the right. Then Tom measured the pox mark itself. It was 0.374 by 0.315 centimeters in area, and it had two smaller circular features within, one of which was slightly raised.

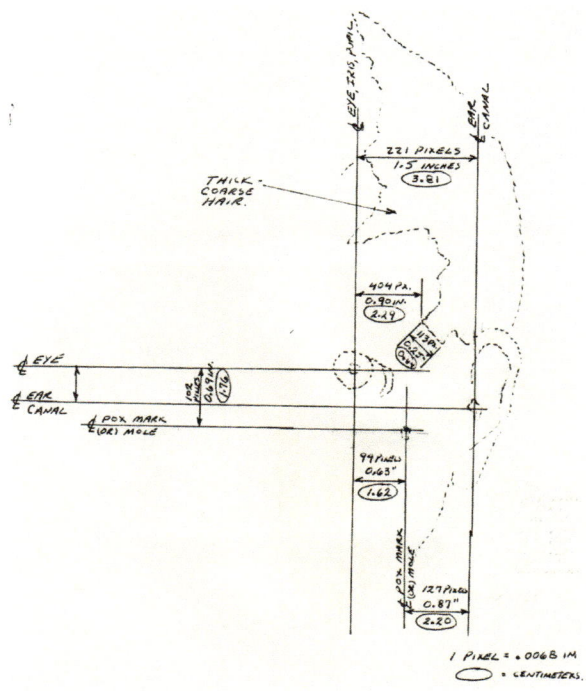

Tom's sketches of the left side of the shooter's face.

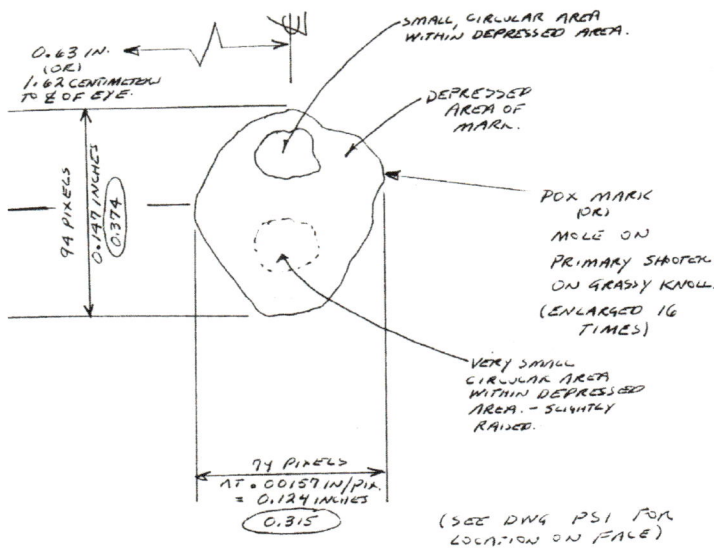

Details of the mole (pox mark) on shooter's face.

Having noted the button next to the badge, the possible electronic earpiece, and the color of the shooter's eyes, Tom decided to step back and take another look at the full picture. He again pulled up the original enlargement and its processed counterpart with several layers removed.

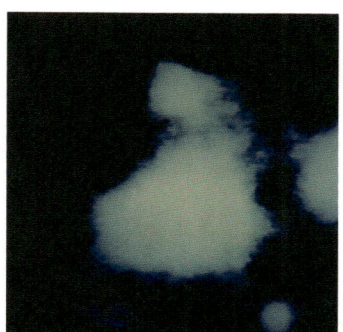

Original enlargement of shooter.

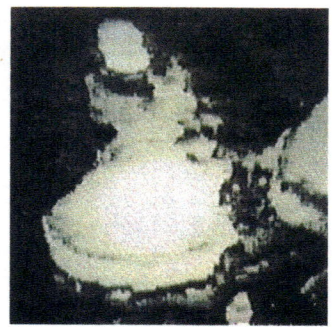

Several layers removed.

Tom's attention was immediately drawn to what appeared to be a second puff of smoke to the right of the shooter (looking at photo). In the processed image, it looked identical to the first puff of smoke. After using several techniques to determine if it might be some sort of reflection, Tom confirmed that it did occupy space and was, in fact, real. Clearly, this meant that there was a second shooter firing at the president from behind the fence.

Enlarging the processed picture, and then producing another image that highlighted varying densities, Tom compared the brightness of the two puffs of smoke. The higher density from the smoke on the right showed that this second rifle was fired a split second after the rifle of the left shooter had fired.

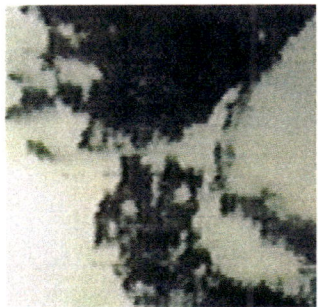 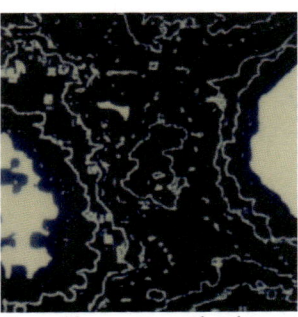

Image processing reveals two puffs of smoke. Several layers removed, enlargement (L); additional processing of smoke densities (R) reveals smoke on right occurred split second later.

Using mathematical calculations, Tom estimated that the two shooters fired one-fifth of a second apart. To fire that close together, they had to have been responding to the same command. Therefore, it was reasonable to assume that both had electronic radio receivers in their ears.

Having now confirmed a second puff of smoke from something that appeared so obvious in the first image, Tom wondered what else he might be able to see if he was a bit more meticulous. With that in mind, he took the overall image with several layers removed, and then stripped another two layers and tagged it with pseudocolor. After perusing the image for a few minutes, Tom's attention was drawn to the upper right corner, which he enlarged.

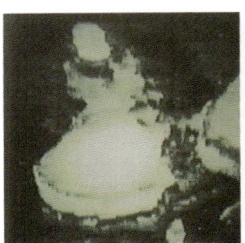 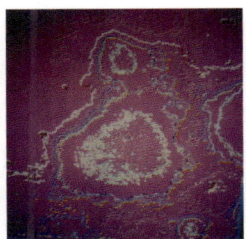 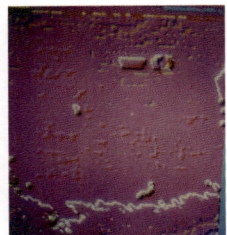

More processing of shooter enlargement – anomaly in upper right corner. Shooter enlargement, several layers removed (L); two layers removed, pseudocolor (C); enlarged(R).

Additional processing and enlargement clarified the images to be that of a nameplate and metal button, probably on the flap pocket of a policeman's shirt. "Was this part of the uniform of the shooter on the right?" Tom wondered. "Could it be from his right pocket? Did it mean that the second shooter was left-handed? Or was this attached to another person's uniform altogether?" These were questions that Tom simply could not answer with the material at hand. He would have to file away this new information and move on to something else.

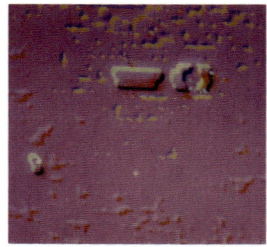 

Additional processing reveals nameplate (L) and metal button (R) on shirt of shooter.

Unable to find any additional detail in the immediate vicinity of the two shooters, Tom decided to look a little farther down the fence line. And he didn't have to go very far before finding another major anomaly. Immediately to left of the primary shooter (as viewed in the Moorman photograph), Tom saw another bright light indicating metal of some kind. It was behind the fence and equal in elevation to the height of the primary shooter's head.

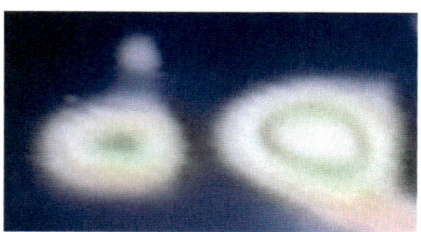 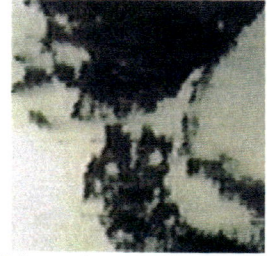

Light from metal object (left); smoke from primary shooter (R).

Primary shooter and smoke (L); second puff of smoke (R).

After trying several processing variations, including pseudocolor and black and white images, it became apparent that the object was a very sophisticated camera of some type (circa 1963). It appeared to have an attached viewfinder at the top, a lens with lens operating adjustments, and an obvious bellows. Tom also determined that a third person behind the fence was holding the camera with his right hand over its right side. As a matter of fact, four fingers of the individual's hand were clearly visible on the edge of the camera.

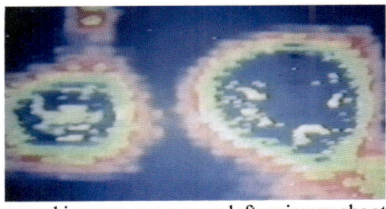 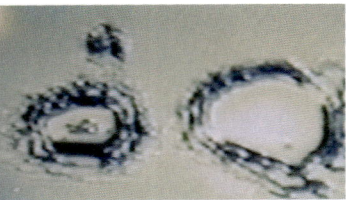

Processed images, camera on left, primary shooter smoke on right; pseudocolor (L); B&W (R).

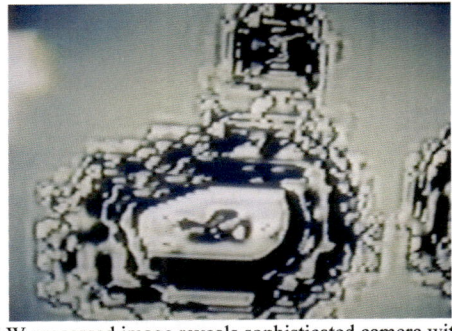

Enlarged B&W processed image reveals sophisticated camera with viewfinder, bellows, and lens. Four fingers of right hand holding camera on left edge.

Tom wondered if this was a type of large format camera or perhaps even an advanced movie camera of some kind. Whatever model and make it was, someone was clearly behind the picket fence intending to capture images of the assassination. But who? And what happened to the pictures that might have been taken?

* * * * *

Even though it seemed that every time he looked at something new, more questions than answers arose, Tom decided to go back and take another detailed look at one of the most emotionally disturbing of his findings – the massive wound in the back of President Kennedy's head. Without stopping to think too much about it, he pulled up the enlarged copy of Zapruder frame #313 and the corresponding processed image of the fourth layer. Then he remembered the extraordinary concentric rings of pseudocolor that left absolutely no doubt in his mind that there was a massive hole in Kennedy's head that had been hidden by halftone or inserted matte photography.

 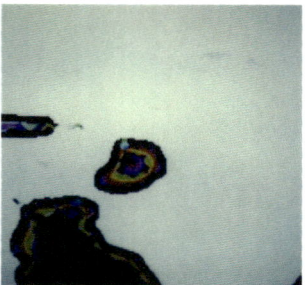

Zapruder frame # 313 (enlarged).   4th layer (pseudocolor; enlarged).

Tom next pulled up the 3-D gray scale image of the wound that revealed the scalp, skull, and brain, and compared it to the fifth layer pseudocolor enlargement. He had not noticed it before, but there was some sort of anomaly in the upper left center of the second image. It was somewhat lighter in color and seemed somehow to be above the other material.

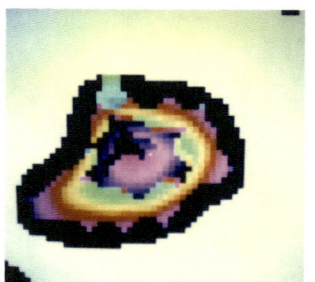 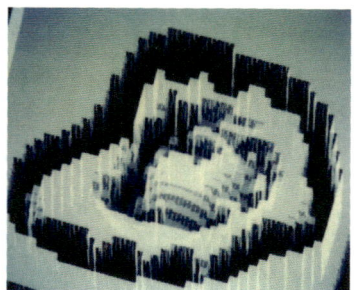

5th layer pseudocolor enlargement (L) and 3-D gray scale image (R) reveal anomaly above other material.

Thinking that another 3-D image and different coloring might allow him to determine just what the anomaly was, Tom produced a three-dimensional view of the pseudocolor fifth layer image, and then retagged the colors with variations of blue and green. And that did it. There was definitely something emerging from the wound. Was this a fragment from the original exploding bullet exiting the head? Or was it part of the skull or brain material that was being blown into the air?

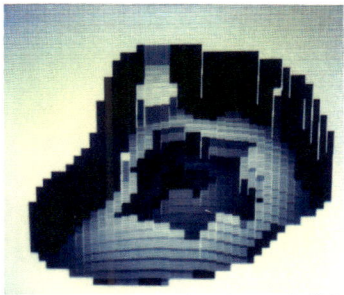

Fifth Layer; 3-D pseudocolor image reveals bullet or skull fragment exiting head.

As Tom stared at this new image, he began to wonder how many layers he could strip away before he lost the spatial data entirely. Would he be able to see far enough down so that he could actually project the area of the head where the bullet entered? He didn't know, but elected to give it a try. After peeling away two more layers, and trying various processing techniques, Tom settled on the fact that the seventh stripped layer was about as far as he could go. After tagging it with pseudocolor, the projectile (or piece of skull) flying out of the wound was still visible. In addition, Tom was able to project far enough down into the wound that he could interpret a likely place that the bullet entered. That projection indicated that the bullet entered in the vicinity of the area just above the right eye.

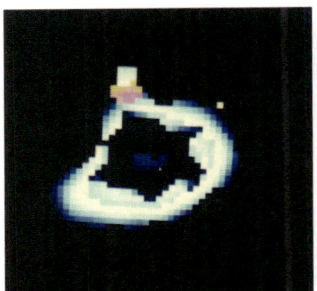 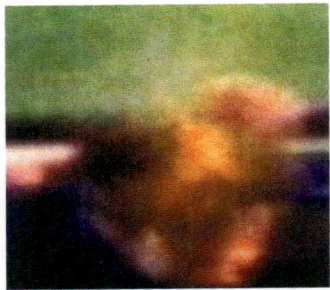

Zapruder #313 final image processing reveals fragment flying out of back head; likely point of entry projected above right eye; 7th layer (L); Frame #313 enlarged (R).

In thinking about that one projectile coming out of the head, Tom's thoughts drifted back to his previous images of airborne head material. "I wonder if there's enough data to allow the computer to calculate angle and direction of flight?" he thought. "Let's take a look."

Tom pulled up the earlier images of airborne head material and began trying various methods of processing. After awhile, he was able to take data from several frames (#s 313-315) of the Zapruder film, feed it into the computer, and have it calculate and display the information he was looking for.

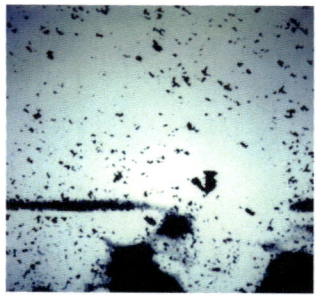

Processing of Zapruder frame #313 revealed airborne head material; 3rd layer; pseudocolor (L); 4th layer; pseudocolor; enlarged (R).

Although an apparent exploding bullet caused head material to eject upward, backward, and forward, the majority of material flew out of the skull at a 15-degree angle (upward and back) from the center point of the head. In addition, several large pieces of skull material moved upward, forward, and rotated clockwise out of the head. Finally, Tom had his computer perform further mathematical calculations that took into account vertical shear angles and the speed of the limousine to verify that the bullet had indeed moved from the right front to the back top of the head.

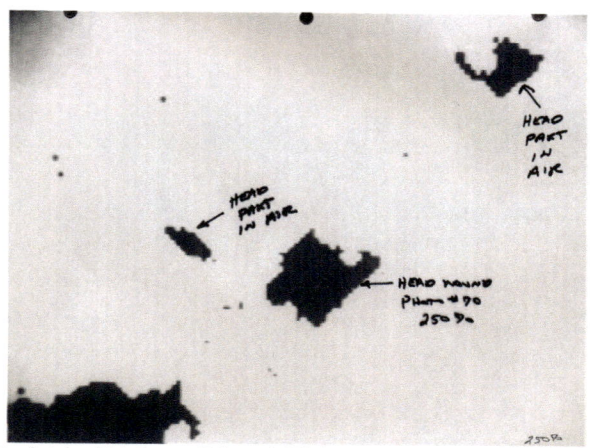

Tom's sketch of 4th Layer; Enlarged; His interpretation of parts rotating in air.

* * * * *

As Tom uncovered more and more new information, he was astounded at how different it was from that of the Warren Commission. Three shots fired from behind the presidential limousine, up high in the sixth floor of the Texas School Book Depository; the single bullet theory; a shot to the back of the head exploding out the front. None of it made sense to him anymore. As a matter of fact, he was angry at both the government for presenting an incorrect scenario to the people all these years, and at himself for accepting those explanations at face value.

However, the more Tom read about the events of November 22, 1963, the more amazed he was to learn that many on-site witnesses had reported the very things that he was now uncovering with his image processing-computer analysis system. For instance, at Parkland Hospital in Dallas, where the president was taken immediately after the wounds were inflicted, several of the doctors and at least one nurse, reported seeing an entrance wound in the front of the neck just below the Adam's apple. Dr. Malcolm Perry described it as "a very small injury [3 to 5 mm] with clear cut, although somewhat irregular margins of less than a quarter inch." Nurse Margaret Henchliffe also witnessed the wound and described it as a fairly inconspicuous one before the tracheotomy procedure (performed in an attempt to save the president's life) obscured it.

Regarding the third and fatal shot to the head, rather than seeing a small bullet wound in the back of the head and a blow-out wound in the front, nearly all witnesses saw *exactly the opposite.* Several doctors at Parkland Hospital, a Secret Service agent, and civilian witnesses reported a small entrance wound in the area of the temple above the right eye. New York's *Herald Tribune* reported that Kennedy was "hit by two shots in the neck and to the right temple." And nearly *everybody* who saw the wounded president reported seeing a large hole in the back of his head, which they interpreted as a wound of exit. "The right posterior portion of the skull had been extremely blasted . . . by the force of the shot," said Dr. Robert McClelland, who was in the Parkland Hospital emergency room. "You could actually look down into the skull cavity itself and see . . . the brain tissue." Other doctors, nurses, government agents, and civilian witnesses gave similar accounts.

Regarding the airborne skull and brain material blasted out the back of the president's head, numerous witnesses testified to such a shocking sight after the fatal shot. Perhaps the most dramatic descriptions came from the two Dallas police officers riding motorcycles at the left rear of the presidential limousine. Bobby Hargis and B. J. Martin both reported having blood and brain material splattered on their uniforms, helmets, and the windshields of their motorcycles.

Virtually all of these witness accounts were ignored or dismissed by the Warren Commission. But Tom's work basically affirmed it all. And now he had what he believed to be hard evidence to back up their statements.

In 1963, photographs and motion pictures were viewed as evidence in formal investigations and courts of law. Back then, however, photographic technology was limited, although images could be manipulated with sufficient expertise and sophisticated equipment. But a quarter of a century later, Tom Wilson had applied the latest in technology and developed a new system that could be utilized as an investigative tool to analyze the photographs and home movies taken in Dallas on November 22, 1963. He had established a method whereby virtually any copy of original photographic material could reveal the truths that lay within – without any distortion or alteration of any kind to the original photograph. As a matter of fact, Tom had worked from videotapes of copies of the Zapruder film using a $3 tape in a $150 video cassette recorder. Anybody with the proper knowledge and a few bucks could do it. But for now, as far as he knew, he was the only one who had unlocked the secrets of these true artifacts frozen in time.

A lifetime of image processing experience had convinced Tom that what was known to date about the assassination of President John F. Kennedy was wrong. And while much more could no doubt be discovered by additional image processing work, Tom felt he had more than enough evidence to prove that both a cover up and a conspiracy existed. It was time to get the word out. The American people had to know. Somebody had to do something about this terrible injustice.

After thinking about it for quite some time, Tom decided the best way to proceed was to go to New York City and reveal his findings to various national media organizations. First, however, he had to prepare a professional presentation, without too much technical jargon that might confuse the real issue. So over the next several weeks, he wrote a rather lengthy report and produced an accompanying video showing all his findings to date.

Tom began by stating, matter-of-factly, that there were *two shooters on the grassy knoll* firing weapons in the direction of the presidential limousine, as verified by his processing of the Mary Moorman Polaroid photograph. These individuals were dressed in police uniforms, and fired at virtually the same instant, wrote Tom. The first shooter was to the left as viewed in the photograph. He was firing a rifle with his right hand on the trigger and right eye looking through a scope. Elements identified with processing were: badge, identification plate, button, partial face (with coarse hair, left eye, mole or pox mark, probable radio receiver earpiece, and smoke from the weapon.

The second shooter was to the left and rear of the first shooter (from the shooter's perspective). Elements identified with processing were: identification plate, button, and smoke from the weapon. Comparison of smoke densities confirm that the second shooter fired approximately 1/5 of a second after the first shooter.

Tom's article next stated that *a minimum of three shots hit President Kennedy*. Two bullets were fired from the front. One was fired from either the front or the back (as yet undetermined). These three shots, he wrote, do not account for any missile(s) that hit Governor Connolly.

In order to provide a meaningful sequential understanding of exactly what happened to President Kennedy, Tom then structured his report and video in the actual sequence of the assassination.

First Shot:
A bullet entered the front of President Kennedy's neck just above his necktie knot and exited the back of his neck. The entrance hole was very small, less than one centimeter (one third of an inch) in diameter.

> *"It was just a little hole in the middle of his neck . . . about as big around as the end of my little finger."*
>
> Nurse Margaret Henchliffe
> Parkland Hospital Emergency Room

The exit hole in the back of the neck was at least twice as large as the entrance hole in the front. It measured slightly more than two centimeters (three-quarters of an inch) in diameter.

> *"In the process of positioning and stabilizing the President's head and pushing up his neck to straighten the airway for easier passage of the oxygen pumping in, my spread fingers felt the hole on the back of his neck."*
>
> Dr. M. T. Jenkins
Chief Anesthesiologist
Parkland Hospital Emergency Room

It was possible to calculate the exact trajectory of the bullet by connecting the entry and exit hole with a straight line. The path of that straight line was on the horizontal, and President Kennedy was struck while he was still in an upright sitting position. An extension of the straight line to the front of the limousine suggests that the point of origin for this shot was in the vicinity of the picket fence on the grassy knoll. The shot definitely *did not* originate from the sixth floor of the Texas School Book Depository.

Second Shot:

A bullet hole was observed in President Kennedy's back. It penetrated his coat jacket and probably measured in the neighborhood of between one to two centimeters in size with an irregular and jagged border. Its location was to the right of the back-of-the-neck exit hole (first shot), and down toward the lower portion of the shoulder. It appeared this shot occurred while the president was still in an upright position.

"It cannot be ascertained at this time whether this bullet hole is one of entry or exit," wrote Tom. "However, the findings of the *two* wounds, associated with the first and second shots, prove beyond any doubt that *the single bullet theory is wrong.*"

Third Shot:

"A bullet fired from the right front of the presidential limousine entered President Kennedy's head just above the right eye in the vicinity of the temple."

> "In the process of positioning and stabilizing the President's head and pushing up his neck to straighten the airway for easier passage of the oxygen pumping in, my spread fingers felt the hole on the back of his neck."
>
> Dr. M. T. Jenkins
> Chief Anesthesiologist
> Parkland Hospital Emergency Room

"This missile exited through the back of his head, leaving a massive, gaping wound measuring approximately 3.0 by 3.0 inches (7.6 cm by 7.6 cm)."

> "The wound was the size of a baseball."
>
> Dr. Charles Crenshaw
> Attending physician
> Parkland Hospital Emergency Room

"The bullet exploded out the back of President Kennedy's head – sending scalp, skull, and brain material airborne."

> "His head exploded, and I was splattered with blood and brain, and all kinds of bloody water."
>
> Bobby Hargis
> Motorcycle Officer
> Riding to the left rear of the limousine

"Image processing of Zapruder frame #313 has revealed part of the brain within the skull, which (along with movement of airborne head material) makes it possible to trace and project *the bullet's path through the head*," concluded Tom. "Preliminary measurement of this trajectory is *front to back* (the shot originated from the front of the limousine*), right to left* (the shot originated to the right of the limousine), and *down to up*. Additional image processing with further measurements are needed to verify these initial findings."

Tom's last major point in his written report and video stated that the *Zapruder film had been altered* for the purpose of hiding and changing certain pictorial details. It was altered using sophisticated, 1963 state-of-the-art equipment to perform both halftone and insert matte photography. Modern image processing technology, combined with computer analysis, could not only detect these alterations, but could see through them in such as way as to establish the original unaltered picture.

"It is possible to detect the actual areas on each frame where the changes were made," wrote Tom. "Specific areas of alteration on President Kennedy include: the front face, the front chest, the right hand, the back neck, and the back head. Mrs. Kennedy's left arm and hand have also been altered, as have portions of the grassy area to the back of the limousine. In addition, the orange-reddish blob at the front of President Kennedy's head (in frame # 313 and several succeeding frames) has been artificially added to the film. The purpose of this alteration, in part, is to hide the large hole in the back of the head, and to give the impression that the bullet had entered from the rear and blown out the top side and front – exactly the *opposite* of what really happened.

"This new information should be disclosed and in my opinion produces the evidence necessary to reopen the investigation into the assassination of President John F. Kennedy," Tom wrote in conclusion. "Although it does not answer the question of who or why, it positively does resolve the question of multiple assassins, cover up, and conspiracy.

"The 26-year-old images of evidence now become the "Rosetta Stone" that will allow the debunking of the grand illusion of a single assassin. The Warren Commission was wrong. Lee Harvey Oswald was not a lone gunman. Our 35th president was assassinated by a team of conspirators."

* * * * *

In mid-April, 1989, Tom Wilson went to New York City armed with his report and accompanying video. He was bound and determined to bring these new findings to the public's attention. His plan was to knock on the doors of the national media, show them his explosive evidence, and let them publish or broadcast it as they saw fit. Tom had no doubts that the sheer magnitude of the story would compel them to take action.

But he was wrong.

Tom first went to the offices of Time-Life, because he thought they owned the Zapruder film. It would be right to start there, he thought, because they would want to know about the alterations. But after being bounced around to several different people, Tom was told that the film had been returned to the Zapruder family. "We're not interested in it anymore," they said.

Undeterred, Tom looked up a friend who worked at NBC. After seeing the report and video, the man became very interested and attempted to set up interviews with several high-level executives. But the executives all refused the requests. And to make matters worse, Tom's friend was summarily fired from NBC for his efforts.

Next on the list was Dan Rather of CBS. Tom knew that Rather had been in Dallas in November 22, 1963, and had narrated a number of programs on the assassination. He would probably jump on this, Tom thought. After numerous phone calls, an assistant finally came down to the lobby at CBS headquarters, met with Tom, and listened to what he had to say. "Well, how much of Mr. Rather's time would you need?" he asked.

"Two hours to make a complete presentation should do it," replied Tom.

"Oh, I could never ask Mr. Rather for two hours. But let me go upstairs and see what he has to say."

Ten minutes later, the assistant called down to the lobby and spoke with Tom. "Mr. Rather said there is no proof of a conspiracy. We're not interested."

"Holy mackerel," thought Tom. "If Dan Rather isn't interested, who will be?"

Over the next week, Tom contacted (or tried to contact) executives from The New York Times, ABC News, Fox, Carroll and Graff Publishers, USA Today, Discover Magazine, and Geraldo Rivera. All refused to take the story.

This was simply mind-boggling to Tom. It never occurred to him that no one would be interested. It was the President of the United States who was murdered, for God's sake. It was the crime of the century. How could people *not* be interested?

Frustrated, dejected, and discouraged, Tom finally went home to Pittsburgh. "What am I going to do now?" he asked Marcie.

Little did Tom Wilson know this was just the beginning of his long journey into the assassination of President John F. Kennedy.

4 / *Five Autopsy Photographs*

Over the next couple of months, Tom mostly moped around the house. It depressed him that no one wanted to hear anything other than the official false story about what had happened to President Kennedy. And he was concerned that his findings would never see the light of day. However, Tom's deep curiosity brought him out of the blues. He went to the public library and began additional reading and study of the assassination. He poured over the 1964 Warren Report and the 1978 findings of the House Select Committee on Assassinations (HSCA). And he read more material from the many researchers and experts who disagreed with the government's lone-assassin conclusion.

It was at this time that Tom ran across the name of Dr. Cyril Wecht who was perhaps the most renowned professional to voice serious disagreement with the Warren Commission's findings. Tom had heard of Dr. Wecht previously, because they both lived in the same area. Coincidently, Wecht just happened to be Pittsburgh's chief forensic pathologist and well-respected county coroner. The two men lived less than twenty miles apart.

In 1964, Dr. Wecht had been asked by the American Academy of Forensic Sciences to study the Warren Report and present a critical discussion. He had also been asked by *Life* magazine to examine the Zapruder film. In 1978, Wecht testified before the HSCA and was one of the nine-member panel of forensic pathology experts to advise the Committee with regard to the JFK autopsy photographs and x-rays. He cast the lone dissenting vote on the major findings of the panel, which agreed with the Warren Commission's original conclusions. Dr. Wecht was adamant that the single bullet theory was not only wrong, but physically impossible. Kennedy, he said, was shot before Governor Connolly and then struck in the head with a frangible (exploding) bullet. He did not believe the President had been assassinated by a lone individual, but rather, that there had been several gunman.

Hoping to receive some help to expose his findings, Tom wrote a letter to Cyril Wecht in mid-June 1989. He explained his background in computer analysis and image processing, his thirty years of experience with U.S. Steel in Pittsburgh, and mentioned the fact that he had retired as chief electrical engineer. "I have recently been applying a new technique to photographs of the Kennedy assassination, and can prove there was a second gunman behind the picket fence on the grassy knoll," wrote Tom. "It's all basic computing and can be reproduced by anybody at any time. Would it be all right if called you to discuss my findings?" As soon as Dr. Wecht received the letter, he called Tom and the two had an extended conversation.

Dr. Cyril Wecht

One week later, on June 21, 1989, Tom was in Wecht's office with a packed briefcase. After explaining the basics of the technology, he presented his findings to date – the metal badge, the two shooters and the camera behind the picket fence, all his work on the Zapruder film, the President's head and neck wounds, the skull and brain matter in the air, how the film was altered, everything. Excited and impressed, Wecht launched into a discussion of his own experience with the Kennedy assassination. He discussed his review of the Warren Commission's findings, his look at the Zapruder film for *Life*, and his tenure on the HSCA forensic pathology panel. Tom's findings, said Wecht, verified his own conclusions that the Warren Commission and House Select Committee were wrong.

Tom listened intently to Dr. Wecht and was impressed that one man could stand up against the government's version of events for twenty-five years. Tom also began to realize that Wecht could be an invaluable resource for him – not only to help him get his message out to the public, but also to explain many of the details and intricacies of the assassination. Conversely, Dr. Wecht realized that Tom's work was groundbreaking and had the potential to reveal many hidden truths about what really happened to President Kennedy. Bonded by their shared vision of illuminating the truth in the Kennedy assassination, Tom and Dr. Wecht began meeting regularly to discuss their thoughts and ideas.

In the meantime, a Kennedy Assassination researcher gave Tom a copy of a recently released two-part documentary called *The Men Who Killed Kennedy*. Produced by Englishman Nigel Turner, and made for the Central Independent Television Company, the two installments (entitled *The Coup d'Etat* and *The Forces of Darkness*) were first broadcast in Great Britain in October 1988. Wecht had been interviewed by Turner and appeared in the first part discussing the implausibility of the single bullet theory and that an additional gunman had fired at the president.

"One of the autopsy photographs is in this video," the researcher told Tom. "It's been hidden away all these years and Turner has made it public. Why don't you run it through your system and see what you can find."

"Okay, I will," responded Tom. "What do you expect me to find?"

"Well, I don't want to influence you, but let me put it this way. The photo shows the back of Kennedy's head intact. It is supposed to have been taken at the autopsy at Bethesda Naval Hospital in Maryland (a suburb of Washington, D.C.) on the night of November 22 – and the government states that it represents the condition of Kennedy's body. However, if you're right, and if the doctors at Parkland Hospital were right, then there's something wrong with the picture."

"Okay," said Tom. "I'll take a look."

Neither the photograph in question nor any other autopsy photo or x-ray were published in the 1964 Warren Report. As a matter of fact, the Warren Commission did not examine *any* of the JFK autopsy photos or x-rays. Instead, it relied on drawings of some of the photos to determine JFK's wounds. None of those drawings nor any actual photos or x-rays were reproduced in the Warren Report or its accompanying 26 volumes. However, fifteen years later, in 1979, the House Select Committee on Assassinations did publish a few sketches, closely cropped enlargements, and a few x-ray images. All the photo and x-ray reproductions, however, were of extremely poor quality, which made it virtually impossible to distinguish any significant detail. The "official autopsy photograph," as it was called by Nigel Turner in *The Men Who Killed Kennedy,* was represented in the HSCA Report as JFK Exhibit F-48. "This is a drawing made from photographs taken at the time of the autopsy showing the back of the President's head . . . ." read the report.

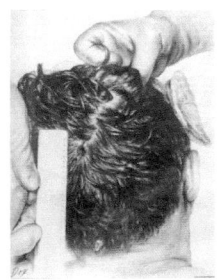

HSCA JFK Exhibit F-48; sketch of "official" autopsy photograph.

It was this particular drawing that was used by the HSCA, in part, to affirm the Warren Commission's finding that President Kennedy was shot in the back of the head. Referring to this exhibit, the Report stated that ". . . an area of the discoloration in the cowlick area of the back of the head of the scalp" was determined to be "an entrance bullet perforation. . . ." The accompanying JFK Exhibit F-50 showed this wound in a tightly cropped version of the actual autopsy photograph. Additionally, the HSCA Report published another cropped portion of the photo stating that it showed ". . . a fragment of dried tissue near the hairline of the President." According to the HSCA Report, it was the "unanimous opinion of all of the [forensic] panel members" that this drawing accurately represented "the location of the wound high in the back of the President's head."

HSCA JFK Exhibit F-50 enlargement, cowlick "an area, entrance bullet perforation."

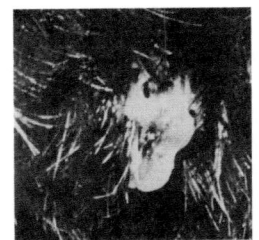

HSCA JFK Exhibit F-51 Cropped Cropped enlargement, above hairline "fragment of dried tissue."

If suspicion about the validity of this autopsy photograph was correct, there may have been an ulterior reason that the HSCA published only drawings and poor versions of the photographs and x-rays. If these pieces of evidence were, in fact, altered in some manner, not publishing the originals prevented scrutiny by experts who might have been able to determine they were forgeries. In stating the HSCA's reason for using drawings and closely cropped photographs, the Report read:

In deciding to release the autopsy photographs, the committee wished to permit public examination of the most important details of evidentiary significance while still maintaining a sense of propriety. In accordance with this desire, the committee decided to display the autopsy photographs to the public in either drawings that represent large areas of the President's body as seen in the photograph or closely cropped photographs that depict the most important areas of evidentiary concern. . . . The committee used photographs . . . in the hearings only to verify the authenticity and accuracy of the drawings and closely cropped photographs. These photographs are not being published. The original autopsy photographs and committee copies are in the custody of the National Archives."

Some of President Kennedy's autopsy photographs were finally released to the public in 1988 – ten years after the HSCA Report, twenty-four years after the Warren Report, and a full quarter of a century after the assassination. The story of these photos, in and of itself, is long and convoluted. On November 23, 1963, Secret Service Agent James K. Fox reportedly developed some of the photographs and, at the time, made a set of copies for himself. In 1982, Agent Fox gave his photographs to a researcher with the caveat that they not be made public until after Fox's death (which occurred in 1987). Then, in 1988, the Fox set was published for the first time in the book *Best Evidence* by David Lifton. Also that year, Nigel Turner aired what he called the "official autopsy photo" in *The Men Who Killed Kennedy*.

On the surface, this particular photograph looks very much like the drawing published in the HSCA Report (HSCA JFK Exhibit F-48). It shows the back of the president's head intact, the entrance hole at the crown, the piece of dried tissue near the hairline, and the skull partially opened (apparently with a saw) for autopsy.

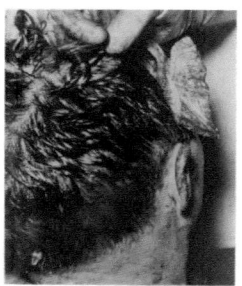

Official JFK Autopsy Photograph (Fox 3).

Tom ran the raw video through his system, stripped the first layer, and displayed it in a processed gray scale. The resulting image immediately revealed a huge area of the photograph with no depth encompassed nearly the entire center and right upper portion of the back of the head. In addition, both the missile entry at the crown and the piece of tissue near the hairline showed no depth at all. In the computer image, this lack of depth appeared as a nice even coat of white, revealing that the photograph had been manipulated. Essentially, the hair, the bullet hole, and the piece of tissue had been painted onto the image. That's why there was no depth. The "paint" was one-dimensional. Therefore, there was, in fact, *no entrance wound* high in the back of the president's head.

Tom next had his computer produce a totally black and white image in which the only part of the photo that was *not* altered appeared in black. After going through many different processing techniques (including removing several layers and displaying them in pseudocolor and 3-D), Tom concluded that every single image he produced was revealing that the photograph had been altered.

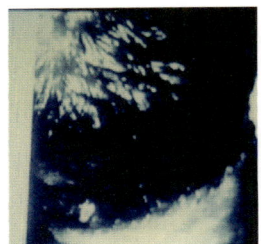
Raw video.

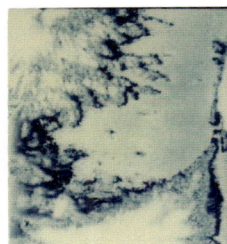
1ˢᵗ layer; no depth=altered.

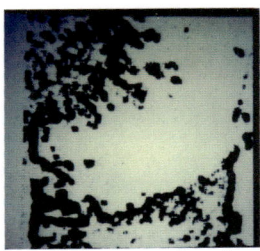
Black area not altered.

Tom next zeroed in specifically on the top of the head and repeated his processing. He wanted to concentrate, in part, on the hand that was holding the top of the scalp to determine if this person was there before or after the photograph was altered. All of Tom's images were conclusive. Much of the top portion of the head had been altered, especially the right side. In addition, the gloved hand shown in the photo pushing the head up and back was part of the *unaltered* portion. Therefore, this person was present when the cadaver was photographed and before the image was altered. "Who was this guy?" wondered Tom. "Was he one of the autopsy doctors?"

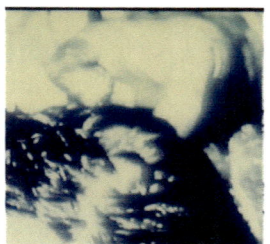 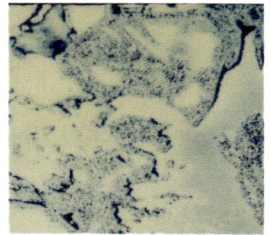

Back of head; raw video (R); Gray; 1st layer (R); no depth = hand present before altering.

After continued image processing, Tom was able to determine that the alterations were performed using three specially prepared matte masks. The first mask was used to wipe out the area to be altered. The second made the altered area look like hair. And the third mask was added the fake missile entry hole in the crown and the piece of flesh near the hairline. Neither were present in the original photograph before alteration. In addition, the bullet hole and the dried tissue were photographed in two stages to provide the illusion of depth.

Tom Wilson felt he had proven that the so-called "official autopsy photograph" as shown in *The Men Who Killed Kennedy* was a forgery. Furthermore, it was his opinion that this photograph had been manipulated for an express purpose. And that was to hide the massive exit wound in the rear of President Kennedy's head and to make it appear that he had been shot from the back rather than the front. It was an outrage, Tom felt. An absolutely terrible criminal act.

* * * * *

After completing his analysis of the "official autopsy photo," Tom arranged a meeting with Cyril Wecht to review the findings. Wecht listened patiently to everything Tom had to say, and then sat stunned for a few moments. He always knew there was a possibility this photo had been altered, but he never dreamed of the extent to which the perpetrators had gone to hide the true nature of President Kennedy's wounds. Wecht was also amazed at Tom's image processing method and its ability to uncover the truth.

Wanting to know more, Dr. Wecht obtained 8 x 10 prints of four additional autopsy photos from the Fox set and made copies for Tom to analyze. These photos included a front head and chest shot, a left profile of the head, a photo of the top of the president's head, and a picture of his back.

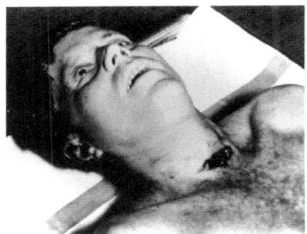
JFK autopsy photo (Fox 1).

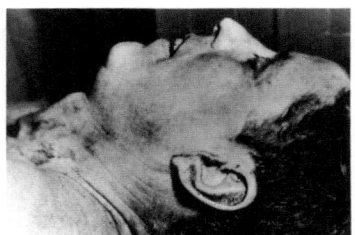
JFK autopsy photo (Fox 4).

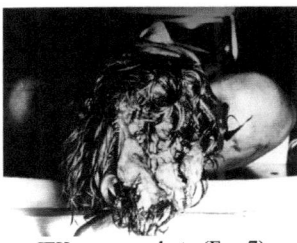
JFK autopsy photo (Fox 7).

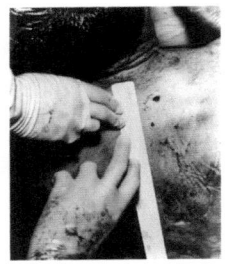
JFK autopsy photo (Fox 5).

Tom eagerly took the photographs and began analyzing them with his image processing system. He started with the front head and chest shot, because he was anxious to see if he would be able to observe the bullet hole at the base of the neck that he had seen in frame #225 of the Zapruder film.

This particular photograph showed no Y-incision in the upper chest area, which meant that the autopsy had apparently not begun when the picture was taken. It also showed the president's body with both eyes open and a large wound at the base of the neck – much larger than the small hole Tom had expected to see.

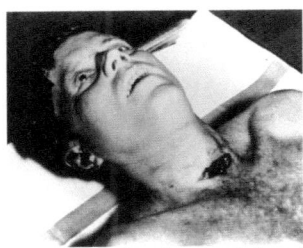
JFK autopsy photo, front head and chest (Fox 1).

Curious to see what the government said about this wound, Tom referred to the 1978 HSCA Report and learned that the doctors at Parkland Hospital in Dallas had performed a tracheostomy on the president in an effort to help breathing. Of the neck wound in this autopsy photo, the HSCA reported it to be "a typical type of tracheostomy incision" . . . with "a semicircular defect at the lower margin . . . which required further evaluation." The Warren Commission, too, had previously described this as a wound of exit from a bullet that had entered "near the base of the back of President Kennedy's neck slightly to the right of his spine." The Warren Report also noted that "by projecting from a point of entry on the rear of the neck and proceeding at a slight downward angle through the bruised interior portions, the doctors concluded that the bullet exited from the front portion of the President's neck that had been cut away by the tracheotomy."

Fourteen years later, the HSCA confirmed the Warren Commission's determination, and added that "the tracheostomy incision, the incision to put in a breathing tube, was made through that perforation of the skin and did modify and change the hole in the manner seen here [in the autopsy photograph] from a circular hole to a semicircle." Essentially, the HSCA was inferring that the large hole was created by the blowout of the bullet wound exiting the neck and that the small semicircle was made by the doctors when performing the tracheostomy.

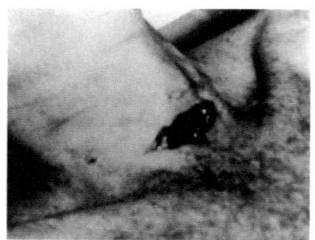
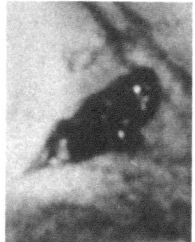

Enlargement, neck and chest (Fox 2).   Enlargement; note semicircle at lower margin.

When Tom performed his image processing, he found that the true nature of this wound was absolutely nothing like what either the Warren Commission or the HSCA had determined. He began by creating a 3-D rendering of the raw video. Then, after tagging the resulting image with pseudocolor, Tom saw two other holes within the larger wound. A bullet hole was in the lower center of the area, corresponding to the HSCA's semicircle. The tracheostomy tube entrance was in the upper right part of the overall wound and less well defined than the smaller, sharper bullet entrance hole.

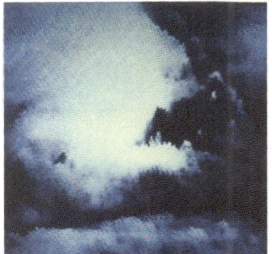
Raw video; 3-D.

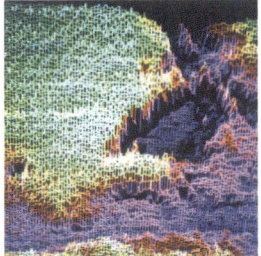
3-D; pseudocolor.

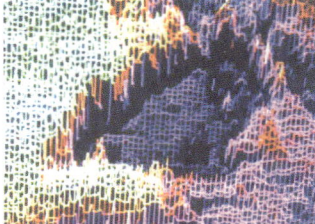
Enlargement; 3-D ; pseudocolor.

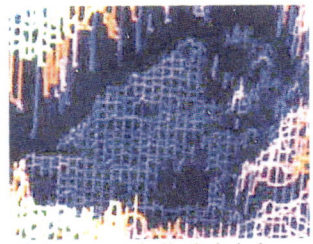
Enlargement; bullet hole in lower center; tube entrance, upper right.

With additional detailed analysis using his layer-stripping techniques, Tom was able to determine that this deformation in the neck was caused in a three-step sequence.

1. The bullet entry hole in the lower center of the neck came first. This hole was smaller than the smallest tracheotomy tube. The bullet passed through the neck on the horizontal, penetrating the tracheal rings and back portion of the posterior wall.
2. In the Parkland Hospital emergency room, the attending physicians made a tracheostomy incision and inserted the tube slightly to the right (looking at the neck from the front) of the bullet entrance hole. The tube was inserted down toward the lungs. This hole is larger and less well defined than the bullet entrance hole in the lower center of the neck.
3. The larger wound was cut sometime after the body left Parkland Hospital in Dallas. It is much larger than a standard tracheostomy incision and, apparently, it was created to make the front neck wound look like a bullet exit hole. However, Tom's image processing revealed that the larger hole did not go deep into the neck – as would be expected from a rear neck entry bullet expanding from back to front. The larger wound is, in

fact, surficial, and was made before the photograph was taken.

Tom next went back and made precise measurements of both this autopsy photograph and his previous processing of the Zapruder film. In comparing them, he found that the location of the small bullet entrance hole in the autopsy photograph's neck wound was identical to the neck wound in frame #225 of the Zapruder film. They were, in fact, one and the same.

Zapruder 225; 3rd layer; pseudocolor (C); Enlarged; bullet hole red (R).

With detailed measurements and analysis of the neck wound, Tom determined that the bullet entered the base of neck, passed through on the horizontal, penetrated the tracheal rings, and exited through the back of the neck. Moreover, the exit wound projection corresponded precisely with the hole in the back of the neck that Tom had previously found through his processing of frame #315 and #316 of the Zapruder film.

 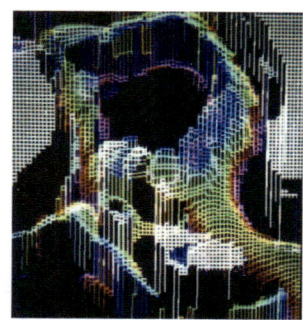

Frame #315; enlarged.   Layer 5; 3-D; digitally expanded

Showing exit hole in back of neck.

After completing his image processing of the center neck wound, Tom went back and took a look at an additional small hole he had observed in the right side of the neck (to the left of center looking at the photograph). He again produced a 3-D rendering of the raw video, tagged the resulting image with pseudocolor, and then focused in on the hole with enlargements.

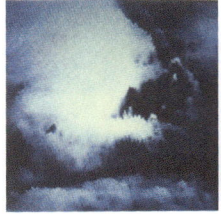 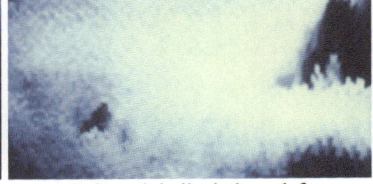 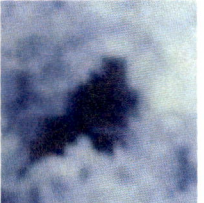

Raw video; 3-D.   Enlarged; bullet hole on left.   Enlarged; bullet hole.

 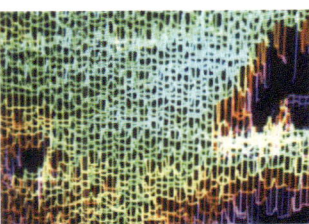 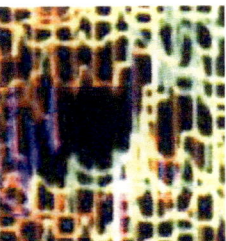

3-D ; Pseudocolor.   Enlarged; bullet hole on left.   Enlarged; bullet hole.

As far as Tom was concerned, the results were conclusive. This was another bullet hole entrance wound. The size and shape was consistent in size with missile entry hole in front of the neck. "My God," thought Tom, "how many other unknown bullet wounds in the body of President Kennedy am I going to find? How many people were shooting at him?"

Disturbed that this new wound had not been reported, Tom went back and reviewed the government's explanation of the President's neck wound. As with the autopsy photos, the Warren Commission had not dealt with the wound in detail and there was no full photograph in either the Report or any the 26 volumes of testimony and exhibits. The HSCA, however, had published a closely cropped picture of the center neck wound from the autopsy photograph (JFK Exhibit F-38). As before, though, the Committee presented only a drawing of the larger picture (JFK Exhibit F-36) and stated that it represented "detail from the photograph showing injury to the front of the neck." Unfortunately, the drawing did not show the bullet entry hole in the right side of the neck. And it had been cropped out of the close-up of the center neck wound.

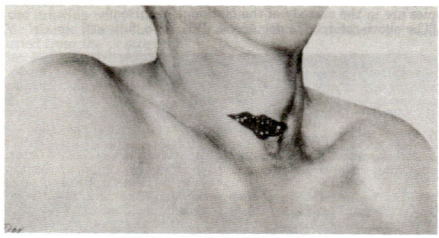
HSCA JFK Exhibit F-36.

HSCA JFK Exhibit F-38.

When Tom saw these renderings, it was obvious to him that the Warren Commission had avoided the issue completely by not producing the autopsy photo, and that the HSCA had purposely hidden the evidence of another bullet wound in the right side of the neck.

* * * * *

Next on Tom's agenda was a look at the left profile and top of head autopsy photos. Despite running a number of different image processing scenarios, he found absolutely no abnormalities in the left profile photograph. In his opinion, it was genuine and had not been altered.

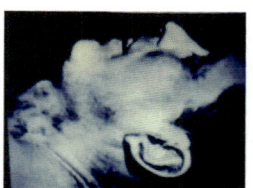 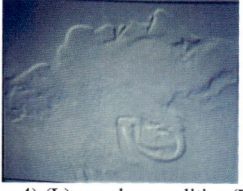
JFK Autopsy Photo, Left Profile (Fox 4) (L); no abnormalities (R).

But when Tom perused the other photograph, his attention was immediately drawn to what looked like a foreign, non-human object within the head amidst the hanging hair and brain material. After running several enlargements, Tom was able to identify a metal object, round on the top with a small cylindrical shaft extending from the round portion on a vertical axis.

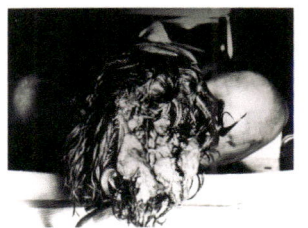

JFK Autopsy Photo, top of head (Fox 7).   Enlargement 1.

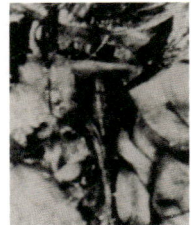

Enlargement 2.   Enlargement 3; close up of metal cylindrical device.

It was obvious to Tom that this device was used to prop up the internal part of the head. But who did it and when was it done? The device certainly wasn't inserted at Parkland Hospital in Dallas. And this particular picture was supposed to be an official autopsy photo taken at Bethesda Naval Hospital before the autopsy began. More importantly, Tom wanted to know *why* it was placed in the head.

After making some precise measurements, which located the cylindrical device above, behind, and to the left (looking at the photograph) of the right eye, Tom decided to take another look at the front head and chest autopsy photograph. He hadn't noticed it before, but there appeared to be excessive swelling above the right eye. And when Tom processed the raw video with a 3-D image, it became even more obvious that the swelling was abnormal and did not appear consistent with the rest of President Kennedy's head and skin.

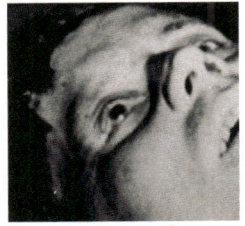
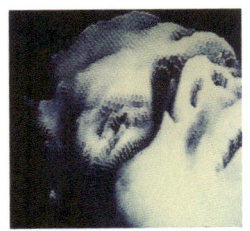

Head and chest autopsy photo, raw video.   Raw video; 3-D.

Tom's previous work had determined that the huge exit hole in the back of President Kennedy's head was caused by a bullet that had entered in the vicinity of the area just above the right eye. So he reasoned that the cylindrical device might have been used to shore up the area inside the head that had been displaced when the bullet passed through.

In addition, as Tom could not see a bullet entry wound above the right eye, he thought the hole might have been filled in or covered over in some manner. In that case, the cylindrical device might also have been used to hold the fill material in place. Of course, at this point, all of this was speculation, and Tom decided to return to the head and chest autopsy picture at some future date to perform a more extended study. Right now, he still had one more autopsy photograph (the back) to analyze for Dr. Wecht.

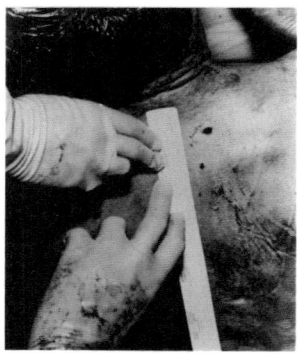

JFK autopsy photo; back (Fox 5).

The first thing Tom noticed about this photo was that there were two individuals holding a ruler on the president's back. One person's partially gloved right hand was holding the top of the ruler while another person's left hand (not gloved) held the bottom part. "Were these the autopsy doctors?" Tom wondered. "Or were one or both of them photographers? Was one of them the same person whose hand was in the other photo?"

Immediately to the right of the top of the ruler, Tom observed three holes (two small and one larger). There was also some dried blood below the holes along with some unusual striations in the skin. At the back of the neck, where Tom expected to see the bullet exit wound he had observed in frame #315 of the Zapruder film, the photo was noticeably darker, there were folds in the skin, and the top hand partially obscured the back of the neck. "I don't see it," he said to himself.

Additional processing verified the presence of three holes in the back (one large, two small). Tom labeled them 12 o'clock, 6 o'clock, and 9 o'clock (with the president's head oriented at 12 o'clock. Detailed measurements revealed that the large hole was in the exact location of the hole (in the back near upper right shoulder) he had documented from his processing of frame #315 of the Zapruder film.

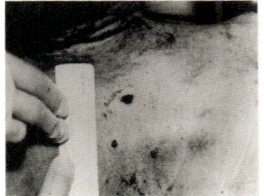

Enlargement; Back (Fox 5).

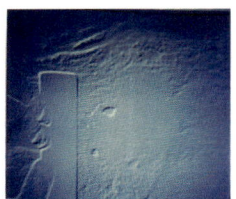

Processing verifies three holes.

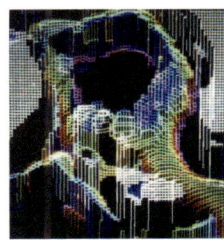

Zapruder film; frame #315; 3-D; Hole in upper back near right shoulder in exact location as 12 o'clock bullet hole in autopsy back photo. Exit hole in back of neck (up and to the left) not visible in photo.

Tom had some lingering doubts that the hole at 6 o'clock might be a spot of blood. But when he had the computer tag only real holes and, he was able to prove conclusively that all three anomalies in the back were holes. With additional processing, Tom was actually able to determine penetration angles and the direction from which the shots came.

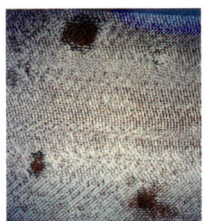

Computer tagged only holes to gray scale and reflectivity.

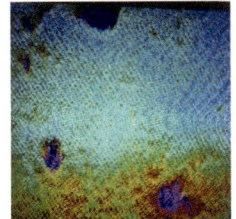

More processing; reveals missile direction and penetration angles.

The hole at 12 o'clock was larger than the other two and had ragged edges, both of which were indicative of a bullet exit wound. Moreover, when Tom went back and took a look at the Zapruder film, he could see that the fibers of the president's coat were pushed outward. More in-depth processing of the autopsy photograph verified that this wound was definitely a bullet *exit* hole that was fired on the horizontal with a very slight downward angle. It must have entered in the front of the chest slightly to the left of center.

Tom also determined that the hole at 9 o'clock, which was small with smooth edges, was an entry hole and that the incoming missile was fired on the horizontal. In looking at a picture taken at the time of the assassination by James Altgens (an Associated Press photographer), Tom believed that the shot was most likely fired from the second or third floor of the Dal-Tex Building (directly behind the limousine). That location offered an unrestricted line of sight directly to the president's upper back.

James Altgens photograph. Dal-Tex Building located on right directly behind the limousine and with unrestricted line of sight to the president.

Tom's image processing and analysis of the hole at 6 o'clock determined that it was produced from a missile entering the president's back at a 45-degree angle to the right and up from the limousine. [This calculation was made by taking into account the posture of the president (as determined from the Zapruder film) and using the spine as vertical axis and the shoulder blade as horizontal axis.] Tom's projection indicated that the shot came from a west window on the upper floor of the Texas School Book Depository. [Note: Both the Warren Commission and the HSCA concluded that all shots fired at President Kennedy came from the *eastern-most* window on the sixth floor of the Texas School Book Depository.]

HSCA Exhibit F-123 (R); Texas School Book Depository and close-up of 6th floor eastern-most window. Analysis shows that 6 o'clock shot to JFK's back originated from a western window on an upper floor (L).

Still concerned that he could not see the exit wound in the back of the neck (from the frontal shot that nicked Kennedy's necktie), Tom surmised that the President's head was manipulated to hide the wound. In the original unaltered portion of the autopsy photo, he believed the head was pushed up and back for the purpose of hiding the wound under the resulting folds of skin. Photographic darkening and the position of the gloved hand holding the ruler father served to obscure the exit wound in the back of the neck.

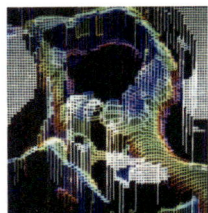 

Zapruder film; frame 315; 3-D; Exit hole in back of neck (up and to the left) not visible in photo.

JFK Autopsy; Back; Enlargement note bullet exit hole; folds in neck.

In addition, Tom went back and looked in more detail at his original processing of the "official autopsy photograph" that he had made from *The Men Who Killed Kennedy*. The neck exit hole was not shown in this photo, but neither were the wrinkled folds. Focusing his series of images exclusively on the back of the neck, it was apparent to Tom that this area had been altered in two stages. The true exit hole was removed with the first matte and then made to look like skin with the second matte.

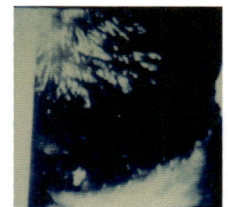
Back of head; raw video (Fox 3).

Enlarged; Neck; raw video.

First processed; no depth=altered.

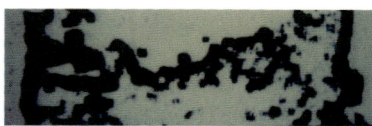
Neck; black area=only area not altered.

Rather than produce the autopsy photograph of the back in its report, the HSCA published a drawing that "shows the back of the President . . . and a perforation of the skin of the right upper back. . . ." In other words, it showed only the bullet hole at 12 o'clock and omitted showing (or even mentioning) the other two bullet holes.

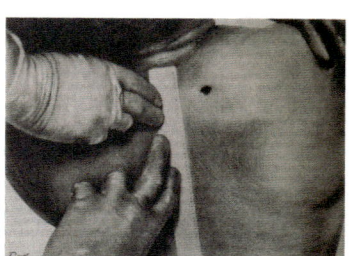
HSCA JFK Exhibit F-20; drawing.

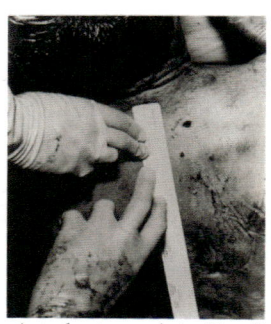
Actual autopsy photo (Fox 5).

A few pages later, the HSCA produced "an enlarged detail" of the autopsy photograph showing only the 12 o'clock bullet hole (omitting the 6 o'clock and 9 o'clock holes). It then concluded that "this perforation was a gunshot wound of entrance characterized uniquely by an abrasion collar, a roughening of the edges around the entrance perforation, which is more apparent in the photographs than the blowup. . . ."

In fact, an "abrasion collar" and a "roughening of the edges" are more indicative of an *exit* wound. An *entrance* wound is characterized by smooth edges.

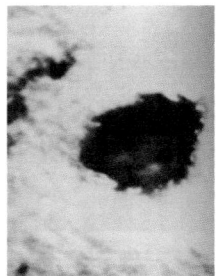

HSCA JFK Exhibit F-22; Cropped photo
showing only 12 o'clock bullet hole.

The HSCA went on to state that the 12 o'clock exit bullet hole in the back was an entrance hole that exited through the "tracheostomy" wound in the center of the president's neck. This was the "magic bullet" that the Warren Commission said went on to hit Governor John Connolly. In essence, both the HSCA and the Warren Commission took two wounds that were caused by two separate shots fired from the front of the president, and then told the American public that both wounds were caused by one shot fired from above and behind.

To reinforce this scenario, the HSCA published two drawings (JFK Exhibit F-46) explaining its version of the neck wounds and their trajectory. The drawing shows "the track that the bullet took through the back, exiting the neck adjacent to the spine, and through the windpipe (or trachea) in the neck," read the report. It shows the direction of the bullet path in the body. This path can be produced by various bullet trajectories, depending on the position of the President at the time the missile struck." The HSCA also cited the original Bethesda Naval Hospital autopsy report, which concluded "that there was a gunshot perforation of entrance in the right upper back and that the exit wound was in the front of the neck."

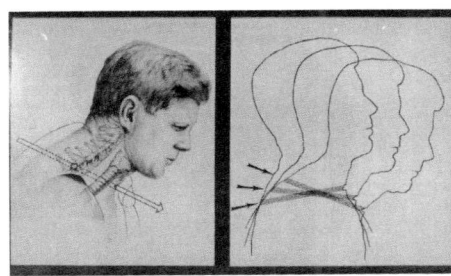 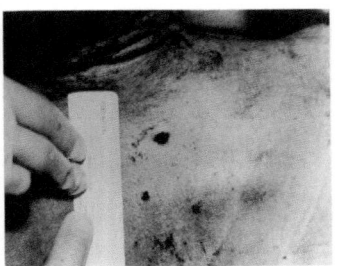

JFK Exhibit F-46   Autopsy Photograph; back.

Because there was so much to be seen in this particular autopsy photograph, Tom sat down and made a sketch of his findings. He drew the vertical spine and the horizontal shoulder blade axes, and then related the bullet holes to them. The larger of the three holes at 12 o'clock was an exit wound, he noted. At 9 o'clock was an entrance wound that came in on the horizontal. At 6 o'clock was an entrance wound fired from a 45-degree angle up and to the right.

Tom noted that he had gone back to look more carefully at the Zapruder film and found evidence for the 6 o'clock bullet hole entrance, but could not see the hole at 9 o'clock. He also sketched in where he believed the exit hole in back of the neck was and how it had been covered by folded skin.

Finally, Tom made it a point to note the two individuals holding the ruler, because they had to have been fully aware of all the president's wounds. The bullet exit and entry holes were obvious – and the photograph had been altered after the picture was taken.

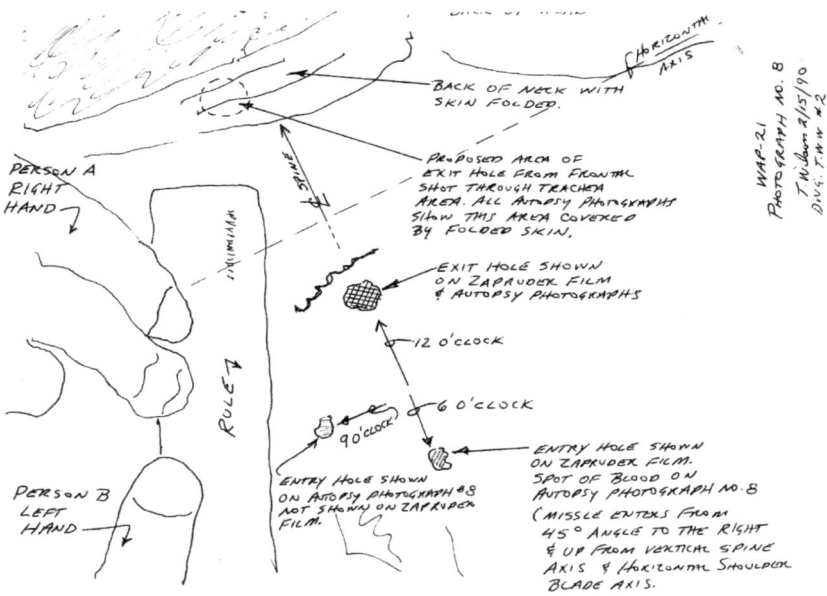

Tom Wilson's sketch of findings after processing and analysis of JFK Autopsy photo of back.

After Tom completed this sketch (on February 15, 1990), he made an appointment with Dr. Cyril Wecht to review his findings. "Some of the autopsy images have been photographically altered to support the official line of a lone gunman firing from behind," he told Wecht. "And I think it's important to point out that the individuals whose hands are seen in the photographs, whoever they were, saw the real wounds, because the photographs were altered in the darkroom after being taken."

While Dr. Wecht listened intently, Tom stated that back in April, when he had tried to get the media interested in his findings, he had assumed that there were only three shots fired at the president. But he was wrong, he said. He could now prove that at least seven shots were fired at President Kennedy – six of which definitely hit him. Then Tom showed him his image processing of all the autopsy photographs.

The evidence proved that at least four shots were fired from the grassy knoll area, he told Wecht. One shot was the entrance hole in the lower center of the neck; two shots came from gunmen dressed as police officers (one of which probably accounts for the bullet entrance hole in the right side of the neck); and one shot entered the president's head above the right eye and blew out the back of the president's head.

Another shot was fired from the front, hit the president in the upper left center of his chest, and exited in the right upper back.

Two shots were fired from the rear of the president. One of these bullets hit the president nearly on the horizontal, and was fired from directly behind the limousine, perhaps from the second or third floor of the Dal-Tex building. The other bullet hit the president at a 45-degree angle, came from above and to the right, and probably originated from of an upper floor on the west side of the Texas School Book Depository.

Finally, Tom gave Dr. Wecht a brief review of his earlier findings with respect to the Mary Moorman photograph and the Zapruder film. "Processing of these autopsy photographs has provided a direct correlation and verifications of my previous findings," he said. "Thanks to modern technology, this 26-year-old piece of evidence, the Zapruder film, now becomes the "Rosetta Stone" that can unlock the key to the truth about the assassination of President Kennedy."

Dr. Wecht paused for a few moments before responding. "Until I saw what you have unveiled, Tom," he finally said, "I never thought I would see the truth come out in my lifetime."

5 / *On The Ground In Dallas*

On November 8, 1990, Tom went to Dallas and walked through Dealey Plaza for the first time. His purpose was three-fold. First, he wanted to take measurements in order to verify the exact positions of President Kennedy and the shooters as seen in his image processing of the Zapruder film and the Mary Moorman photograph. He knew that precise presentation and verification of evidence was important in a court of law. Second, he hoped to verify that one of the shooters behind the fence fired the fatal headshot. And third, Tom wanted to see the scene of the crime for himself – to stand behind the picket fence, to look up at the Texas School Book Depository, and to see the location on Elm Street where John F. Kennedy's life ended.

One of Tom's photographs of Dealey Plaza showing the picket fence on the grassy knoll.

Tom's initial reaction to being on the ground in Dealey Plaza was that everything seemed smaller than what he'd seen in the photographs. The distance from the shooters behind the picket fence to the center of Elm Street didn't seem that far at all. Mary Moorman and Abraham Zapruder were much closer to the President at the time of the shots than he'd realized. It must have been traumatic for Mary Moorman, especially, Tom thought, to have witnessed the president's head explode just a few feet in front of her. What *did* seem far away to Tom was the distance from the so-called sniper's nest on the east side of the Texas School Book Depository to Kennedy's position on Elm Street at the time of the final head shot. Simply standing in the middle of Dealey Plaza made Tom realize the assassination scenario presented by the Warren Commission and the HSCA was highly unlikely.

After looking around and getting the lay of the land, Tom got to work. Using a manual measurement system (tape measure extension, angle error correction, etc.), he took extensive readings of various fixed points in the assassination images. He pinpointed locations of key individuals, including Abraham Zapruder, Mary

Moorman, the shooters behind the picket fence, and President Kennedy at the time of the fatal headshot.

After completing his measurements, Tom returned home, entered all the new information into his computer, and compared it to the extensive mathematical data he had previously captured from the images. He was surprised to find, however, that the measurements taken on the ground in Dallas did not fit with the positions he'd obtained from the assassination images. For instance, Tom could not place President Kennedy at the spot in Zapruder frame #313 when the shooters behind the picket fence were firing, because the projectile trajectory between the two locations was incorrect. And when Tom placed the president four feet farther down the road where the shooters could hit him, Mary Moorman's location was incorrect and Abraham Zapruder was out of place. Tom simply could not make anything fit.

After thinking about it for some time, Tom reasoned that the human measurements he had made were simply inadequate for scientific verification. He was going to have to go back to Dallas and run more tests – only this time he would use a more precise measuring system, one that he would design to be scientifically accurate so as to minimize human error.

Over the next several weeks, Tom created special optical and image processing equipment that would check all angles and locations within Dealey Plaza. For example, he made two types of optical reflectors along with homemade targets that were nothing more than simple metal pie pans with fabric and glass attached to them. Tom also designed a location plan that took into account all of the structures in Dealey Plaza that were still standing in 1990. For instance, he established a fixed datum center at the top apex of the concrete wall on the grassy knoll, which would allow both precise measurement to each important location and accurate comparison of one assassination image to another. Finally, Tom would feed all of his captured data into the computer for analysis.

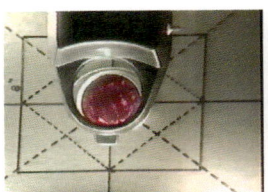 

The two optical reflectors Tom designed to aid in photometric triangulation at Dealey Plaza.

Once all the information was in the computer, rather than using frame rates on the Zapruder film for synchronization of events, Tom would use measured photometric angles. By doing so, he believed he was removing unreliable mechanical devices (such as the camera used by Abraham Zapruder) from the equation. Essentially, Tom eliminated what he called "the fallacy that projecting movie camera speed can accurately be converted into exact location of events." In truth, Tom did not care about the speed of the Zapruder film. Instead, he used actual photometric triangulation gleaned from images frozen in time.

After completing all his preparations, Tom returned to Dealey Plaza on December 17, 1990. And this time, he took his wife, Marcie, who would serve as his field assistant. Once onsite, the two set about establishing a triangulation of viewer, shooter, and victim. Tom brought copies of key frames of the Zapruder film to help in establishing the positions of Mary Moorman (frame #303) and President Kennedy at the time of the fatal headshot (frame #313).

Zapruder film frame #303
Moorman's position (Blue Raincoat).

Zapruder film frame #313
President's position; headshot.

In addition, Tom brought along a copy of the Moorman photograph for use in ascertaining the exact locations of the shooters behind the picket fence, a witness named Gordon Arnold (who claimed to have been standing just in front of the shooters), an unidentified man on the steps, the top apex of the pergola wall, and the pedestal upon which Abraham Zapruder stood.

Mary Moorman photograph
President Kennedy's position.

Upper portion of Mary Moorman photograph.

Man on steps   Shooter   Apex of wall   Zapruder

That morning, Tom was all business. He had Marcie stand in each of these key positions and hold the targets in front of her face while he snapped photographs from various angles.

Dealey Plaza in 1990. Tom's assistant took various positions with target and reflectors.

      On steps   Behind fence   Apex of wall   Zapruder

It must have looked odd to casual observers that day. Tom and Marcie scurrying all over the grassy knoll. Him positioning her in various spots. Her holding pie plates up in front of her face. Marcie even stood in the middle of Elm Street at the location where President Kennedy's fatal headshot occurred. She would stand there during breaks in the flow of traffic while Tom clicked his camera as fast as he could. When the traffic picked up again, she would run to the curb until there was another break.

Tom and assistant at work in Dealey Plaza on December 17, 1990.

Standing on the sidewalk in front of the Texas School Book Depository, and watching this odd scene, was motion picture director Oliver Stone. He was onsite for his new project (titled *JFK*). Before long, a member of the production crew approached Marcie as she moved between locations. "Do you mind if I ask what you're doing?" asked the crewmember.

"Sorry, but I can't tell you," replied Marcie.

Tom had insisted that he and his wife maintain strict secrecy about their work, in part, because he did not want to discuss his findings until he had verified them. But Tom also didn't want to be bothered.

Director Oliver Stone on the set of *JFK*.

During a break for lunch, Tom approached Stone and introduced himself. He explained that he was doing some research on the assassination. Stone, in turn, told Tom that he was making a movie on that very subject. The two then got into a discussion about Tom's image processing system and the kinds of things that could be discerned. "Well, what do you think about a shooter behind the picket fence?" Stone asked.

"There was definitely at least one man firing a rifle at the president from that position, probably two," replied Tom. "They were wearing police uniforms."

"Well, how do you know that?"

"You've heard of the shooter behind the picket fence in the Mary Moorman photo, haven't you?"

"Sure," replied Stone.

"Well, I verified it. In fact, my system produced much more detail than had previously been revealed. There's no doubt in my mind about it. I've seen it. It's proof positive."

During their extended discussion, Tom told Stone about some of his basic findings. The director, in turn, seemed mesmerized – and fascinated that someone had done so much work that had never been made public. The two stood there talking for quite a while as Marcie and members of the movie crew listened. Finally, Stone said that he was hungry and, pointing to a sidewalk vendor a few yards away, said: "Let me buy you a couple of hot dogs."

As they were eating, Tom looked at Stone and grinned. "Is this what they call a Hollywood power lunch, Oliver?" he asked.

After a laugh, Stone said: "Hey, Tom, maybe you can verify some things for us."

"Be glad to help," Tom replied. "Here's my card. Call anytime."

The next day, Tom and Marcie flew back home to Pennsylvania. A few weeks later, Tom received a call from Stone asking him to consult on the movie. "We'd like you to take a look at a bunch of photographs, tell us what you see, and also authenticate some of the things we're seeing," he said.

"Okay, I'm ready, Tom replied enthusiastically.

* * * * *

In the weeks prior to receiving Oliver Stone's call, Tom input all his data into the computer system, processed it, and came up with three major conclusions: 1) The position of the presidential limousine was farther down Elm Street than had previously been represented; 2) The direction of the fatal head shot did not turn out as Tom had expected; and 3) the witness, Gordon Arnold, was definitely standing in front of the picket fence and his account of what happened was probably true.

On November 22, 1963, Gordon Arnold was 23 years old and at home on leave after completing Army basic training during which he spent time on the infiltration course with bullets whizzing over his head. That morning he'd heard about the presidential motorcade and decided to drive downtown with his movie camera and film the event. After parking his car in the lot behind the picket fence on the grassy knoll, Arnold (who was dressed in his Army uniform) walked to the southwest corner and decided a good vantage point would be on the train overpass. As he walked up there, he was approached by a man in a suit wearing a sidearm who pulled out a badge, identified himself as Secret Service, and ordered him out of the area. Arnold then walked back to the fence and looked for a good vantage point when the agent came back up to him and again told him to get out of the area. The young soldier then walked the entire length of the fence, saw the motorcade coming, and began filming.

Gordon Arnold standing in front of the picket fence 25 years after the assassination.

Just as the presidential limousine got right in front of him on Elm Street, Arnold explained that a rifle was fired from behind him, a bullet whizzed past his left ear, and he hit the ground – just as he'd been trained to do in Army basic training. "The next thing I knew, a police officer was standing there over top of me asking me what the hell I was doing," said Arnold. "I told him I was staying down so I wouldn't get hit." The officer, who had dirty hands and was not wearing a hat, then kicked Arnold, asked if he'd been taking a picture, and then demanded the film, which Arnold handed over. The young soldier also described a second policeman standing over him. This individual was holding a rifle, his face was streaked with tears, and he was shaking as if very upset. Arnold said that both policemen then went off to the left behind the pergola. Terribly frightened, he went straight home and, two days later, was in Alaska at his new duty assignment.

Tom Wilson was very interested in Gordon Arnold's story, especially the part where he had described two uniformed officers.

If true, this witness had confirmed Tom's findings that two men dressed as policeman had fired shots at President Kennedy from behind the picket fence. Further research revealed that U.S. Senator Ralph Yarborough, who had been riding with Vice President Lyndon Johnson two cars behind President Kennedy, reported seeing a soldier throw himself to the ground at this very location. "He was down within a second of the time the shot was fired," said Yarborough, "and I thought to myself, 'there's a combat veteran who knows how to act when weapons start firing.'"

Like the shooters behind the picket fence, Gordon Arnold was not readily visible in the Mary Moorman photograph. However, enlargements showed images of one shooter wearing a police uniform and, to the left (looking at the photo), a fuzzier outline of Arnold standing up and wearing a pointed Army cap.

 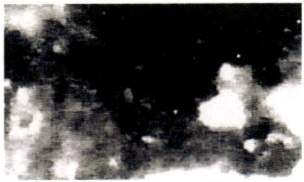

Moorman photograph (L); Enlarged: Arnold image left of shooter (R).

While in Dealey Plaza, Tom carefully checked out the position where Gordon Arnold said he was standing, which coincided with his image in the Moorman photo. As Tom tied the exact spot to fixed geographic points, he measured Arnold's position to the datum target, to the shooter behind the fence, and to Kennedy's position at the time Mary Moorman snapped her photograph. After inputting all the data and processing it, Tom was able to confirm beyond any doubt that Gordon Arnold was standing exactly where he said he was, and that his story about a bullet whizzing past his left ear was true.

Tom's assistant in shooters' position (L); Arnold's position (R).

Through detailed image processing, Tom was also able to demonstrate why critics doubted the presence of both Gordon Arnold and the shooter behind the fence in the Moorman photograph. "They were hidden behind the higher reflective energy of the daylight coming though the image," Tom explained. "Human vision could not see them. Only a computer image processing system could strip away the first layer of visual information to expose the shooter and clarify the figure of the witness."

Tom next turned his attention to analyzing the exact position of the presidential limousine, which he believed to be paramount in verifying the paths of the incoming bullets. Among the many measurements he made included those from the datum target to the shooter, the shooter to Kennedy, the datum target to Kennedy, and Abraham Zapruder's location to that of Mary Moorman, Kennedy, and the datum target.

Tom's precise measurements included
shooter position and datum target to Kennedy's position.

In addition to using the Moorman picture and frame #313 of the Zapruder film, Tom had also obtained a copy of another home movie filmed by assassination witness Orville Nix. At the moment of the crucial headshot, the Nix film showed President Kennedy from an angle behind and to the west of that located in the Moorman image. Triangulation of these three photographic images taken at different angles was far more accurate than counting movie frames, Tom believed. It provided the exact location of the president from three different vantage points at the time of the headshot.

Nix film just before head shot (L), at headshot (C), after headshot (R).

Tom's precise measurements and computer analysis revealed that the when the bullet struck President Kennedy's head, the limousine was farther down Elm Street and closer to the picket fence than depicted in the Zapruder film. Both the Nix film and the Moorman photo showed the limo in the same place, which Tom determined was its true location.

Split screens: Tom's assistant on left, Mary Moorman photo on right. Tom's precise measurements demonstrated that the fatal headshot occurred farther west on Elm Street.

The computer count and verification analysis showed the actual point of bullet impact to Kennedy's head was 7 feet 6 inches farther west than indicated in Zapruder frame #313. In Tom's opinion, this misplacement occurred when the Zapruder film was altered either because of human error, or because the limousine was deliberately moved back for some as yet unknown reason.

 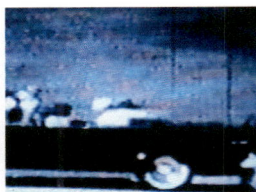 

Headshot at same location in Moorman (L) and Nix (C), but 7' 6" farther west in Zapruder (R).

Fatal shot to JFK's head occurred 7' 6" farther down Elm Street than Zapruder film indicates.

When Tom realized the limousine was farther down Elm Street than the Zapruder film indicated, it caused him to sit back and reanalyze his thinking about the exact point of origin of the headshot. In that position, a shooter behind the picket fence could not have fired a shot that hit President Kennedy in the temple and exited through the back top of his head. Tom had overlooked it all this time, but now it was clear to him. The fatal headshot came from the *front* of the president, not the side. He could not tell exactly where, but there had to be another shooter in the right front of the president's limousine. As this realization sunk in, tears began to well up in Tom's eyes. "For God's sake, how many shooters did they have out there, anyway!" he wondered.

After completing his analysis of the data taken from his time on the ground in Dealey Plaza, Tom catalogued and organized all his information, equipment, and images. He made several detailed diagrams showing the measurements, and he prepared a lengthy video that documented all his work to date.

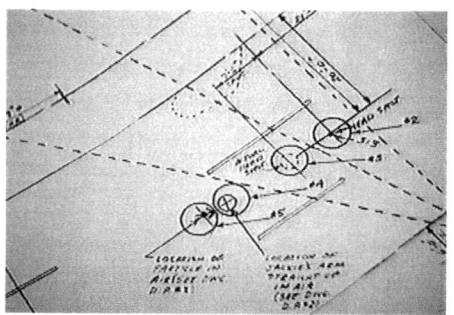

One of Tom's detailed diagrams showing Moorman field of view (dashed lines) and correct location of Presidential limousine.

* * * * *

Armed with knowledge that the Zapruder film was altered, Tom went to Washington, D.C. to perform extensive research at the National Archives. He wanted to view all the copies of the film to see if they were the same. Perhaps there was an outside shot that one copy of the original film might not be altered.

From June 6-10, 1991, Tom was at the Archives facility at College Park, Maryland where the films of the assassination were housed. His first step was to register for formal researcher status, and he was assigned Researcher ID #A91-10670. But when he asked to see the original Zapruder film, he was told that it was not available for viewing. "It is kept in a special storage facility and no one is allowed to see it," he was told. "However, you are free to view all of our copies, Mr. Wilson."

So over the next several days, Tom sat down and reviewed in detail every copy of the Zapruder film in the National Archives. And based on his past image processing analysis of other copies, it was apparent to him that all the Archives copies were altered versions.

Especially obvious was the covering up of President Kennedy's massive head wound.

Tom next turned his attention to where the Zapruder film copies in the Archives had originated. Were they received directly from the Warren Commission, from the House Select Committee on Assassinations, or from Time-Life? Where did they come from? But when Tom began asking for documentation that substantiated the authenticity or provenance of these copies, he ran up against a brick wall. The first member of the staff Tom encountered gave him a copy of a National Archives news release fact sheet on all Kennedy assassination materials. But it did not answer any of Tom's questions. He was subsequently shuffled off to several other offices, but no member of the staff on duty had any idea where such information might be obtained. One individual told him point-blank that there was simply nothing available – not even simple transmittal sheets. "But there must be some documentation," replied Tom. "The American people have a right to this information. We have a right to know the truth."

Back home in Pennsylvania, on July 2, 1991, Tom wrote out a specific request for information from the National Archives. Citing the Freedom of Information Act, he asked for information on the Zapruder film and all other films of the assassination, including the Orville Nix home movie. Among other things, Tom's letter included:

What original films were the copies made from?

Where are these original films located now and are the originals accessible for viewing?

What is the chronological history of the original films, and any copies that your copies were made from? I would request dates, names, locations, and processes used on the making of films and/or videotapes.

Where were your specific copies processed? What type of equipment was used for copying? Who specifically made these copies? Are these the only copies that are and have been made available for viewing at the Archives?

I realize this is quite a large request, but it is mandatory in order to establish the authenticity of these pieces of public evidence. I would appreciate any information that our department has.

The National Archives responded to Tom's letter in a communiqué dated July 16, 1991, which stated that it was "unable to answer completely all questions." Information it did relate included the following:

None of the originals are available for viewing. Only copies can be viewed.

Warren Commission exhibit copies are 8mm copies indicated as 1st generation dupes of the original, plus various 8mm copies and 16 mm enlargements.

The individual who made copies for *Time-Life, CBS,* and others stated that the first copy he made was a 16mm for *Time-Life* and that he improvised because there was no equipment available to copy the 8mm film. From those, he then made contact prints.

The copy of the Zapruder film you viewed was a 16mm enhanced copy received as part of the files from the 1978 House Select Committee on Assassinations.

In our holding, we also have: the original 8mm Zapruder film (held in courtesy storage for the Zapruder family); and various 2nd and 3rd generation copies as received as a donation from *Time-Life.*

The National Archives response then concluded by stating:

We hope this information is helpful to you and we would be happy to answer any additional question within reason. However, you must realize that while we can trace the provenance and our continuous possession of these materials since they arrived in our custody, we cannot after these many years provide names, dates, and types of equipment or copying processes.

After receiving this letter, Tom sat down and jotted down a few notes in his ledger.

"All the images I have analyzed to date have been copied from the same altered film," he wrote. "Is it possible that what they think is a true copy of Abraham Zapruder's film is, in reality, a cleverly contrived forgery and that every image to date is a copy of a copy? The so-called original in the Archives had better not have the head wound altered, or I am afraid there is no original to be found.

"This leads to one question: Is there an original pristine film anywhere?"

6 / *Suspicious Images in Dealey Plaza*

On two separate occasions, February 17-20 and March 6-11, 1991, Tom went back to Dallas and met with Oliver Stone and/or his team of researchers about the assassination of President Kennedy. After extensive discussions, he agreed to use his image processing system to analyze a number of photographs taken in Dealey Plaza on November 22, 1963. Stone's group provided copies of the images, notes about specific areas to focus on, and a list of questions they hoped could be answered.

Back home in Pennsylvania, Tom spent the next six weeks analyzing various aspects of ten separate photographs. He documented his findings at the end of April 1991.

Photo of Three "Tramps"
Approximately ninety minutes after President Kennedy was shot, a freight train leaving the rail yard behind the picket fence was stopped by tower operator Lee Bowers so it could be inspected. Three men, often described as winos, derelicts, or tramps, were pulled off one of the boxcars and taken into custody. As they were being escorted to the police station, George Smith, a photographer for the Fort Worth Star-Telegram snapped their picture. Shown walking were the three "tramps," two police officers with weapons, and a civilian going in the other direction.

George Smith's photo of the three "tramps".

Tom was asked to take a close look at the civilian walking in the other direction, the nameplate on the lead police officer, and whether or not the second tramp was wearing an earpiece. Regarding the man moving in the other direction, Tom was asked specifically if he had an electronic device in his left ear and whether or not he was wearing a class ring on his left hand.

In his analysis, Tom detected a thin piece of wire coming from the rear area of this man's left eyeglass temple piece. The wire went along the bottom of his hairline and into his shirt collar just below the right ear. Tom also determined that this man was wearing bifocals with a conventional straight horizontal line separating the distance correction on the top from the reading correction on the bottom.

  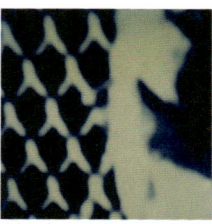

Processing revealed this man had a wire extending from his glasses into his shirt collar.

Tom's analysis also showed the ring on the man's third finger was not a class ring. Rather, it was a solid metal gold or silver wedding band (approximately 1/8 to 3/16 of an inch in width. The man also had a small scar between the ring and his knuckle.

 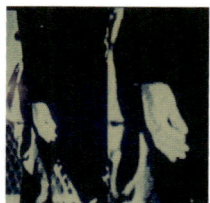 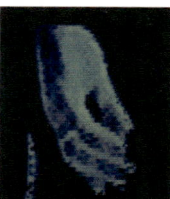

This man also wore a wedding band and had a small scar between the ring and his knuckle.

Regarding the nameplate on the uniform of the lead police officer, Tom reported that it could not be read, because the sharpness of the photo had been reduced when the original negative was created.

Lead policeman's nameplate could not be read due to poor quality of original negative.

Finally, Tom's image processing analysis determined that there was no earpiece in the right ear of the tramp in the back end of the photo. [Note: the third tramp is obscured from view behind this man.]

No earpiece detected in the right ear of the tramp at the back end of photo.

Photo of Deputy Sheriff Buddy Walthers Picking Up Possible Bullet from the Grass.

Dallas car salesman James Tague was caught in traffic that had stopped when the presidential motorcade moved through Dealey Plaza. Stopped on Commerce Street (going in the opposite direction of the motorcade), Tague got out of his car near the triple underpass to watch the procession. No sooner had he turned toward President Kennedy's position coming down Elm Street than he heard shots ring out. Apparently, a bullet hit the curb in front of him, sprayed debris into the air, and one of the pieces of concrete struck Tague in the face.

Moments after the shots were fired, Deputy Sheriff Buddy Walthers was on the scene interviewing James Tague. Joined by a uniformed policeman and a blond-haired man claiming to be an FBI agent, Walthers inspected the curb, and observed the mark apparently made by the bullet. A few minutes later, he was up near the positions of Mary Moorman and Jean Hill on the south side of Elm Street when he noticed something in the grass. By this time, reporters and photographers were swarming all over Dealey Plaza. In a batch of pictures taken by William Allen of the *Dallas Times-Herald* and Jim Murray of Blackstar Photo Service, one shows Walthers leaning down to pick up the object in the grass on the south side of Elm Street, immediately across from the grassy knoll.

Deputy Sheriff Walthers (in fedora hat) leans over to pick up something out of the grass.

Deputy Sheriff Walthers initially stated that he had found a bullet and given it to the FBI agent. In later formal testimony, however, he said it was a piece of the president's skull.

Tom Wilson was asked to determine whether or not there was a bullet in the grass. With his image processing system (programmed to detect metal), Tom quickly pinpointed a possible bullet just below Walther's hand.

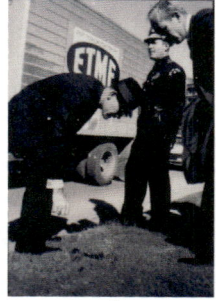  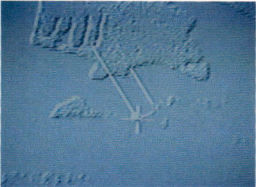

Image processing pinpoints metal object just below Walthers' hand.

"There is a metallic object longer in length than in diameter in the grass," wrote Tom in the write-up of his findings. "It is located at five o'clock between the dark shadow and the curb." Tom produced additional images that focused in on the metallic object, which appeared to be elongated directly in line with the camera angle. "Further analysis with additional work on the negative could prove it was a bullet," Tom stated.

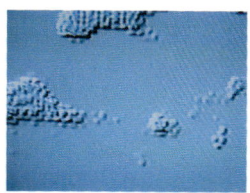 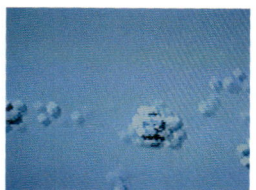 

Progressive enlargements of processed image reveals probable bullet in grass.

Photo of Man Walking Away

Phil Willis, a former World War II Army veteran and amateur photographer, came down to Dealey Plaza with his wife and two young daughters to see President Kennedy. Standing on Elm Street across from the Texas School Book Depository, Willis snapped this photograph (one of several dozen taken) within a minute after shots were fired. It shows the last of the cars in the motorcade near the triple underpass, the press bus passing by, and the backs of a number of people as they walked or ran toward the area where Kennedy was shot.

Photo taken by Phil Willis within a minute of shots being fired.

One of those individuals, the closest to Willis when he took the picture, was later identified as a Navy veteran from Arkansas named Jim Hicks. Some researchers believed Hicks might have been part of a communications team involved in the assassination. Tom was asked to take a look and see if his image processing could identify a handheld two-way radio in his back pocket.

Through enlargements of the photographs and preliminary processing, the man was determined to have light hair with a crew cut. A black object was also seen extending about three inches above his back left pocket.

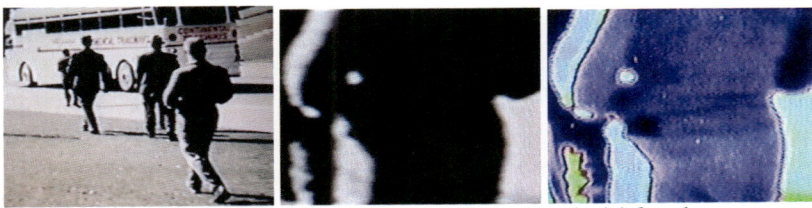
Enlargements and processing focus on object in man's back left pocket.

"Further processing reveals beyond any doubt that the object in his pocket is a communications radio," wrote Tom in his observations notebook. "The radio extends down to the bottom of the pocket and is tilted slightly to the left. The antenna, probably a pull up (not a "rubber ducky"), is slightly off center to the right of the centerline of the radio. The knob of the antenna is sticking up from the top of the radio approximately 1.5 to 2.0 inches."

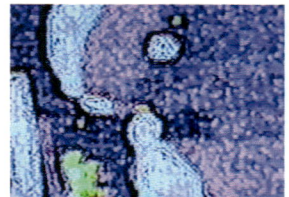 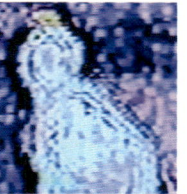

Further processing revealed the object to be a communications radio.

Photo of Man Sitting on Curb

As the ninth car in the motorcade (press car) passed through Dealey Plaza only moments after the shooting, *Dallas Morning News* Staff Photographer Clint Grant (riding in the car) snapped this photograph looking back up Elm Street.

Photo taken from press car by Clint Grant.

At the far right of the picture, a Hispanic-looking man wearing a soft cap and dark glasses is sitting next to a Caucasian man on the north side of Elm Street. As Kennedy's limousine approached the Stemmons freeway sign, this second man opened up his umbrella and furiously pumped it up and down several times. In frame #332 of the Zapruder film, the Hispanic-looking man can be seen standing and holding his right fist in the air just as the first shot hit Kennedy in the neck. Some researchers have suggested that this gesture was some kind of taunt or sign of revenge – and that the umbrella movement was a signal of some sort.

Frame #332 of Zapruder film. Notice man gesturing with fist on right; umbrella on left.

Immediately after the shots were fired, these two men calmly sat down on the sidewalk curb. Many have pointed out that this was strange behavior as other bystanders were either ducking for cover or rushing toward the picket fence.

Enlargements showing two men sitting on sidewalk curb.

Essentially, Tom was asked to take a close look at the Hispanic-looking man to determine if there might be something under his jacket. Because of the poor quality of the photo, however, he was unable to reach any verifiable conclusions. "The different contour levels of the man's jacket are not folds of clothing," Tom noted. "There is an item or items of specific dimensions underneath." He then proceeded to draw a simple sketch of as part of his documentation.

 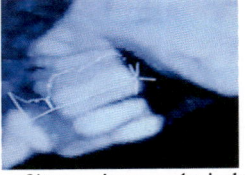

Enlargement and processed image of item or items under jacket.

Tom's sketch of man sitting on sidewalk curb.

Photo of Man Walking Down Elm Street

Several minutes after shots were fired at President Kennedy, a civil engineer from Dallas named Jim Towner took the following photograph as he stood on the south side of Elm Street. As people run toward the triple underpass and the picket fence, the Hispanic-looking man who had been sitting on the curb (as shown in the previously analyzed photograph) is now observed to be calmly walking west on Elm Street. His hands are behind him and he appears to be holding something in his left hand.

Jim Towner's photo taken minutes after the shots.

Tom was asked to take a close look at this man to see if it could be determined what he was holding behind his back. Although the photograph was of poor quality, through enlargements and several variations of image processing, a small camera and a communications radio were detected.

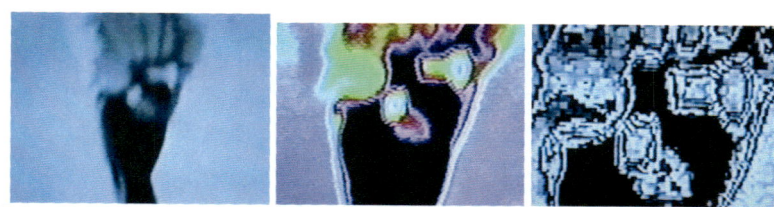

Enlargements, pseudocolor and B&W processing reveal camera and communications radio.

"The man is holding a communications-type radio," wrote Tom in his notebook. "His left hand fingers are wrapped partially around the radio. The palm of his hand is on the device and the back of his hand is against his pants. The antenna is on the right side of the radio as viewed and is in the retracted or down position." Tom also documented details of the small camera. "A strap is visible over his right shoulder. It is connected to a camera that is located about waist height. Attached to the camera is a round metallic flash attachment with an unused flash bulb in the socket of the attachment. His right hand is at his right side. There is nothing in his right hand." All these findings were then documented in another sketch.

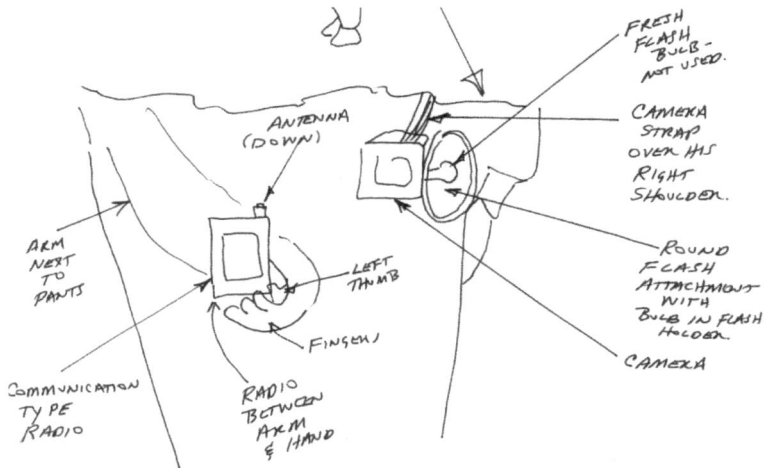

Tom's sketch of the man's back showing radio device and camera.

James W. Altgens Photograph #5

James W. Altgens, a 44-year-old Coast Guard veteran of World War II, was covering President Kennedy's visit to Dallas for Associated Press (for which he had been a professional photographer for twenty-five years). Believing that his best view of the presidential motorcade would be from the top of the triple underpass, Altgens walked up there, but was refused access to the bridge by two uniformed Dallas police officers. After moving to various other locations, he took up a position across from the grassy knoll on the south side of Elm Street (approximately twenty to thirty feet west of Mary Moorman). As the presidential limousine approached, Altgens stepped off the curb into the street and, using a telephoto lens, snapped the fifth of seven pictures he took of the motorcade.

This photograph was taken just a few moments after President Kennedy was struck in the neck by the first shot. It corresponds to somewhere between Zapruder frames #253 and #263. Looking through the windshield of the limo, the president can be seen with his arms up to his throat, his wife's gloved hand holding his left arm. Immediately behind the limousine is the Secret Service car with four agents riding on the sideboards, and three Dallas motorcycle policemen acting as escorts. In the left background is the Texas School Book Depository and, in the right background, is the Dal-Tex building.

James W. Altgens photograph #5 taken moments after Kennedy was struck in the neck.

Tom's assignment was to focus on two specific aspects of this photograph. First, some researchers claimed there was a bullet hole in the windshield of the presidential limousine, and that it may have accounted for the shot that hit Kennedy in the neck (coming from the right front). Could Tom confirm a bullet hole in the windshield?

Using photo enlargements and a series of expanded raw imaging and false color processing, Tom was indeed able to confirm the existence of a bullet hole. It was located in the upper left center of the windshield, and was in a perfect place to have hit the president. If this hole was created by a bullet, it was obviously fired from somewhere in front of the presidential limousine.

  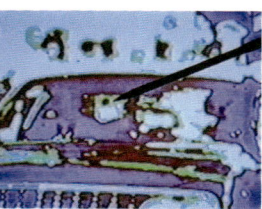
Enlargement and processing show location of bullet hole in windshield of limousine.

  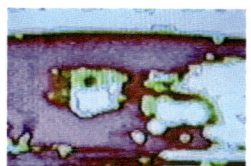
Enlargements, expanded raw imaging, and false color processing confirmed bullet hole.

Tom was also asked to see if he could confirm the suspicions of researchers who believed that one or more shots were fired at the president from the second floor of the Dal-Tex building. They suggested he focus in on one particular open, darkened window on the second floor. This request reminded Tom of his earlier work on the bullet wounds in President Kennedy's back. Afterwards, he had located this same Altgens photograph and surmised that the more horizontal entry wound in the president's back may have been caused by a shot that originated from a lower floor of the Dal-Tex building. Now Tom learned that an early researcher named Harold Weisberg had noted that a man on the fire escape directly above the open window appeared to have fallen backwards. And yet, seconds earlier in a different photographic image, he had been sitting in a normal position. Because of this man's close proximity to this window, Weisberg suggested that a gunshot may have startled him.

Enlargements focus in on man on fire escape just above dark open window.

Tom's first instincts were to simply make a series of enlargements focusing in on the open window. He next created several raw black and white processed images that filtered out some of the extraneous light. With this, he noted in the very bottom portion of the window an unusual elongated device and what appeared to be the left profile of a man.

 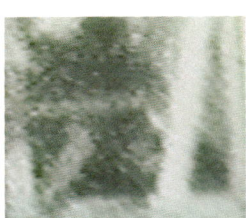 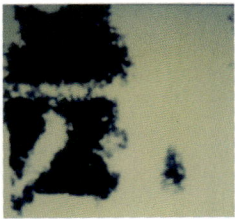

Enlargements and raw processed images of darkened open window reveal an elongated device and the left profile of a man.

Further enlargements and image processing using false color tagging produced more definitive images of both the device and the individual operating it. Tom produced a sketch of his findings and his documentation notebook read as follows:

There is nothing in the left window as viewed. I can see the far wall inside the room. There is some sort of picture on this wall.

In the next partially open window to the right as viewed, there is a profile of the left side of a man's face. He has a beard. His left eye is closed and he is looking through a telescope-type viewer. The telescope-type device is at a 45-degree angle to the vertical axis of the window frame. The device has a small oval tube at the end nearest the window. There are two small protrusions coming out of the device on the side away from the man. The device is apx. 6 to 9 inches in diameter and is apx. 36 to 48 inches long with a 90-degree eyepiece. It may be some sort of long-range accurate weapon, although I am unsure at this point. Currently, I am conducting research to identify the device.

Enlargements and false color tagging reveals man with beard pointing at President Kennedy a telescope-type device that may be some sort of long-range accurate weapon.

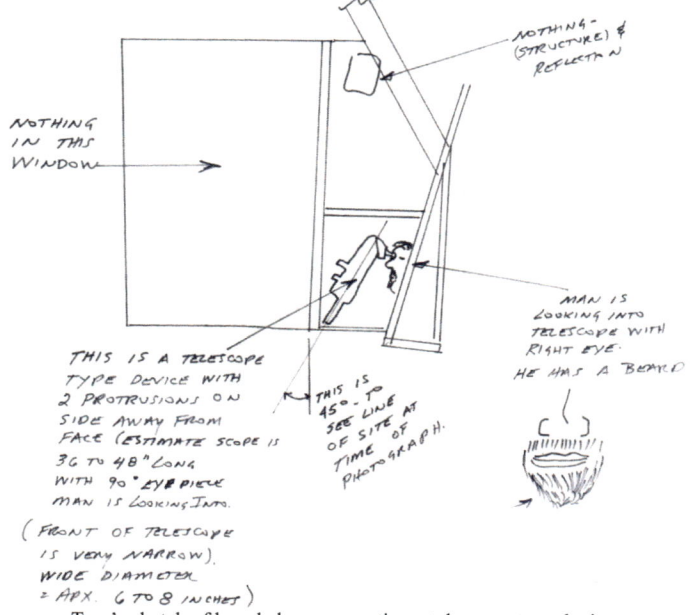
Tom's sketch of bearded man operating a telescope-type device.

Mary Moorman Polaroid Photograph

As if Tom hadn't already spent enough time looking at the Mary Moorman Polaroid, he was now asked to evaluate the windshield of the presidential limousine – both for a bullet that struck the metal trim and for a hole and crack in the glass.

Full-frame, uncropped Mary Moorman Polaroid photo.

Moorman's photograph, some researchers believed, showed clearly that a bullet struck the metal trim just above Secret Service Agent Roy Kellerman's head. Sure enough, when Tom focused in on the area with several enlargements, he could definitely see two deformities, one large, one smaller. In an intermediate enlargement, however, Kellerman can be seen holding some sort of notebook in front of his face. "What is he trying to shield himself from?" wondered Tom.

Enlargement #1 Kellerman shielding face.   Enlargement #2; Agent defect in trim.   Enlargement #3;

Further image processing using black and white, pseudocolor, and layer removal revealed a bullet fragment in the larger deformity. There was no doubt about it. A shot had been fired that missed the president and landed there.

 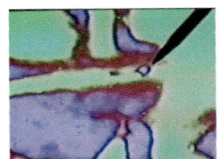 

Enlargement #3, B&W.   Enlargement #3, false color.   #4, 2nd layer, bullet visible.

Employing additional enlargements using the same image processing techniques, Tom was able to focus in specifically on the bullet fragment.

Enlargement #5; layer removed; B&W (L); pseudocolor (C);
Enlargement #6, pseudocolor, fragment visible (R).

Focusing next on the windshield itself, Tom's enlargements delineated a deformity in the glass just to the left of Agent Kellerman. He also observed a cloudy fan-shaped irregularity extending down and to the right. "What's this?" Tom wondered. "It looks like the tail of a comet or something."

Enlargement #2.   Processed B&W white; hole in windshield more visible.

After processing the image using black and white imaging and layer removal, Tom came to the conclusion that he was, indeed, looking at another bullet hole and that the cloudy fan-shaped irregularity was actually a crack in the glass extending away from the hole. In his notebook, Tom noted that if the exact height of the rearview mirror was known, then the exact location of the hole could be pinpointed.

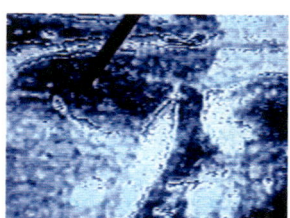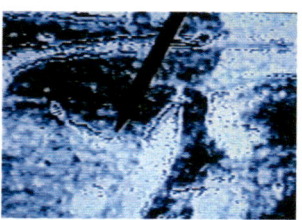

Processed B&W; layer removed; pencil pointing to hole (L), end of crack in windshield (R).

Knowing that he had access to other photographs that showed the windshield at various points in the motorcade, Tom turned his attention to evaluating the timing of the shots. Remembering that Nigel Turner's video *The Men Who Killed Kennedy* showed film of President Kennedy's limousine leaving Love Field in Dallas, Tom pulled out the appropriate image from the video and took a close look. His analysis showed that there was no dent in the trim of the windshield and no bullet holes in the glass. This proved conclusively that there was no damage to the windshield before the motorcade procession began, and that the shots occurred after the limo left the airport, but before Mary Moorman snapped her photograph.

 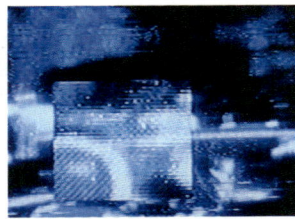

Images of the presidential limousine leaving Dallas Love Field show no damage to the windshield's trim or glass.

Tom then went back and took another look at James W. Altgens fifth photograph. Although he had already proven the existence of one bullet hole in the left front windshield, Tom could not see a bullet hole and crack in the right front (as observed in the Moorman photo). Therefore, the bullet hole and crack must have occurred from a shot fired *after* Altgens snapped this picture and *before* Mary Moorman took her photo – a time span of approximately six seconds.

Tom also noted the relative positions of Secret Service Agent Roy Kellerman in the two photographs. In the Altgens image, Kellerman is sitting in the front passenger seat very close to the limo's door. But in the Moorman photo, he is in the middle of the front seat. Therefore, sometime within a span of only six seconds, Kellerman slid to his left and put a notebook up in front of his face for protection. It was during this time span that the second hole (and crack) in the windshield was created. After making these observations, Tom couldn't help but ask himself the questions: "Did Roy Kellerman somehow know when and from where the shots were being fired? Was he using the notebook to protect his face from splattered glass?"

Altgens #5 (L); no bullet hole in left front windshield; Kellerman seated next to door. Moorman (R); bullet hole in left front glass; Kellerman in middle of seat, shielding face.

James W. Altgens Photograph #6

Moments after the fatal shot to President Kennedy's head, James W. Altgens (still standing on the south side of Elm Street opposite the grassy knoll) turned to his left and snapped the sixth of his seven-shot sequence in Dealey Plaza. The resulting photograph showed the presidential limousine just before it passed through the triple underpass. Secret Service Agent Clint Hill (who had been riding in the next car) can be observed standing on the back bumper pushing Jacqueline Kennedy into the back seat. After the fatal headshot, Mrs. Kennedy had climbed onto the trunk to retrieve a piece of her husband's skull, and Hill had rushed to her aid from the next car.

Altgens #6 taken moments after fatal headshot to President Kennedy. Agent Clint Hill pushes Jacqueline Kennedy back into seat.

Tom's primary reason for taking a close look at this photograph was to confirm or deny the existence of the bullet hole he had documented in the Mary Moorman image. Using the same image processing techniques (enlargements, black and white and false color tagging), he was able to clearly observe the bullet hole in the left front windshield. The position of Agent Clint Hill, however, blocked a view of the right side of the windshield, so Tom was unable to confirm the bullet hole he had observed in the Altgens #5 photo.

 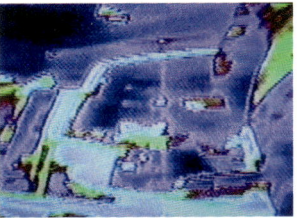

Enlarged and false color tagging reveals bullet hole in windshield glass.

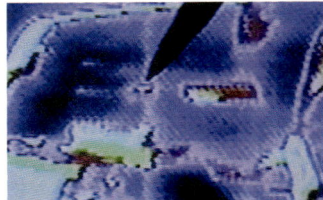 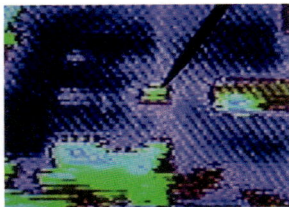

Further enlargement and processing confirms bullet hole in same location as that seen in Mary Moorman photograph.

<u>Photo of "Sniper Window" on Sixth Floor of the Texas School Book Depository</u>

Seconds after shots were fired at President Kennedy, James W. Powell (standing approximately a hundred feet south of the corner of Main and Elm Streets) snapped a picture of the upper south face of the Texas School Book Depository. Powell, trained in investigative photography, was a military intelligence officer assigned to the 112th Intelligence Corps Group's Field Office in Dallas. This photograph revealed a clear view of the southeast corner window on the sixth floor, which has been labeled the "sniper window."

Photo taken by James W. Powell shows clear view of "sniper window" moments after shots were fired.

Tom knew that Powell's photo was of critical importance, because both the Warren Commission and the HSCA had concluded that all the shots that hit the president came from this building. "The shots which killed President Kennedy . . . were fired from the sixth floor window at the southeast corner of the Texas School Book Depository," read the Warren Report, "[and they were] fired by Lee Harvey Oswald." Similarly, the HSCA Report stated: "Lee Harvey Oswald fired three shots at President John F. Kennedy . . . from the sixth floor window of the southeast corner of the Texas School Book Depository Building."

According to government records, Powell turned over his photograph (a 35 mm color slide) to the FBI on January 2, 1964. However, it did not appear in the Warren Report or the Warren Commission's Exhibits. The FBI eventually released Powell's photograph in 1976 and it eventually was entered into the files of the House Select Committee on Assassinations. Although no detailed photograph image analysis was performed, the final HSCA Report did include a copy (Exhibit F-123).

Texas School Book Depository
Arrow pointing to "sniper window."

HSCA Ex. F-123; Powell photo.

Because some researchers believed they could see the faint image of a person in the window, Tom was asked to focus in on the "sniper window" to see if anybody was there. If so, could the individual be identified as Lee Harvey Oswald? Or was it someone else?

Powell Photo enlargements focusing in on "sniper window."

With another enlargement and image processing removal of the first layer, the left profile of an individual came into view. Tom's initial reaction at seeing this image was that the area in the right portion of the window had been faked. However, as he continued with his work, he concluded that there was no forgery involved. Rather, the optical processing and enhancement for human eyes, along with gray-scale separation and enlargement, actually destroyed and distorted about 80 percent of the spatial gray scale information. The image was real – and the left profile was, indeed, a person.

 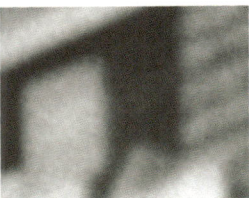 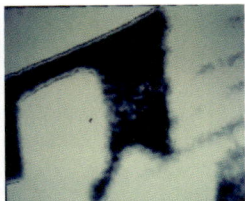

Additional enlargement and image processing reveals the left profile of an individual.

After extensive image processing analysis, Tom documented the following in his notebook:

A male figure in the right portion of the window is looking down to his right. A line of site analysis shows he is looking at approximately the area where Mary Moorman is standing.

He is wearing a military-type beret that has a large spread eagle sewn on it. The eagle is made of cloth and its color is white or very light tan.

He is wearing a military-type oval earphone made out of rubber and plastic. The headphone set has a small microphone attached to the headband that goes under the beret. Wires are seen going from the microphone to the earpiece and up the headset headband.

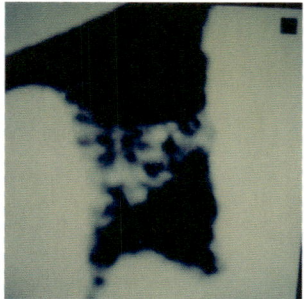 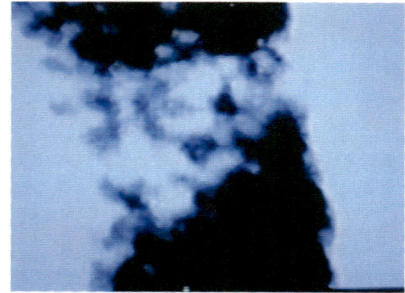

Further image processing reveals a man wearing a beret, headphone, and microphone.

As his analysis continued, Tom focused in on the face of the individual. "He has a very large bulb-type nose (similar to the actor/comedian W.C. Fields)," wrote Tom. "His left eyelashes are very long. His left cheek is slightly puffy. He has a tattoo or sticker patch on his left cheek. The tattoo is: 'F9' with a smaller 's' below. The '9' is about two-thirds the size of the 'F' and the smaller 's' is at an angle (perhaps italicized)."

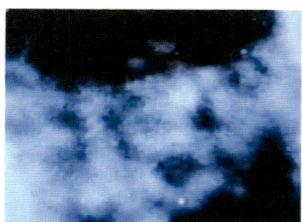 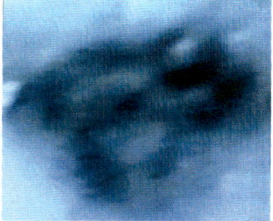

Man with bulb nose, long eyelashes, tattoo (L); Close-up of tattoo: "F9" with small "s" (R).

Upon completion of his analysis of the Powell photo, Tom looked at the man in the sniper window and shook his head negatively. "Well, this is certainly not Lee Harvey Oswald," he said to himself. "He is obviously a military man of some sort. And with all this communications gear, and given the vantage point from this window, he may have been coordinating the shooting with others in Dealey Plaza." Rather than speculate beyond this comment, Tom decided to draw a sketch of his observations and leave it at that – at least for now.

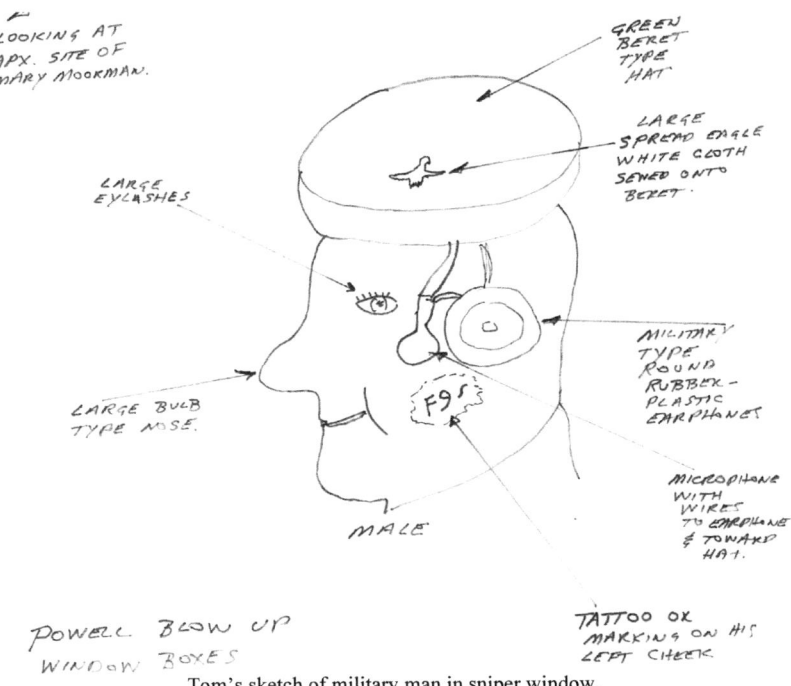

Tom's sketch of military man in sniper window.

Once Tom had performed image processing of all the photographs, he recorded a video of his findings and sent a summary report to Oliver Stone. During this phase of Tom's journey into the assassination of President Kennedy, he had evaluated ten photographs and identified what he considered to be both suspicious people and new evidence in Dealey Plaza.

Tom's identification included numerous men with communications devices, Secret Service Agent Roy Kellerman's movements in the front seat of the presidential limousine while shots were being fired at the president, and a telescope-type device (possible weapon) on the second floor of the Dal-Tex Building. His new evidence included two bullet holes in the glass windshield of the presidential limousine, a bullet fragment and dent in the trim of the presidential limousine, a bullet in the grass, and a military man in the sniper window of the Texas School Book Depository who was definitely not Lee Harvey Oswald.

As Tom began to digest the fact that Oswald might not have fired any shots at President Kennedy, he became curious. "Just where was Lee Harvey Oswald when the shooting was going on, anyway?" he asked himself. "Was he really a patsy, as he claimed when he was in police custody? And what about those famous pictures of Oswald in *Life* magazine with the rifle and revolver? Were they really faked as some researchers believed? Hmmm. I wonder what my image processing system might reveal?"

7 / *The Oswald Backyard Photographs*

According to the Warren Commission, sometime between March 2 and April 24, 1963, Lee Harvey Oswald's wife, Marina, took two pictures of her husband in the backyard of the small house they were renting at 214 West Neely Street in Dallas. He was dressed in black, wearing a pistol, and holding a rifle and two communist newspapers (the *Worker* and the *Militant*).

The two backyard photographs discovered by local police on November 23, 1963.

Six or seven months later, on November 23, 1963 (the day after President Kennedy was killed), police officers "obtained a search warrant and examined Oswald's effects" at the home of Michael and Ruth Paine in Irving, Texas, where the Oswalds had been staying. During the search, officers discovered the backyard photographs in the garage. However, the black clothes worn in the pictures were not found and the photos, themselves, were not listed on formal inventory sheets of Oswald's possessions.

"These photographs were shown to Oswald on the evening of November 23 and again on the morning of the 24th," read the Warren Report. Oswald replied that he had never seen the photographs before and that he did not own a rifle. The photographs, he said, were composites. Noting that he had been photographed by the police while in custody, Oswald speculated that someone must have superimposed his head over someone else's body. He knew something about photography, he said, and at the proper time he would show that the pictures were fakes.

These backyard photographs played a major role in convincing Americans that Lee Harvey Oswald was the lone assassin who killed the president. They portrayed him as a gun-toting communist who might kill for political reasons. They linked him to the supposed murder weapons of both Kennedy (rifle) and Police Officer J. D. Tippit (pistol). And the timing of these photographs indirectly tied him to the order, purchase, and delivery of the rifle. Moreover, the photos were consistently kept in the public eye. The Dallas Police Department, for instance, released the backyard photographs to the press on November 23, 1963 – the very day they were found. Then, on February 21, 1964, *Life* magazine placed one of the pictures on its cover with a caption that read: "LEE OSWALD with the weapons he used to kill President Kennedy and Officer Tippit." Seven months later, when the Warren Report was released (September 27, 1964), the backyard photos were found front and center in Chapter IV: The Assassin. "The Commission has concluded that the rifle shown in these pictures is the same rifle which was found on the sixth floor of the Depository Building on November 22, 1963," read the report. "The rifle used to assassinate President Kennedy was owned and possessed by Lee Harvey Oswald."

Cover of *Life* magazine; February 21, 1964.

Warren Commission Exhibit No. 134.

In an attempt to thwart speculation that the photos might be fake, the Warren Commission specifically addressed the issue of authenticity. It noted that FBI Special Agent Lyndal L. Shaneyfelt, a photography expert, "photographed the rifle used in the assassination attempting to duplicate the position of the rifle and the lighting" in the photographs. Subsequently, Shaneyfelt "linked the actual rifle with the rifle in the photograph. . . " and then testified that, by creating a simulation photograph, he was able to determine "the photographs were not composites of two different photographs and that Oswald's face had not been superimposed on another body." As a result, the Warren Commission determined that "the authenticity of these pictures has been established."

However, over the next decade, photographer and JFK Assassination researcher Jack White of Fort Worth, Texas produced compelling evidence that both of the backyard photographs were, indeed, forgeries. His work, in part, led to the creation of the House Select Committee on Assassinations (HSCA), which spent several years (1976-1979) investigating the assassination. During that time, a photographic evidence panel scrutinized the pictures using stereoscopic techniques, photogrammetry (the science of ascertaining the positions and dimensions of objects from measurements of photographs), and computer digital image processing.

HSCA Figure IV-37: Edge analysis of CE 133-B utilizing digital image processing.

In its final report, the HSCA stated: "The photographic panel found no evidence of fakery in the backyard photographs," and that "Lee Harvey Oswald owned the rifle from which the shots that killed President Kennedy were fired." Therefore, both the Warren Commission and the HSCA investigations judged these incriminating photographs to be authentic.

* * * * *

After spending considerable time studying the history of the backyard photographs, Tom sent out several letters to the U.S. Government requesting information under the Freedom of Information Act. He asked the National Archives to send him anything they had on the simulation photograph created by the FBI for the Warren Commission. Two weeks later, he received a reply stating that they had no data or documentation, but would send them a copy of the photo. Tom then fired off a letter to the Director of the FBI requesting copies of all data and information related to the backyard photographs. After six weeks passed with no response, Tom sent another letter in which he reiterated his request, but this time he was more specific. "Please send me Agent Lyndal L.

Shaneyfelt's files on the analysis of the Oswald photos and the rifle," he wrote.

While waiting for a response from the FBI, Tom spent considerable time communicating with Jack White about White's work on the backyard photographs (White was one of the researchers on Oliver Stone's team). Through those discussions, it became apparent that one of the big controversies about the backyard photographs was the inconsistency of shadows cast by the sun on Oswald's figure. "Well, if there are inconsistencies in the shadows," thought Tom, "that means they cannot be used to determine the time of day the photographs were taken."

In his research, Tom learned that the time the photographs were taken had been critical to the Warren Commission's determination that Lee Harvey Oswald was the lone assassin of President Kennedy. "The dates surrounding the taking of this picture and the purchase of the rifle," read the Warren Report "reinforce the belief that the rifle . . . was shipped from Klein's [Sporting Goods] in Chicago on March 20, 1963, at a time when the Oswalds were living on Neely Street." After stating that the Commission had determined the dates on the two communist newspapers, the Report went on to point out that Marina Oswald testified that she had taken the photographs on a Sunday afternoon about "10 days prior to the attempt on Major General Edwin A. Walker's life (April 10, 1963)." The Warren Commission then inferred that the backyard photographs were taken on March 31, 1963, at a time when "Oswald had undoubtedly received the rifle shipped from Chicago on March 20, the revolver shipped from Los Angeles on the same date, and the two newspapers which he was holding in the picture."

More than a decade later, the HSCA verified the Warren Commission's timing, in part, based on its own study of shadows in the backyard photographs. "Given the view shown in the backyard photographs, it is possible to estimate that the camera was aimed about 70 degrees east of north," read Volume VI of the findings. "The shadows in the photographs indicate that the sun was behind and to the right of the camera. Since this would place the sun in the southwestern sky, it was afternoon, and the sun was going down."

As Tom looked closer at the photograph labeled WC Exhibit 133-A, he noticed that the sun was reflecting off Oswald's black shoes. "I wonder if I can calculate the actual timing of the photograph based on these reflections?" Tom thought to himself.

Warren Commission Exhibit 133-A; enlargements showing sun reflecting off shoes.

Image processing quickly revealed that the shoes had been polished with a military-type spit shine, which enhanced the sun's reflections. After isolating the reflections and viewing them in three dimensions, Tom was able to calculate that the sun was, indeed, the one source of light creating them. This determination was based on a concise plot of the sun from sunup to sundown in the Dallas area on March 31, 1963 (data obtained from a well-known science center). "The reflection of the sun on the shoes were correlated to the angular zenith of the sun's travel," wrote Tom in his notebook. "Correlation of this data with the reflection date shows that if the photograph was taken on Sunday, March 31, 1963 in Dallas, then the exact time of day was 9:12 a.m."

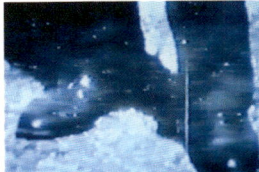 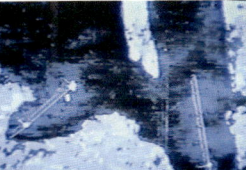 

Processing shows military spit shine on shoes. Sun reflections then isolated and measured.

Because Tom's findings were so at odds with both the Warren Commission and the HSCA, he felt that the time of day that the backyard photographs were taken was now in question. And since the exact date had never been nailed down, it was also in question. Therefore, Tom reasoned that the photos could have been taken at any time. The background could have been obtained well after the Oswalds lived on Neely Street. And if Oswald's face had been superimposed on another body, as he stated during his interrogation by Captain Will Fritz, then it could very well have been done within a couple of weeks of November 23, 1963.

As Tom continued his detailed analysis of both backyard photographs, he found additional inconsistencies bolstering the argument that they were, indeed, forgeries. The four major inconsistencies in Tom's analysis were:

1. <u>The height of the individual taking the pictures.</u>

When the centerline of the focal plane of the photographs and lens of the camera to ground level was checked, the camera was at waist level of a person approximately 5 feet, 11 inches tall. Marina Oswald, who was alleged to have taken the pictures, was only 5 feet 3 inches tall.

2. <u>Physical dimension of rifle versus the Oswald figure don't match.</u>

Using the rifle dimensions related in the Warren Report as the measurement basis, the computer count (of consistently sized units) shows that Oswald's physical dimensions do not agree. And using Oswald's physical dimensions given in the Warren Report as the measurement basis, then the rifle dimensions do not agree.

3. <u>Communist newspapers, the *Militant* and the *Worker*.</u>

The newspapers being held by the Oswald figure are longer than their actual length and do not agree with any other measurements provided by the Warren Report (including the size of the rifle and Oswald's height).

4. <u>The heads in the two photographs are of different size.</u>

Measurements in consistent computer-counted units do not match. Comparison measurements included: distance between the eyes, between the ears, across the neck, and from the top of the head to the bottom of the chin.

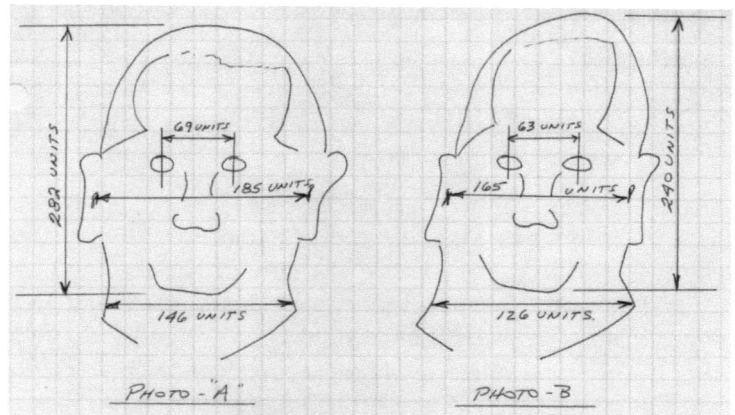

Tom's sketch of measurements showing size of heads in two photographs are different.

During his ongoing image processing analysis, Tom was able to conclusively demonstrate that both pictures (WC Exhibit 133-A and WC Exhibit 133-B) had been photographically altered. The face of

Oswald had, indeed, been superimposed on another head and body – and other areas of the figure were a combination of two different photographs.

After performing his work, Tom concluded that the following parts of WC Exhibit 133-A had been either altered or added: most of the face, the shadow under the nose, part of the mouth, portions of the ears, the entire chin, part of the neck, the newspaper (in its entirety), part of the right arm, all of the right hand, and the fingers of the left hand.

Processing of Photo 133-A reveals additions to include: face, arm, hands, chin, neck, portions of ears and rifle, and the entire newspaper.

In addition, the following parts of WC Exhibit 133-B had also either been altered or added: most of the face, the shadow under the nose, part of the mouth, portions of the ears, part of the neck, the entire chin, part of the rifle (stock, end, and strap), the newspaper (in its entirely), part of the left arm, and the fingers of the right hand.

Processing of Photo 133-B reveals additions include: portions of face, mouth, chin, rifle, fingers of right hand, left arm, rifle strap, and neck.

Next focusing in on the face, Tom tried various image processing effects until he could see the alterations in solid white. On Photo 133-B (as in 133-A), it appeared as some sort of mask. "Why, that looks like something a hockey goalie might wear," Tom muttered to himself. The eyes were cut out, as were part of the shadow beneath the nose and part of the mouth. These areas might not have been altered. The white areas, however, definitely represented changes, including most of the face, the chin, part of the mouth, and portions of the ears.

 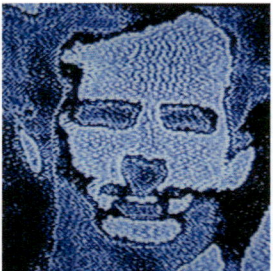 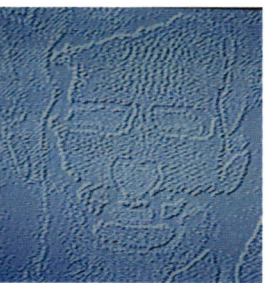

Original; 133-B (L); Mask of face (C), note eyes, shadow under nose and mouth not altered; Additional processing (R) confirms alterations.

Additional processing of the mask image (using pseudocolor), revealed the eyes under the mask. The right eyeball in both photographs appeared white and was obviously abnormal. Tom's preliminary investigation suggested that it might be artificial, possibly glass. This abnormality of the right eye proved that the figure in both of the Oswald backyard photographs was the same person – but it was not the Lee Harvey Oswald arrested in Dallas on November 22, 1963.

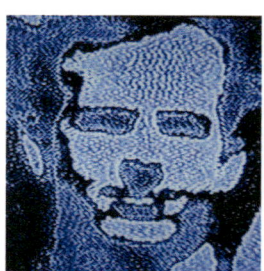 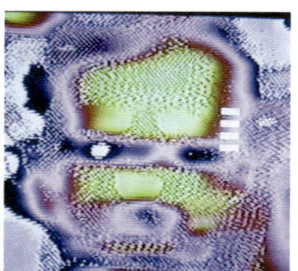

Additional processing reveals eyeballs under mask of face. Chin gone and right eye is abnormal, appears white, and artificial (possibly glass).

Tom subsequently took the image of the mask and removed an additional layer. The new image showed various white patches that obviously denoted specific additional areas of alteration. The eyes were darkened to hide the abnormal right eye. Part of the shadow under the nose was darkened or changed in some way. Also appearing altered were the cheeks, the lower part of the left ear, and the area under the chin.

  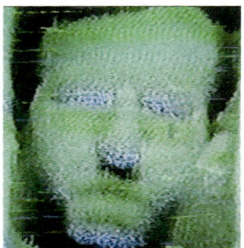

Original; 133-B.   First layer removed. revealing mask effect.   Second layer revealing alterations below mask.

When the next outer layer of information was removed, a closer representation of the true face of the overall body was revealed. In a video prepared to document his findings, Tom gradually removed this next layer from left to right. The following photographs reveal that removal in quarter stages.

 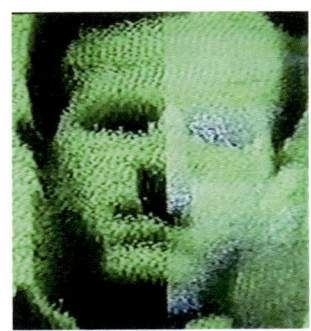

Third layer: 1/4 removed.   Third layer: 1/2 removed.

Third layer: 3/4 removed.   Third layer: all removed.

Removal of this layer revealed a man that had a larger nose, puffier cheeks, and a significant difference in the lower portion of both ears. He looked even less like Oswald's arrest mug shot.

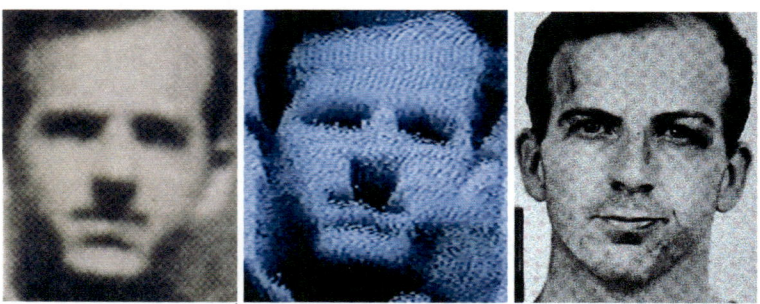

Original photo (133-B) (L); 3rd layer removed (C); Mug shot taken on November 23, 1963 (R).

The overall quality of the images prevented Tom from removing additional layers of information. However, he was able to conclusively demonstrate that the backyard photographs were fakes. More pristine copies, combined with more advanced image processing techniques, he believed, could eventually reveal a complete and accurate representation of the real face attached to the body in the Oswald backyard photographs.

* * * * *

In the fall of 1991, Tom was invited to speak at the Assassination Symposium on John F. Kennedy in Dallas, which was held from November 12-17, 1991. It was his first chance at a legitimate forum where he could showcase his findings. With the endorsement of Dr. Cyril Wecht (who also spoke at the conference), and with his experience as a consultant for Oliver Stone now on his resume, Tom was given a key presentation slot.

Prior to the Dallas Conference, tremendous interest in the Kennedy Assassination had been generated due to the impending release of Oliver Stone's movie *JFK*. Leading up to the film's December debut, much of the mainstream print media launched blistering attacks against Stone for even suggesting that Lee Harvey Oswald was not the lone assassin. *The New York Times, The Washington Post,* the *Los Angeles Times,* the *Miami Herald,* the *Chicago Tribune,* and *Time* magazine all ran negative articles trashing the film before it hit movie theaters across the country.

Tom was shocked at all the personal attacks on Oliver Stone, so he vowed to make as good a presentation as he possibly could. Before leaving home, he prepared a videotape of called "Montage of Conspiracy," which included only images, as he decided to provide the sound with his own voice during the talk. Then, after receiving a letter from Oliver Stone granting him permission to publicly release any and all of the consulting work he had performed for the director, Tom packed up and paid his own way to Dallas.

On November 15, 1991, Tom presented his work to an audience of approximately 200 people interested in the assassination of John F. Kennedy. Despite the fact that there was loud noise raging from a party of U.S. Secret Service agents in the next-door ballroom, Tom mesmerized his audience for more than two hours. He talked about smoke from behind the picket fence, two gunmen firing one-fifth of a second apart, the camera to their right, the police uniform, the badge, the mole on one shooter's cheek, and the eye of that shooter. "I can tell you right now that his eyes are brown," said Tom. Then he went through his other research: the altered autopsy photographs, the bullet wounds in President Kennedy's body, the direction of the shots, his analysis of the Zapruder film with its matte inserts masking the president's head wound, the parts of brain and skull flying through the air, the head wound itself, the faked backyard photos, and most of his other findings.

Reactions to the presentation were mixed. Many in the audience came up and congratulated Tom on his groundbreaking research. The next day (November 16, 1991), a story appeared in the *Dallas Times Herald* in which Cyril Wecht called it "beautiful work." Mark Potok, the article's author, probed the methodology. "Nothing is theory," replied Tom, "Nothing is speculation. The process is like looking at a photo of a darkened door leading into a hallway, which looks black to the human eye." The writer went on to state: "His method 'peels away' the layers of gray, going deeper and deeper and picking up shades invisible to the eye. In the end, with the computer [processing of] the grays to make them visible, you will see the man who is standing at the end of the hall."

Potok sought out the reaction of David Belin, one of fourteen assistant counsels to the Warren Commission, who had been savagely attacking Oliver Stone's *JFK*. "It's a series of massive lies," the *Times-Herald* quoted Belin as saying of Tom's work. "The man is basically making an outrageous claim." Also tracked down for comment was G. Robert Blakey, who had served as chief counsel and staff director for the House Select Committee on Assassinations. Potok quoted Blakey as saying about Tom's work: "You know the saying among computer people, 'garbage in, garbage out'? This is garbage."

When Tom read these comments, he became angry. "I know I've presented evidence that contradicts findings of both the Warren Commission and HSCA, but that's no reason for them to attack me personally," he told Marcie. "Besides, I don't believe either one of them have seen my work. They weren't at the presentation yesterday. Heck, I don't think they were even in Dallas!"

After being contacted by a local attorney who *was* in the audience, Tom filed a defamation lawsuit (under Texas law) against Belin and Blakey that made national headlines. He brought the suit for two reasons. First, Tom wanted the defendants to pay for the outrageous remarks they had made about him and his work. And second, he believed that the lawsuit might provide a legal forum for him to present the new evidence he had uncovered about the assassination.

The lawsuit lasted for years and many depositions were taken. Among them was one by Oliver Stone, who stated: "Belin has made speeches, given public appearances (including appearances on network television), and has written letters and articles that were published in newspapers and magazines around the country which have attacked me, the movie *JFK*, and people associated with the movie. He has unjustly called us liars and profiteers."

Tom's lawsuit was eventually dismissed for jurisdictional reasons by a local judge who ruled that the defendants had insufficient ties to Texas. And even though the appeals process went all the way to the Supreme Court, Tom lost in the end.

* * * * *

Upon returning home to Pennsylvania, Tom was surprised to be contacted by some national media outlets. A representative of *Newsweek* magazine interviewed him in the lobby of the Sheraton Hotel in downtown Pittsburgh, after which Tom sent pertinent information for the story that he was told the magazine would be printing. Representatives of the ABC news magazine *20/20* also contacted Tom and asked for key information regarding his findings, which he sent along. However, neither *Newsweek* nor *20/20* ever published a story, nor did Tom ever hear from them again.

Meanwhile, in his never-ending quest to obtain government data on the Oswald backyard photographs, Tom finally received a reply from the FBI stating that they had reviewed his "FOIA Request #362,349 with personnel familiar with the JFK assassination" and had been unsuccessful in locating any information. However, they further stated, "We have 202,134 pages in the file and if you send us a check for $20,203.40, we will copy the documents and forward them to you."

As if all he had been through in dealing with the United States Government and its supporters of the lone assassin story hadn't been enough, Tom was sitting at his workstation on January 12, 1992 at 2:00 p.m. when the telephone rang. "Is this Tom Wilson?" asked a man with a heavy Spanish accent.

"Yes, it is," replied Tom casually.

"You and Dr. Wecht should not talk about the shooter like that. You will be hearing from us."

"What is your name, sir?" asked Tom.

The caller hung up.

8 / _X-Rays and More_

In the wake of Tom's Dallas presentation, he was contacted by a number of concerned citizens and credible researchers familiar with various aspects of the Kennedy assassination. They provided him with additional autopsy photographs and two x-rays purported to be of the president, and requested an evaluation of the actual condition of the body. "Are these images genuine?" they asked. "Or are they altered?"

Similar to other autopsy materials he had studied, Tom found that these new images did not reflect any of the damage to the president's face, eyes, and head that he had observed in the Moorman photograph and the Zapruder film. But upon generating an early processed image of one of the new photos, he was especially stunned to observe what appeared to be restorative artwork on the head. "What's this?" Tom wondered. "The face, the right temple area, the back of the head – all appear to have been altered. Could it have been done by professional morticians?"

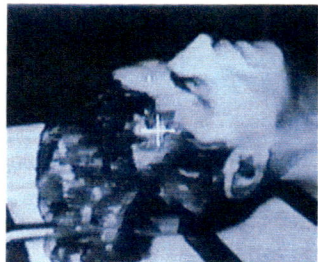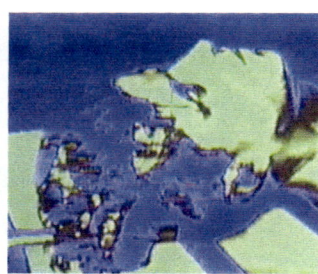

Early image processing of autopsy photograph appeared to reveal restorative artwork.

Rather than speculate on what he was seeing, Tom decided to undertake an image processing study of restorative art on cadavers. If this was, indeed, what happened to President Kennedy's body, he wanted to prove it beyond any doubt by comparing his full range of imaging optics and computer protocol on known cadaver art restoration with those of the autopsy photographs.

With Dr. Cyril Wecht providing guidance and assistance on gathering information and subject materials, Tom obtained books, videos, and certified photographs of work performed by licensed professional practitioners in all stages of the craft. He studied techniques used on cancer victims, burn victims, accident victims, and specifically analyzed images of such restorative materials as wax, powder, artificial devices and other cosmetics. With the face of one individual, for example, Tom was able to isolate the various stages of restoration by stripping away the layers and tagging pseudocolors to the resulting images. Wax stood out as a clearly definable material when applied to parts of the head, including the ears, eyes, nose, and other areas of the face. After extensive experimental study, Tom found that his image processing system could clearly detect the difference between natural parts of the body and the non-human materials that had been added.

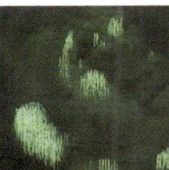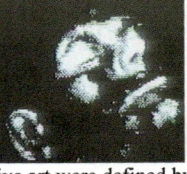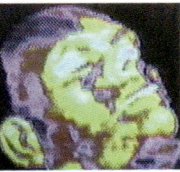

Various stages of restorative art were defined by image processing, including materials used (such as wax).

Overall, Tom was amazed at how well and how quickly a restorative art professional could restore a body to a completely natural and realistic-looking state. It was as if scars, bruises, broken bones, bullet wounds, and other defects had never existed at all.

When the processed images from the study were compared to that of the new autopsy photograph, it immediately became apparent that restorative work had been performed on the president's head. Obvious areas of disguise included the right ear, the entire face, and some hanging scalp material on the back part of the head. The right temporal area, which Tom believed was the entrance area of an incoming missile, was also filled with mortician's wax. This material covered the actual bullet hole while, at the same time, gave the appearance of internal swelling. Tom had previously observed and made note of this swelling in his analysis of JFK's front head and chest autopsy photo.

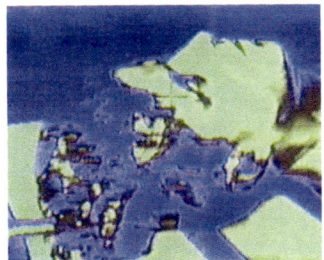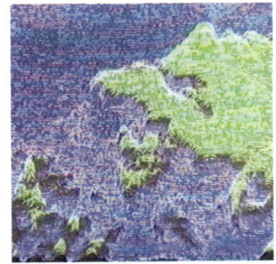

Image processing (pseudocolor [L] and 3-D pseudocolor [R]) reveal restorative work performed on ear, face, right temporal area, and hanging scalp.

As Tom continued his image processing by peeling away more layers, he determined that not only was restorative art performed, but that this particular photograph was also a composite of at least two separate images. A third stripped layer showed the actual base of the president's head in white, while non-human material (on the face, the ear, in the temporal area, and on the back scalp) was represented by darker colors. Tom's analysis proved that the hanging scalp material was added using a half-tone process similar to what he observed had been used in altering parts of the Zapruder film. Upon making this observation, Tom shook his head negatively. "I wonder if the same people did both alterations?" he mumbled to himself.

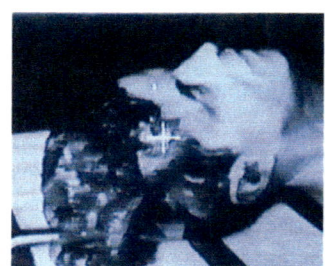 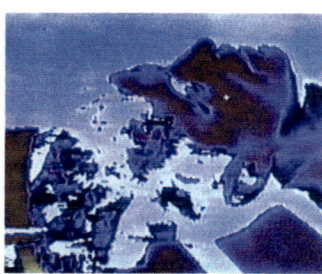

Original photograph (L). 3rd layer reveals composite photograph (R).

Along with his image processing work on previous images, Tom now had more compelling evidence that some of President Kennedy's so-called "autopsy photographs" were not only altered via photographic manipulation, but were taken *after* restorative art had been performed on the body. Furthermore, it was obvious to Tom that these deceptive changes were made for one reason and one reason only – to hide the real wounds inflicted on President Kennedy.

With such results, Tom decided to take another look at the JFK front head and chest autopsy photograph. Previously, he had concentrated on the throat wound, but had also observed some swelling above the right eye. Now he wanted to study the head more closely in regard to both the wound in the right temporal area, and for possible restorative art. Sure enough, after removing only a few layers, Tom was able to determine conclusively that restorative art had, indeed, been performed on the president's body before this picture was taken.

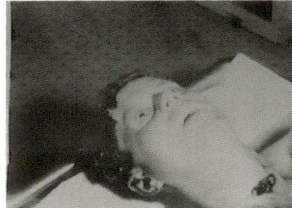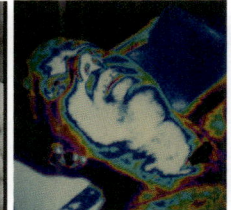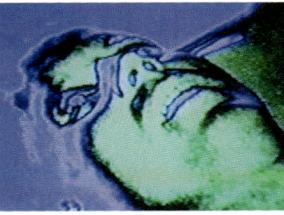

Processing of frontal head and chest photo reveals restorative artwork.

In scrutinizing these images, it was apparent that some sort of anomaly existed in the area of the right eye. As Tom took a closer look and tried various image processing techniques, he determined that the eye was not real. In fact, it was painted on, which meant that this autopsy photograph was another composite. "What in the world is going on here?" Tom asked himself. "What happened to Kennedy's eye in the first place? Did the bullet to the temple damage it? What?"

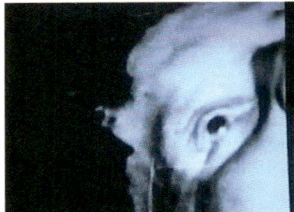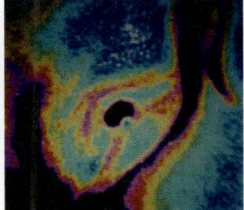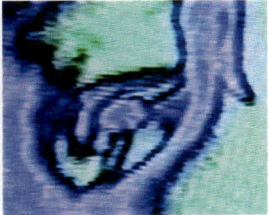

Close-ups and image processing revealed that the right eye is painted onto this photograph.

Startled at this finding, Tom decided to back up and take another look at the overall head. His intent was to gradually focus in to see if he could isolate the bullet wound in the right temporal area. However, his attention was immediately drawn to the area on the back right of the head, which appeared very dark, virtually black. This darkness also extended farther off the head area and appeared to be a shadow on the tiled floor below the autopsy table. But as Tom stripped the layers away and processed the image, it became apparent that this dark area was not a shadow at all. Rather, it was a remnant of photographic blackening designed to cover up the massive hole in the back right of President Kennedy's head. The alteration was especially obvious with Tom's tagged pseudocolor image in which the covered up area appeared white.

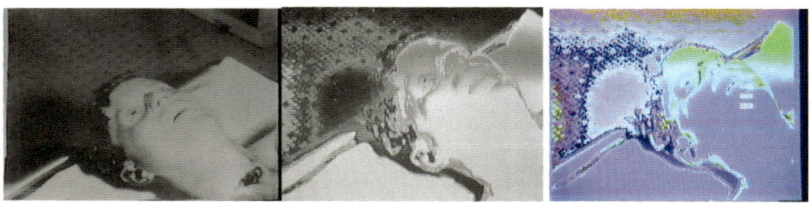
Photographic blackening used to cover massive hole in back of head.

In this same processed image, enlargements detected that the bullet hole to the right temporal region had been revealed beneath the photographic blackening. "No doubt about it," Tom said to himself. "It's there, plain as day."

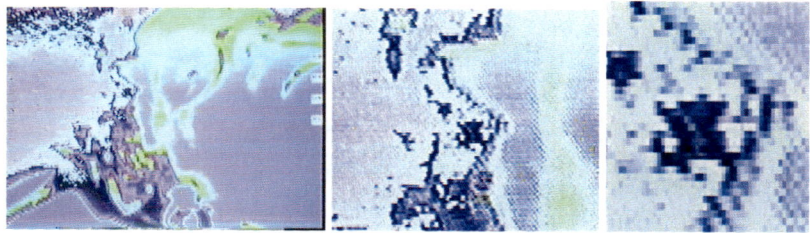
Pseudocolor enlargements reveal bullet hole in right temporal area.

The final autopsy photograph evaluated by Tom was both difficult to discern and somewhat gruesome in nature. It was a picture of the president's skull with a massive hole in it. At first glance, Tom wasn't sure of the orientation of the picture or exactly what he was looking at. But after awhile, it became apparent that when the photo was taken the camera lens had been above and slightly behind the top of the skull. The center suture line of the cranium, for example, ran from the lower left side of the photo up to the top at a slight angle from vertical. That would place the forehead and face just out of view at the top border of the photograph. Tom also noticed that an individual was holding a small ruler at the lower right portion of the picture – partially obscuring the area of the hole in the back of Kennedy's head that he had observed from his study of the Zapruder film.

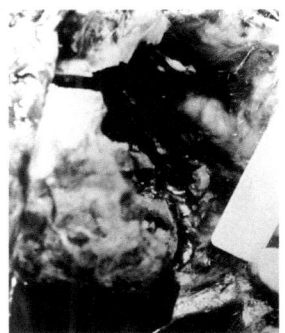

Right side of skull with massive hole (Fox 8). Center suture of cranium visible on the left. Forehead and face just out of view at the top border.

Clearly, Tom was shocked at the size of the hole shown in this photograph. "This is much, much larger than the hole that can be seen just after the shot to the head," he wrote in his notebook. "Such a massive cavity cannot be explained from the photographic evidence contained in the Zapruder film."

In researching the history of this photograph, Tom noted that it did not appear in the Warren Report. However, an indirect reference to it in a drawing (Warren Commission Exhibit 388) was buried within one of the volumes of the Hearings and Exhibits without any narrative comment. This same drawing appeared in Volume I of the HSCA Report as JFK Exhibit F-68 and was described as representative of the president's position "before the explosion of the head" as "derived from Zapruder frame #312."

The HSCA also published two more drawings in an effort to explain its determination of President Kennedy's massive head wound and what caused it. JFK Exhibit F-65 indicated "the path of the bullet entering the right upper head region approximately 1 inch to the right of the midline of the body and approximately 4 inches above . . . the external occipital protuberance," read the report. "This bullet then proceeds from back to front exiting in the area of the . . . coronal suture line." For JFK Exhibit F-66, which illustrates the massive hole in the head, the HSCA explained that this diagram "shows the entrance perforation in the upper posterior right side of the skull, and the bullet path proceeding forward causing extensive fractures of the skull bones on the right and then exiting the right frontal area." The HSCA then described the massive exit hole as "a semicircular defect in the frontal bone of the skull."

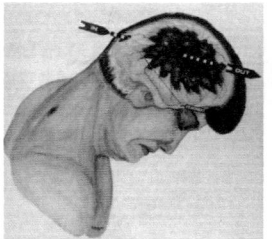 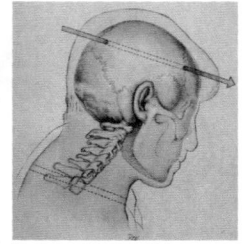 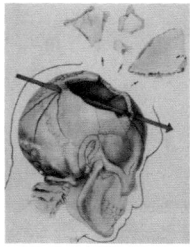

WC Exhibit 388 / JFK Exhibit F-68 (L); JFK Exhibit F-65 (C); JFK Exhibit F-66 (R).

The HSCA Report listed this autopsy photograph as JFK Exhibit F-59 but did not publish it. Instead, a poor quality, heavily cropped enlargement was printed (JFK Exhibit F-60 and Figure 25) and described as a "closeup photograph of the semicircular exit defect in the margin of the fracture fragment in the right parietal region." Unfortunately, the cropping of this photo eliminated the center cranial suture line, the ruler used for scale, and what was left of the original exit hole at the lower left of the photograph. Tom felt it was a very poor representation of the overall image – one that an average viewer couldn't possibly make heads or tails out of.

 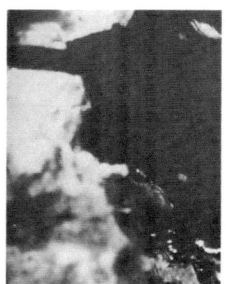

Original Photograph.   JFK Exhibit F-60 / HSCA Figure 25.

In his analysis of this photograph, Tom made two key observations. First, it was an original image. There were no alterations made, nor was it a composite photograph. Second, there was no brain material visible inside the cranium. That meant the brain had been removed before the picture was taken.

Overall, this autopsy image was confusing to Tom. Not only was it difficult to orient, but the massive hole could not be explained from evidence he had garnered from the Zapruder film. It was possible that the original exit hole in the back of the head may have been extended to include the top right portion of the skull. But Tom wasn't the first person to speculate on such a possibility. Other researchers had also published their findings that this more massive hole must have been created after the shooting, but prior to the autopsy.

* * * * *

After Tom's November 1991 presentation in Dallas, several researchers sent him copies of two x-rays reportedly taken at President Kennedy's autopsy – the anterior/posterior (AP) x-ray and the lateral x-ray.

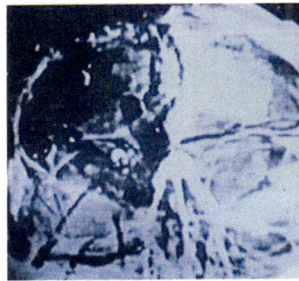
Tom's copy of the AP X-ray.

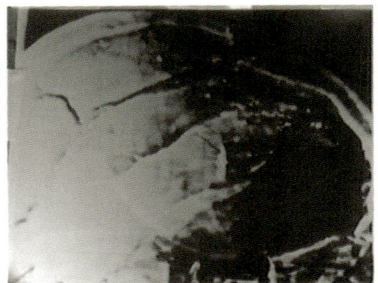
Tom's copy of the lateral x-ray.

The history of all the Kennedy x-rays is murky. None were published in the Warren Report or its accompanying twenty-six volumes of hearings and exhibits. As a matter of fact, there is some controversy as to whether or not the members of the Warren Commission even viewed the x-rays. Fifteen years later, the HSCA published photographic copies of only four of "the original 14 autopsy x-rays kept at the National Archives." Even then, the copies it produced were very poor quality enlargements that were significantly cropped. In explaining the reasoning for publishing these images, the HSCA Report stated the following:

"The committee wished to permit public examination of the most important details of evidentiary significance while still maintaining a sense of propriety. In accordance with this desire, the committee decided to display the autopsy x-rays to the public in a cropped fashion. In the hearings the committee used the original x-rays only to verify the authenticity and accuracy of the cropped counterparts; the entire original x-rays are not being published."

The technician who took the x-rays at Bethesda Naval Hospital used a portable x-ray unit. The anterior/posterior x-ray is a view looking directly into the face. In the HSCA Report, the AP x-ray is represented by two images, both of which are photographic copies. JFK Exhibit F-55 is an "unenhanced" enlargement of very poor quality. JFK Exhibit F-56 is also an enlargement described as a "computer-assisted image enhancement."

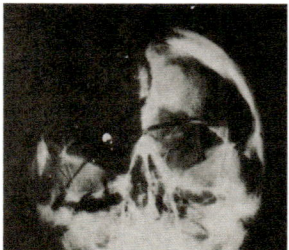 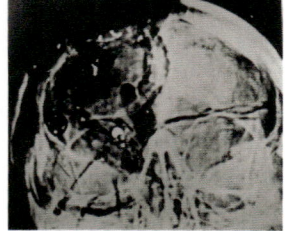

JFK Exhibit F-55   JFK Exhibit F-56

Of particular interest to Tom was the appearance in both images of a white, almost circular object located in the vicinity of the right eye, which the HSCA called "a missile fragment." It was glaringly apparent even in JFK Exhibit F-55, which was unusually dark and devoid of almost all detail on the upper right side of the head where there was significant skull damage. The HSCA's darkening, cropping, and enhancing of the original x-rays definitely hid most of the skull's revealing images. However, even though the image Tom obtained was a photographic copy rather than an original x-ray copy, it still contained sufficient detail, especially when put through his image processing system.

As Tom peeled away a couple of layers of gray from his copy, a white rectangular area in the back right of the skull became visible (upper left when looking at image). This was the area that had been blasted out from the fragmentation of the bullet entering the right front temporal area. The 90-degree angles of the rectangle reflected how the surface broke along preexisting lines of weakness in the skull itself. As Tom continued to remove layers all the way to the rear of the head, the rectangular area appeared black, because the skull was lying on the x-ray cassette film and there was no bone left in this area.

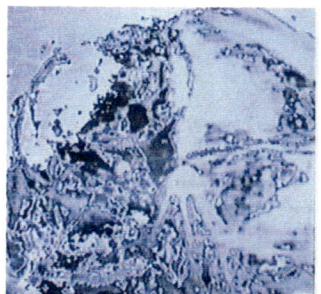 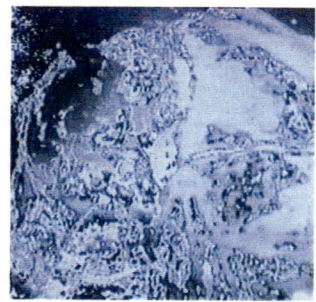

Processed images of AP x-ray reveal rectangular area in back right of head blasted out. As more layers removed, exit area appears black (no skull present).

After removing layers of gray all the way to the back of the head and tagging the resulting image with pseudocolor, Tom was able to specifically define areas where the skull was missing. He also observed that the president's right eye had been damaged internally, and he could still see the large artifact (called a missile by the HSCA). An additional three-dimensional image not only revealed which portions of the skull were still remaining, but seemed to indicate that the "missile fragment" was actually lying on top of the eye.

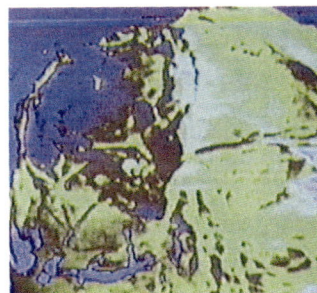
Layers of gray removed all the way to back of head, tagged with pseudocolor; 3D image (R)..

With additional image processing and enlargements, Tom was able to locate and isolate the bullet entry hole in the right temporal area. This location corresponded exactly with the swollen area above the right eye that he had observed previously in JFK's frontal head and chest autopsy photograph.

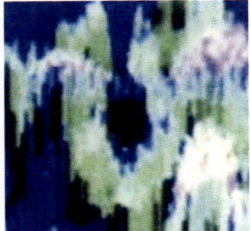
More processing and enlargements locate and isolate bullet entry hole in right temporal area.

Overall, Tom's analysis of the AP x-ray showed that President Kennedy had been struck by a bullet in the right temporal area that instantly fragmented and blew out the back right side of his head. Additionally, Tom did not observe the presence of any brain material in the head, which confirmed his finding that the brain had been removed prior to the taking of the AP x-ray.

Tom next took a careful look at the lateral x-ray, which was published in the HSCA Report as JFK Exhibit F-52 and JFK Exhibit F-53. Unfortunately, in its narrative description of this important piece of evidence, the HSCA did not state specifically whether the image was a right lateral or left lateral x-ray. The difference, it turns out, is crucial to the interpretation of President Kennedy's wounds. Both exhibits (again poor quality photographs of the original x-ray) were inferred to be right lateral, meaning that the viewer was looking at the right side of the head. For example, JFK Exhibit F-52 was described as "an enlarged copy of that specific x-ray showing a side view of the skull of the President with the back of the head to your left." "Right lateral" meant that the x-ray technician placed the film plate behind the right side of the head and the x-ray source on the left side. If true, this lateral x-ray should have revealed the blown out portion of the back right side of the president's skull. But the back of he head was clearly shown to be intact, if heavily fractured. JFK Exhibit F-53 was described as "a lateral view of the president's head" and a "computerized enhancement," which the HSCA said it created because it brought "out some of the details of the x-ray more clearly."

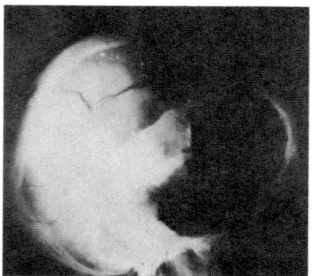
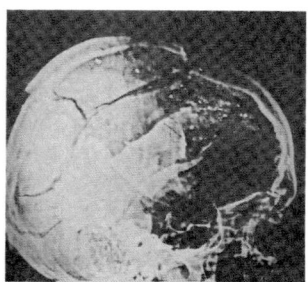

JFK Exhibit F-52   JFK Exhibit F-53

Of particular interest to Tom was the HSCA's observation of "many small white areas in the x-ray that are metallic fragments resulting from a bullet having passed through the skull and fragmenting to some small degree." Upon close inspection of JFK Exhibit F-53, Tom could clearly see these bullet fragments. However, he was confused when the HSCA Report also stated that they were "consistent with a bullet having entered the President's head high on top of the head and passed through [the skull]." The path of the fragments seemed to end at the right eye, which coincidentally was where the bullet fragment was located in the AP x-ray. Obviously, the HSCA wanted the reader to believe that the bullet path traveled from the upper back of the head to the lower right front. From his other image processing work, however, Tom knew that such an interpretation was incorrect. "I could tell that something was wrong with this lateral x-ray," Tom wrote in his notebook. "And I had to find out what the problem was."

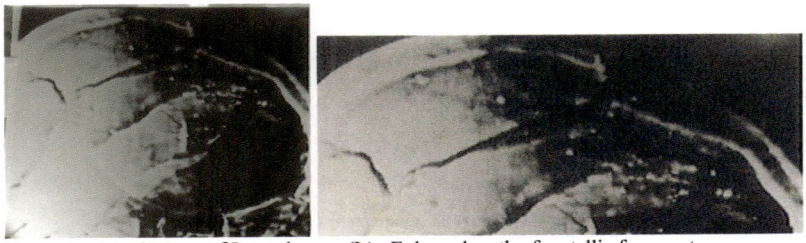
Tom's copy of Lateral x-ray (L). Enlarged; path of metallic fragments.

Tom's meticulous image processing work revealed that the black area on the right side of the lateral x-ray was not missing skull material. The rest of the head was actually there. Apparently, the image had been darkened in this area to hide crucial details.

Processing reveals details of skull in black area on right side of x-ray.

As his system continued to process the x-ray image, Tom was able to delineate significant information hidden within the darkness. Finally, the bullet hole in the right temporal area became apparent, and Tom was able to isolate, describe, and precisely locate it.

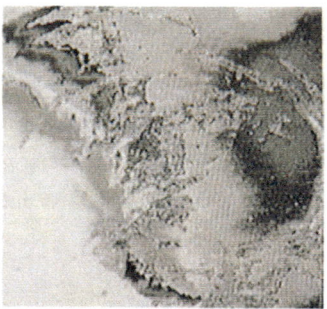 

Bullet hole in right temporal area is located.

Even though Tom had found the bullet hole in the right temporal area, he was still puzzled by the lateral x-ray in general. If the bullet entered at the right temple and blasted out the back right side of the head (as clearly shown in the AP x-ray, then why did this lateral view still show so much of the skull present? And why was the massive hole in the top right side of the head (as shown in the autopsy photograph) not visible?

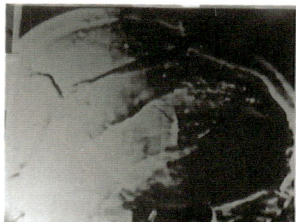 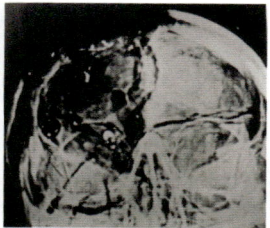 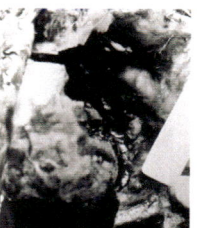

Why did lateral x-ray not show missing skull material as in AP x-ray and autopsy photograph?

Tom stared at these images for hours and hours, trying to figure out what was wrong, thinking about how to reconcile all his conflicting observations. "Is this really the right lateral x-ray?" he wondered. "If so, where is the original? Is it at the National Archives?"

Now, Tom started thinking in terms of hard evidence. His analysis had been performed on photographic copies of the x-rays. If he could prove they were made from the authentic x-rays, then he could prove that both the Warren Commission and the HSCA were totally wrong in their findings and conclusions as to how President Kennedy was assassinated. But this evidence was kept under tight security at the National Archives. Access was strictly limited and, technically, it was all the property of the Kennedy family.

"How can I get in there?" Tom wondered.

9 / *The Fatal Headshot*

In 1994, Tom obtained a pristine copy of the Mary Moorman photograph from a credible source. Certified as having been made directly from the original Polaroid shortly after the assassination, this particular copy was accompanied with written documentation to prove who owned it from the time of its inception. This "chain of evidence" would make it admissible and verifiable in a court of law should the need ever arise.

After receiving the negative, Tom had a number of professional enlargements made so that he could scan it into his computer with the maximum amount of detail. In looking closely at one of the enlargements for the first time, he was amazed at the clarity of the image. The large finger- or thumbprint on the right side of the photograph was especially pronounced, but it obscured some detail in that area. *[Note: Mary Moorman has long maintained that the print was neither hers nor that of her friend, Jean Hill. The original Polaroid, she said, was in the hands of the FBI and Secret Service for a short time before the image was released to the public. The fingerprint was made during the time the government had it and was present when the photo was returned to her.]*

Pristine copy of Mary Moorman Polaroid photograph.

Tom looked carefully at the area behind the retaining wall and the picket fence, the pedestal that Abraham Zapruder and Marilyn Sitzman were supposed to be standing on, and Secret Service Agent Roy Kellerman shielding his face with a notebook. But when he took a close look at President Kennedy, Tom was startled. This photograph clearly showed a massive hole in the rear of the President's head. Visible to the naked eye, it could be seen without the aid of a computer or even a magnifying glass.

Massive hole in back of President Kennedy's head visible to naked eye.

With each enlargement, the hole became more and more pronounced, providing additional detail and evidence supporting the fact that this was the bullet exit wound Tom already knew existed. Upon further inspection, two smaller holes appeared to be present within the larger one. Tom inferred that these might have been exit points for a bullet that fragmented into two pieces.

Enlargements reveal two smaller holes within the larger one – perhaps exit points for fragmented bullet.

The shocking clarity of the hole in the back of the President's head caused Tom to wonder why it had never been noticed before. So he went back and looked at early versions of the Moorman photograph that had been printed in major publications around the country in the immediate aftermath of the assassination (1963 and 1964). To be sure, one reason the hole hadn't been identified before was because the original photo was a Polaroid with President Kennedy's head only a small portion of the overall scene. However, it was also clear to Tom that some of these early versions also had the back of the president's head blackened in. It reminded Tom of what had been done to x-rays taken at the autopsy – darkened so as to obscure any visible deformities. "This is outrageous," Tom wrote in his notebook. "Surely, somebody within the government noticed this hole. It's just too obvious to miss. However, there is nothing that I can find in the available record that shows the FBI, the Warren

Commission, or the HSCA ever did anything with this photograph – and yet it appears to be a crucial piece of evidence."

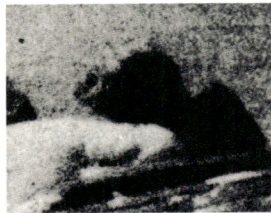  

Three early printed versions of Moorman photograph with back of JFK's head darkened in.

With this finding, Tom now had confirmation of the massive exit wound in the back of President Kennedy's head. He had previously documented it in his analysis of Zapruder frame #313. Now, he had two sources from two different angles almost 180 degrees apart – one from the Zapruder film looking south and one from the Moorman photograph looking north. The Moorman image, however, provided even more detail – showing the two smaller exit holes within a rectangular area similar to what he had seen in the AP x-ray. Obviously, when the bullet exited the back of the head, the skull had partly fractured at right angles along preexisting lines of weakness.

 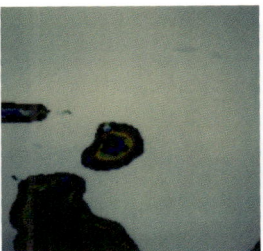 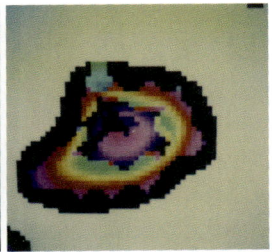

Zapruder # 313 processing verifies exit wound in back of JFK's head.

Moorman photo verifies exit wound in back of JFK's head. Note rectangle in right image.

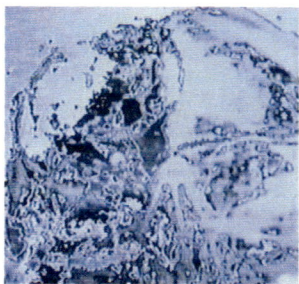 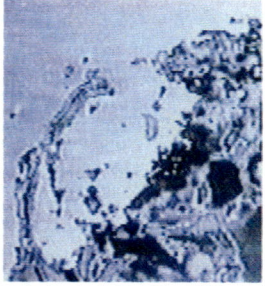

Processed images of AP x-ray show rectangular area in back right of head blasted out by bullet.

Due to the exceptional clarity of this pristine photograph, Tom decided to perform a detailed computer scan (similar to a medical Catscan) of the wound. From the data obtained, he then planned to construct a three-dimensional model in order to calculate the flow of forces within the head, the path of the bullet as it fragmented, and the amount of displaced head material. Over the course of a month, Tom performed 8 vertical and 750 horizontal scans of the head wound, which resulted in 6,000 points of mathematical data. The resulting computer printout of all this information came in the form of a chart that was six inches wide and fourteen feet long.

 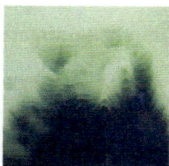  

Detailed computer scan (similar to a medical Catscan) generated 6,000 data points.

After having his computer print out a template for each slice of data, Tom physically cut out all the templates and meticulously pieced them together. The resulting model was an exact replica (not to scale) of the rectangular portion of President Kennedy's head wound.

Computer scan of wound.   Exact model replica of wound.

Because the president's head was tilted down and to the left toward his wife, the orientation of the model seems horizontal but, of course, it is not. The back of the head is toward the viewer, the front of the head away. The holes of the left and right bullet fragments are easily visible – and their paths converge into the head (away from the viewer) to the point of entrance in the right temporal area. With the help of this three dimensional model, Tom was now able to see the scope of damage done to President Kennedy by the bullet as it fragmented into two pieces, traversed his head, and exited at the top right – blasting skull, scalp, and brain material into the air.

As Tom stood back and looked at his model, he realized that he could not only see the material left in the head, but he would be able to definitively measure the amount of material blown out. He performed this calculation by constructing a separate plastic mold and measuring the open void by volume. The amount calculated was 36 percent – almost exactly what one of the doctors in Dallas had estimated.

> *"I was in such a position that I could very closely examine the head wound, and I noted that the right posterior portion of the skull had been extremely blasted.... You could actually look down into the skull cavity... and see that... a third or so, at least, of the brain tissue... had been blasted out."*
>
> Dr. Robert N. McClelland
> Attending physician
> Parkland Hospital Emergency Room

To further document his findings, Tom superimposed the rectangular model of the wound on a generic anatomical head in the position of President Kennedy at the time of the Moorman photograph. Then he rotated the head to the vertical position to obtain a more conventional view. To further demonstrate the mechanics of the fatal headshot, Tom placed the entrance wound in the right temporal area on a front-facing image and put the exit wound in its proper place as if the viewer could see through the head. And finally, a cross-sectional generic diagram was constructed showing the missile entry and exit points. This last image clearly illustrated that the path of the bullet was from front-to-back and down-to-up – precisely opposite of what both the Warren

Commission and the House Select Committee on Assassinations had concluded.

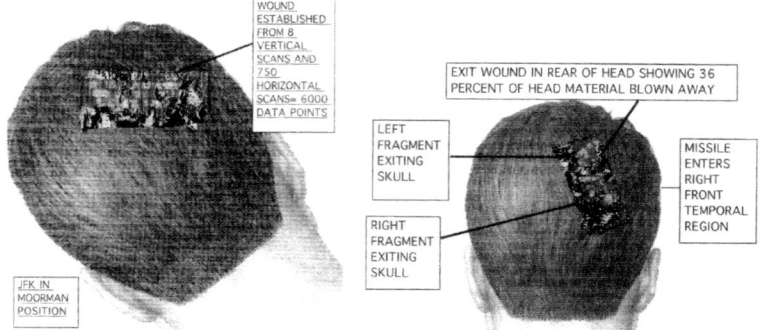

Model of back head wound placed in correct anatomical position (at time of shot (L), and rotated to vertical position (R). Exit points of left and right missile fragments also noted.

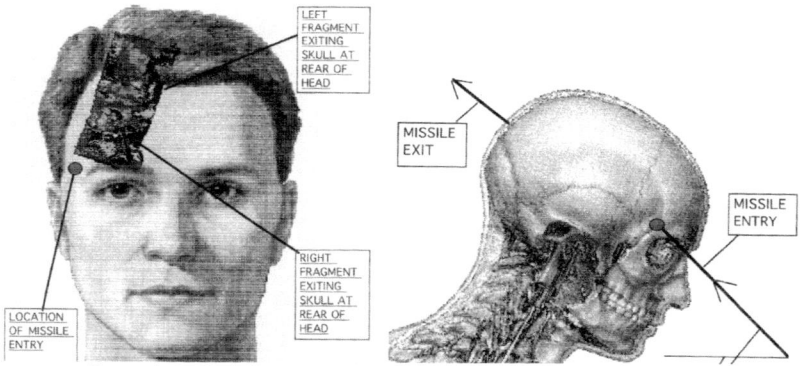

Front view of missile entry and exit points (L); Cross-sectional view (R).

In looking at the cross-sectional image he had just created, Tom realized something that he had previously overlooked. He had never gone back and determined exactly where the bullet originally came from. He'd only focused on what it did to the president's head. Now, however, it was obvious that the bullet path was at an angle coming not from the area of the picket fence on the grassy knoll, but from out of the ground. Somewhat bewildered, Tom's initial thought was that he had somehow made a mistake. "How can this be?" he wondered aloud.

Seeking further scientific proof to either confirm or deny his findings, Tom performed meticulous measurements on the model of the president's head wound. Using his computer and image processing system, he traced the paths of the right and left bullet fragments through the head and found that they converged on a single point, which was the exact location of the bullet entry wound in the right temporal area that he had previously pinpointed. Obviously, the missile was an exploding bullet that had immediately fragmented upon entering the head. Tom next measured the angle of the left and right bullet fragment paths as being 16 and 17 degrees, respectively, down from the horizontal (from the president's head position at the time of the shot in the Moorman photograph).

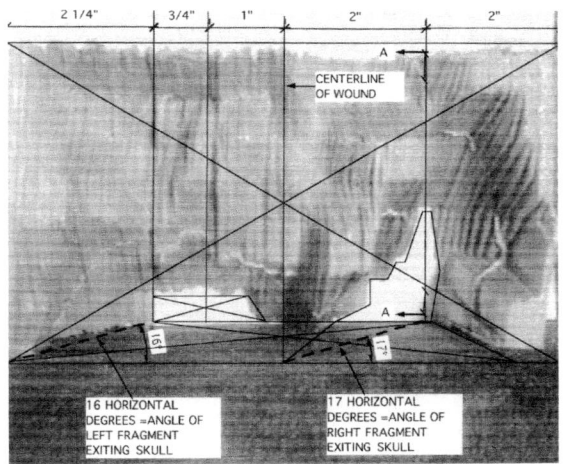

Measurements of head wound mold (corrected for proper scale). Bullet exit toward viewer. Paths of left and right fragments converge into head (away from viewer) to entry of original bullet in right temporal area.

Tom now had enough information to pinpoint the exact location of the shooter that fired the fatal headshot. From his field measurements while on the ground in Dealey Plaza, he had already determined that the position of the president at the time of the shot was 7 feet 6 inches farther down Elm Street than indicated in the Zapruder film. So Tom placed the president in the proper position and then projected the path of the bullet fragments starting at the exit wound, through the head to the point where they converged at the entry point in the right temporal area, and then down into the ground. "The origination point of that bullet corresponds exactly to the location of the storm sewer drain at the base of the steps on the north side of Elm Street," Tom wrote in his notebook. "The assassin who fired the fatal headshot was hiding in the storm drain. There is absolutely no doubt in my mind. It is a proven scientific fact!"

Sewer drain where fatal headshot fired. Taken from Moorman position.

Photo of sewer drain taken from position of President Kennedy at time of fatal headshot (L). Moorman photo enlargement (R).

* * * * *

Tom Wilson was not the first person to allege that a shot had been fired at President Kennedy from the storm sewer on the north side of Elm Street. Over the years, a number of Kennedy assassination researchers have suggested the very same thing. Their evidence is based, in part, on the eyewitness testimony of Sam Pate, a news reporter for radio station KBOX in Dallas. On November 22, 1963, Pate was covering the Kennedy motorcade as it weaved its way through downtown Dallas. Equipped with Channel 2, the radio frequency used by the Dallas Police, he monitored progress while driving in and out of the procession in his bright red 1963 Pontiac Catalina, which had giant-sized lettering on the side that read "KBOX RADIO NEWS 1480."

KBOX newsman Sam Pate and his mobile news 1963 Pontiac Catalina.

Pate was traveling west on Elm Street and had crossed Houston Street to move in front of the motorcade just before the President's limousine made its left turn at the Texas School Book Depository. KBOX had just ended its 12:25 to 12:30 PM CST newscast and turned the microphone over to Sam Pate for an update on President Kennedy's location. Pate's car was moving at a speed of about 20 to 25 miles per hour and was approximately 40 to 50 yards in front of the motorcade when shots rang out. Startled, Pate stopped broadcasting, but left his radio recorder running. Looking in his rearview mirror, he saw the presidential limousine slow down as it came to the curve in front of the grassy knoll. Then he observed a puff of smoke come from the storm sewer and watched as the limo picked up speed and headed toward him.

Listening to Channel 2, Pate heard Dallas Police Chief Jesse Curry (traveling in the lead car of the motorcade) issue an order to move all available men "into the railroad yards and try to determine what happened." Curry then stated: "It looks like the President has been hit. Have Parkland stand by."

At that point, Sam Pate picked up his radio microphone and became the first news reporter to broadcast that shots had been fired at President John F. Kennedy. "There is trouble in the motorcade," he announced. "I repeat, there is trouble in the motorcade. Parkland has been notified to stand by."

Later that afternoon, at about 3:30 or 4:00 PM CST Pate stopped to have lunch at the Lucas B&B Restaurant on Commerce Street in downtown Dallas." While there, the owner, Pete Lucas, came up to Pate and told him that the man who killed President Kennedy had gotten away. Lucas went on to say that the assassin's name was Bruno, that he was short and stocky, and that he had been positioned in the storm sewer and "blew Kennedy away with a .45 automatic."

> "I described it as though someone was shooting a revolver into a hard object – it seemed to have some type of an echo."
>
> Secret Service Agent Clint Hill
> who jumped on the back of the presidential
> limo just before the fatal headshot.

The shocked Pate continued to listen as Lucas further told him that Bruno had made his escape through the sewer, emerging at a point near the Post Office, and then got into a car which drove him to the airport for a flight out of town. Bruno, he said, was from Chicago and an organized crime associate of Jack Ruby. Lucas did not say how he came by this information, but Pate knew that he was a friend of Ruby, who regularly frequented the restaurant.

The very next morning, November 23, 1963, Sam Pate was fired from his job. "Due to budget reasons, we're going to have to let you go," he was told. The news came as a complete surprise, because just the day before Pate had been praised by his superiors at the radio station for his outstanding work in reporting on the assassination. Equally unexpected was a call from the radio station a few days later requesting Pate to record a reenactment tape of his live KBOX bulletins from the day of the assassination. "There's a problem with the original tapes," he was told, "and we need your voice-over for a new video that's going to be titled *Four Days That Shook The World*." Hoping to get his job back, Pate agreed to re-record his bulletins from memory. It was at this point that Sam Pate's famous following statement was made: "It appears as though something *has* happened in the motorcade route."

Over the next four months, Pate spoke to the FBI several times regarding his observations of events on November 22, 1963. In his March 10, 1964 interview with Special Agent Robert P. Gemberling, for instance, Pate "wished to make it known that the majority of his portion of [the broadcast] tape is not an authentic one, but is a tape that he was asked to make several days after he was dismissed from KBOX radio station."

Because Sam Pate went on record calling into question the authenticity of the original tape, the FBI was forced to address the issue to the Warren Commission. [Presumably the tape could be used to account for the number of shots fired at President Kennedy.] In a letter dated June 10, 1964, FBI Director J. Edgar Hoover wrote the following to Warren Commission General Counsel J. Lee Rankin:

A detailed examination of the KBOX tape covering the critical period of the assassination failed to indicate the presence of any sounds, which could be interpreted as gunshots. There is more of Mr. Pate's broadcast recorded on the tape than was incorporated in the record. However, that critical portion of the tape, which is included in the record, does not appear to have been altered.

* * * * *

Over the years, Sam Pate published several stories about the true facts of President Kennedy's assassination. He also survived two car bomb blasts, one of which went off as he turned the ignition switch.

To date, no federal government organization has shown any interest in the Mary Moorman photograph as possible evidence in the assassination of President John F. Kennedy. And yet, as Tom Wilson recorded in his notebook, "It is probably the single most important artifact of the assassination scene."

As of 2008, the original Moorman Polaroid image was sold in an online auction. It is severely faded.

Condition of the original Moorman Polaroid Photograph as of 2008.

10 / _Autopsy X-Rays in the National Archives_

After his detailed image processing of the autopsy photographs and x-rays, Tom made a concerted effort to gain entrance to the National Archives to view original evidence contained in the Kennedy family's Deed of Gift. He hoped to determine whether or not the photographic reproductions he'd analyzed were authentic copies of the original x-rays and photographs, and he wanted to view the originals, which were sure to contain additional detail.

On March 23, 1994, Tom sent a formal request to Yale University Professor Burke Marshall who, on behalf of the Kennedy family, controlled access to the Deed of Gift. In June 1995, after gaining a favorable recommendation from Cyril Wecht, Tom finally received permission from Professor Marshall to view the original autopsy materials. There were, however, strict rules involved. He would not be allowed to photograph or make copies of the evidence. However, he would be able to bring his own reproductions, diagrams, and measurement tools, and he could also take extensive notes about what he observed. Tom was also told that a member of the Archives staff would be with him at all times to ensure adherence to the rules.

Immediately upon receiving the letter of approval, Tom began extensive preparations for his visit to the Archives. First, he created a detailed workbook of all the autopsy photos, x-rays, and computer processed images. Then he designed a special pair of stereo glasses that would allow him to view everything in three-dimensions for more precise comparison to the originals. Tom also conducted thorough research about x-rays, including proper shooting methods, types of films, processing, and interpretation. And because he was concerned about recognizing poor quality x-rays from good quality ones, Tom also studied the effects of overexposure, radiographic density, distortion, blackening in an exposed film, and general image enhancement techniques.

As part of his preparation, Tom wanted to gain as much information as he could about what actually happened at the president's autopsy. After reading a series of books on the subject and speaking with Cyril Wecht, he learned that the technician who took and developed all of the autopsy x-rays worked in Pittsburgh at Presbyterian Hospital. The man's name was Jerrol F. Custer and, as fate would have it, he resided less than two miles from Tom's home.

On November 22, 1963, Jerrol Custer was a 22-year-old Hospital Corpsman Third Class (E-4) on duty at Bethesda Naval Hospital. He had received all of his formal education through the Navy, which included two years of school and one year of training. Tom Wilson conducted three separate interviews with Custer in hopes of learning about the specifics of the autopsy and gaining as much information as possible about the original images in the National Archives. The first session explored all the specific tasks Custer performed at the autopsy. Tom also informed Custer that he had received permission to view the original photos and x-rays in the Archives, and he would be able to verify all statements made. In the second interview, Tom showed Custer his image processing findings and asked for the former x-ray technician's feedback and recollections as to whether or not they coincided with his experiences. The third and final session occurred after Tom's review of items in the Deed of Gift and focused on his observations while there. All three interviews were recorded on audiotape and transcribed into a certified 116-page affidavit.

* * * * *

Before Tom left Pittsburgh for Washington, D.C. to visit the National Archives, he listened to the audiotapes and summarized Jerrol Custer's recollections as to what actually happened during the autopsy of President Kennedy. *It was performed on Friday night, November 22, 1963, at Bethesda Naval Medical Center in Bethesda, Maryland, just outside Washington, D.C.*

At around 5:30 p.m., Custer was in the cafeteria just finishing dinner when he was approached by the duty chief and told that the autopsy of the President would be performed at Bethesda and that, as the radiology technician on duty, Custer was to take the x-rays. "The body was first taken to Walter Reed Compound and will be brought over here shortly," *the chief said. The officer on duty (a different person) later made the same statement about the body first being taken to Walter Reed. [Walter Reed Army Medical Center (in Washington, D.C.) is located less than 4 miles (as the crow flies) from Bethesda Naval Medical Center.]*

Bethesda Naval Medical Center where the autopsy of JFK was performed (L). Walter Reed Army Medical Center where Custer was told JFK's body was first taken (R).

Custer immediately met with Lieutenant Commander John H. Ebersole, Bethesda's resident radiologist on call. Ebersole was in training to become a board-certified radiologist and had little or no experience on criminal murder cases. "I've been told that, for security purposes, the president's body will be contained in the morgue," Ebersole said to Custer. "So you're going to have to use the portable unit to take the x-rays."

"But we can take higher quality film upstairs in the x-ray department," Custer replied.

"We're not interested in entry and exit wounds," replied Ebersole. "We'll only be looking for any bullet fragments remaining in the body. So the portable unit will be sufficient."

"Not interested in entry and exit wounds?" Custer thought to himself. "This is a murder case and it's the President of the United States, for God's sake. Why wouldn't we want to take the best possible films we could get and search for as much detail as possible?" Custer, however, did not question his superior officer and simply followed orders. He quickly hooked up with his assistant, Ed Reed, a student in training, and the two moved the portable x-ray unit (along with all materials they would need, including film cassettes, aprons, measuring tools, etc.) down to the basement morgue, and waited for the president's body to arrive.

About a half-hour later (at approximately 6:15 pm), the duty officer told Custer that the body had just arrived at Bethesda by helicopter and would be loaded into an ambulance and brought over to the morgue. A few minutes later, Custer heard a commotion and went down the hall to the door of the loading dock. He saw the assembled honor guard pull the president's casket out of a black ambulance, carry it into the morgue, and place it on the floor between the dissecting table and the gallery. It was a plain metal shipping casket, light gray in color.

Air Force One arrived at Andrews Air Force Base at 6:08 p.m. At approximately 6:15 p.m., a gray ambulance left Andrews with Jacqueline Kennedy, Robert Kennedy, and the president's body (in a formal bronze casket) for the 45-minute drive to Bethesda Naval Hospital. This was the same time that the helicopter landed at Bethesda with President Kennedy's body, which (according to Jerrol Custer) had been flown over from Walter Reed Army Medical Center.

After the honor guard left the morgue, Custer, along with several others, helped lift the body out of the shipping casket and place it on a moveable table that had just been wheeled in. The president's body was completely nude. The face was not visible, because the head had a plastic bag and a bloody sheet wrapped around it

The casket was taken into the adjoining "cooler" room, and the table with the body on it was moved closer to the gallery. Custer and his assistant were then asked to leave the morgue and wait for a phone call from Dr. Ebersole. At this point, both the floor of the morgue and the gallery were crowded with people – doctors, photographers, civilians in suits, and high-ranking military officers.

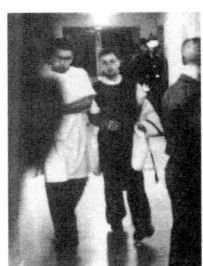

Jerrol F. Custer (left) and assistant Ed Reed
in hallway outside morgue at time of autopsy.

* * * * *

At 9:00 a.m. on September 25, 1995, Tom Wilson arrived at the National Archives in College Park, Maryland (just outside Washington, D.C.) and was met by Steven D. Tilley (Special Access Chief). Mr. Tilley escorted Tom to the area where the Deed of Gift was kept, presented him with a list of materials, and asked him to choose which items he would like to view. Those items would then be brought in for his inspection, taken away after he was done, and the next requested items would be retrieved. Tom was also given a pair of white gloves for handling of the artifacts and evidence. Tilley's assistant would remain in the room at all times.

"I'd like to begin with the x-rays, please," said Tom, who had made this decision beforehand. As Tilley and his assistant retrieved the materials, Tom reviewed his notes about what happened in the autopsy room upon Jerrol Custer's return after about an hour's absence.

* * * * *

When Custer came back, the president's body was on the dissecting table, the autopsy Y incision had been made, and the Navy pathologists (Dr. James J. Humes and Dr. J. Thorton Boswell) were standing by their tables sautéing various organs. "They were looking for bullet fragments," said Custer. "Boswell was cutting up the liver like a piece of meat. They had already pulled the lungs out. The large intestines were out. The kidneys were out. Actually, most of the organs were already out of the body."

Custer also observed that the plastic bag and bloody sheet had been removed from the president's head. But when he looked at the face, Custer did a double take. "Kennedy was virtually unrecognizable," he recalled. "The face was drooped – like somebody had pulled the scalp back and the face down. The right eye was slightly popped out – protruding more than the left one. And there was a large, gaping wound in the neck."

In preparation for taking x-rays, Custer performed an initial examination of the president's head. "The skull was a mess," he noted. "It looked like somebody had taken the scalp and sheared it right off. It was laying back, loose, and partially shredded." Custer also observed a "king-sized hole" in the top right region of Kennedy's head that ran from the back all the way to the front. "It was big enough hole for me to put both my hands into the skull," he said. The brain was already out of the cranium, and Custer was told it was being infused. He noticed a small amount of white material, possibly plaster of paris, inside the skull along with an artificial apparatus that was apparently being used for stability. On the outside of the skull, Custer saw "a suture between the temporal bone and the parietal bone" in the area of the right temple. "There were serrated edges and it looked as if it had been sawed," he noted. "It flapped out."

Backing off for a moment, Custer turned and looked toward Dr. John Ebersole who was supposed to be directing him in the process of taking the x-rays. *"Take whatever films you feel necessary,"* said Ebersole.

At that point, Dr. Humes piped up and said, *"Remember, you're taking x-rays to find bullets."* Ebersole then essentially repeated that message. *"Yes,"* he said, *"we're here to find any bullet fragments within the skull or body."*

Custer did not understand this order, because he knew that a forensic pathologist performing an autopsy and the radiologist taking the associated x-rays would always try to find out how the murder victim was killed. They would look for entrance and exit wounds, trace the paths of bullets, and do whatever else it took to find the cause of death. But that didn't seem to be what they were doing on this occasion. Although disturbed, Custer did not question this direction from his superior officers, and simply responded, *"Yes, sir."*

Taking another look at the president's body, which had already been cut open and dissected, Custer knew that none of the body x-rays would show anything. The brain would be gone from the head shots, the lungs wouldn't be there for the chest x-rays, and so on. *"Why didn't we take the x-rays before the Y incision?"* Custer asked.

"Mind your own business and get to work," Dr. Ebersole responded.

> *"That is right,"* [the x-rays were taken before any incision was made in the body]. *"The primary purpose of doing that [was] to avoid the fluids getting on to the cassettes. . . . The skull films were definitely taken before the autopsy [Y incision]."*
>
> Dr. John H. Ebersole
> Testimony before the HSCA
> March 11, 1978

"Okay, then I suggest we start on the skull films, because that's where all the damage is." When Ebersole agreed, Custer began his initial preparations.

The president's head was resting on an inverted *"C"* – a four-inch-wide metal bracket that had to be removed, because it would have interfered with the x-rays. Just as he and Ed Reed started to lift the head in order to take off the bracket, one of the Navy pathologists (Humes or Boswell) told Custer not to move the body too much due to the unstableness of the cranium. *"Yes, sir,"* he replied.

It turned out that using the word "unstable" in describing the president's head was an understatement. As Custer lifted the skull, it was so fractured that the bones moved back and forth, sideways, and up and down. "It was like somebody took a hardboiled egg and just rolled it around until it was thoroughly cracked," said Custer. "Part of the head would bulge out, another part would sink in. The only thing that held it all together was the skin. And even that was loose."

Because the head was in a 30-degree upward tilt, Custer tried to straighten it out a bit, but was unable to do so, because rigor mortis had set in. "All right, Ed," Jerry said to his assistant, "let's begin with the AP view." With the head tilted so much, he knew that the orbits would be slightly elongated on the final film, but there was really no other choice. So Custer and Reed proceeded with the taking of the head x-rays.

With the body laying face-up on the dissecting table, Jerry Custer gently lifted the president's head while Ed Reed placed the x-ray cassette underneath. Then, realizing that the flap of bone, hair, and scalp in the right temporal region would have created double density on the x-ray if left open, Custer closed the flap back onto the skull. Upon doing so, he noticed a small bullet hole on the top of the flap. In his opinion, it was clearly a wound of entrance.

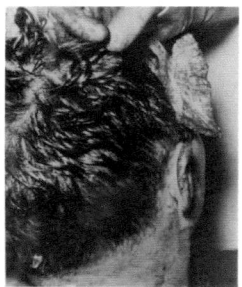

Autopsy photo showing flap in right temporal area.
The x-ray technician witnessed a bullet entrance hole on top of the flap.

Custer and Reed next put the portable x-ray machine in position. It was an old, bulky GE unit, weighing between 1500 and 2000 pounds. The base was approximately three feet by three feet wide, stood three feet high and, of course, was on wheels. The main tower, which projected the radiation source, was approximately six feet long. Custer placed the source 44 inches above the head and then took the x-ray.

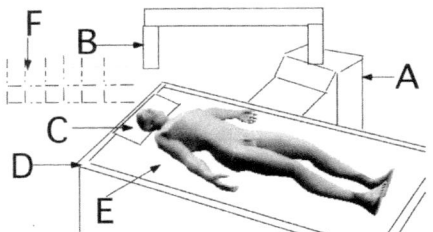

Placement of body and equipment for AP (anterior-posterior) x-ray (#1). Portable x-ray unit (A), x-ray source (B), x-ray cassette film (C), metal framework of table (D), body lying on table (E), bar fence in front of viewing gallery (F).

As Custer lifted the president's head so Reed could remove the exposed x-ray cassette beneath, he noticed that the skull seemed to be growing more and more unstable each time it was handled. So he gently set the head back down and began preparations for the right lateral x-ray. He positioned a new cassette vertically on the right side, and moved the radiation source to the left.

But now Custer had a problem. For the AP x-ray, the radiation source was pointing down. For the lateral x-rays, however, it had to be pointing horizontally, which meant that people had to moved out of the path of the radiation. Custer's problem was that there were more than 50 people in the morgue. "The gallery was loaded from pillar to post," recalled Custer. "People were all over the place, taking notes, poking their noses into everything, making comments, shouting orders. The commotion was astronomical. The decibel-level was extremely high. It was pure mayhem."

Custer had to scream at people to get them to move out of the way of the x-ray source. But with Ed Reed helping to physically move people, they were finally able to take the right lateral x-ray.

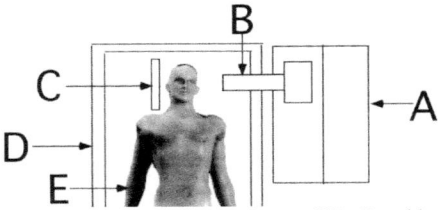

Placement of body and equipment for right lateral x-ray (#2). Portable x-ray unit (A), x-ray source (B), x-ray cassette film (C), metal framework of table (D), body on table (E).

For X-ray #3 (left lateral), the portable unit was wheeled to the other side of the dissecting table so the radiation source could be placed on the right side of the president's head. But when Custer placed the x-ray cassette on the left side, he saw that the base of the skull was slightly sunken. Trying to lift the head higher, he also noticed that the canvas top on the table (stretched out on the table's metal frame) had sagged slightly. To make matters worse, this time he had to shoot over a small bar on the side of the table. The combination of those three things would actually cause the back of the head to be cut off on the resulting x-ray. But there was really nothing that could be done short of moving the entire body to another table – and the pathologists weren't going to allow that, because the body had already been cut open. So Custer simply lifted and straightened the president's head as best he could.

As with the other x-rays, Custer placed his personal measuring tool (a rectangular metal plate with 6 circles) at the lower right so it would be visible on the exposed film. Although he had been told not to place a nameplate underneath each image, he felt certain there would be no objection to this tool. After all, he had used it on virtually every x-ray he had ever taken. Its purpose was to not only identify who took the image, but also serve as a useful indicator for image distortion. After setting the measuring tool and getting people out of the way, Custer exposed the film for the left lateral x-ray.

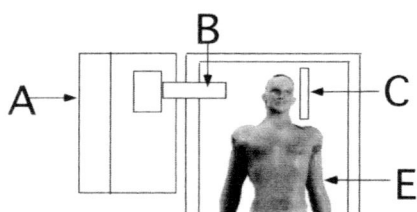

Placement of body and equipment for left lateral x-ray (#3). Portable x-ray unit (A), x-ray source (B), x-ray cassette film (C), body lying on table (E).

For the final two skull x-rays, the portable unit was moved to the front end of the table so that the radiation source would be above and behind the top of the head. Custer then took two oblique views, the first of which focused specifically on the massive hole in the right side of the head. The second was called a "Towne" x-ray. Angled at 30 degrees toward the feet, the radiation source entered the head at the level of the hairline to provide a clear image of the occipital region of the skull.

After taking these two x-rays, Custer and Reed gathered up all five exposed cassettes and left the morgue to go up to the x-ray department on the fourth floor to develop the films. One of the federal agents in the room was assigned to escort them upstairs. Their route was somewhat circuitous in that they had to get on the *elevator, go up to the first floor, walk down a corridor past the main lobby, and take another elevator up to the fourth floor.*

Just as the three men came up to the lobby, a large group of people (including members of the press) entered through the main doors. The federal agent immediately stopped Custer and Reed and ordered them to wait. *"I don't want them to see you,"* said the agent. Custer then noticed that it was the presidential party that had just arrived from Andrews Air Force Base. Jacqueline Kennedy was there, still dressed in the bloody dress that she had worn in the Dallas motorcade. Custer also saw Robert F. Kennedy, the president's brother. *"They got on to the elevators and went up to the towers,"* Custer remembered. *"Then I was allowed to pass, and go up to the x-ray department."*

Jacqueline Kennedy and Robert F. Kennedy, shown here at Andrews Air Force Base, had just arrived at Bethesda Naval Hospital and were passing through the main lobby when Custer saw them. At the time, he was carrying the undeveloped x-rays of JFK's head.

Once there, Custer took all the cassettes into the darkroom for processing. When the federal agent tried to follow him, Custer pushed the agent back. *"Wait a minute,"* said Custer. *"You can't come in here."* The agent waited outside.

Developing and processing of the x-ray films lasted only five minutes. Custer viewed each film, but did not label them, because he had been instructed not to do so. Then he and Reed gathered the images and, escorted by the same federal agent, proceeded back downstairs to the basement morgue. *"The entire time elapsed from leaving and getting back with the developed head x-rays was less than half an hour,"* Custer recalled.

On the way back into the autopsy room, they had to go through the smaller *"cooler"* room. *"As we passed through, I saw a second casket sitting next to the shipping casket that the president's body had come in,"* recalled Custer. *"It was a bronze ceremonial casket and it was closed. At the time, I wondered where it came from. Now I know it was the casket that had arrived with Mrs. Kennedy."*

Upon return with developed head x-rays, Custer saw a gray shipping casket (similar to the one at L) and a more formal bronze casket (similar to the one at R) on the floor of the "cooler" room next to the morgue. Apparently, the bronze casket had arrived with the entourage that came from Andrews AFB.

"Then I walked through the cooler room and handed the x-rays to Dr. Ebersole, who had never left the morgue."

> *"I personally carried the cassettes containing the x-rays to the x-ray department, which was on the fourth floor of the hospital. [Once there, they were] handled by a darkroom technician, given back to me, and hand carried by me to the autopsy room."*
>
> Dr. John H. Ebersole
> Testimony before the HSCA
> March 11, 1978

According to Custer, Dr. Ebersole was waiting for the x-rays *"like a man that was starving for a meal."* He grabbed the films, shuffled through them, and quickly placed the AP x-ray up on the light board. Then he took his glasses off for a closer look.

Almost immediately, Custer pointed out a tiny bullet sliver near the right eye. *"No, no, that's just an artifact,"* Ebersole replied.

Now pointing to the right temporal area, Custer said: *"Well, Doc, don't you think this looks like an entry wound?"*

"Listen, interpreting these films is not your job," replied Ebersole. *"You're here to take x-rays only. Do not ask questions. Just do what you're supposed to do."*

As Doctors Humes and Boswell came over to view the AP image with Ebersole, Custer stood aside. After they pointed at the x-rays and made comments, the doctors went into a conference with several people in the gallery (who could also see the image from where the light board was positioned). There were two men, in particular, who were involved in the discussion and seemed to be giving directions. *"One was a high-ranking military official, a four-star general in uniform,"* recalled Custer. *"The other was a civilian who I took to be JFK's personal physician [Admiral George G. Burkley], because of the way he talked. He said things like:* 'The Kennedy family would not like that route followed up.' These two men were clearly in charge."

After the conference broke up, Ebersole pulled the AP x-ray down from the view box and started to examine it in front of a portable light attached to one of the tables in the room. "Please do not put the film too close to that bulb, Doc," cautioned Custer. "It's hot and you could burn it."

Ebersole ignored the warning and continued moving the x-ray around the bulb. Custer again made the comment, "Please don't get it too close." But no sooner had he said the words than the x-ray started to burn – breaking down the chemical base, exposing the silver, and crinkling the film.

"The whole morgue witnessed this happen," said Custer. "One of the doctors even made a comment. 'Little careless, John,' he said. The worst part about it was that the burn occurred exactly in the area that I suggested was an entry wound at the right temple."

> "I don't know. It [the burn mark] may have happened that night and I may have been the guilty party . . . ."
>
> Dr. John H. Ebersole
> Testimony before the HSCA
> March 11, 1978

* * * * *

At the National Archives in College Park, Maryland, Tom Wilson was prepared and waiting for Steven D. Tilley and his assistant to bring in the original x-rays. On his worktable, he had placed his own copy of the AP image (with which he planned to start), transparencies of all his processed images, the published versions from the HSCA report, his homemade stereo glasses, and his spiral-bound workbook for taking notes.

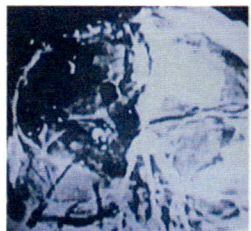 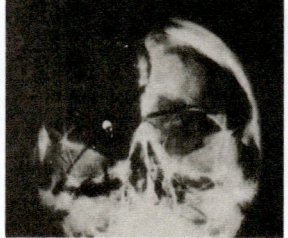 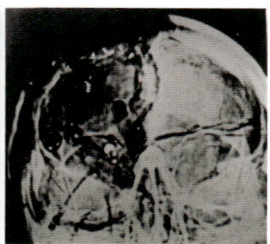

Tom's copy of the AP X-ray (L); JFK Exhibit F-5 (C); JFK Exhibit F-56 (R).

The materials brought in were contained in a series of consecutively numbered folders, and Tom was surprised at how many images were contained in each folder. He was expecting to see only one original of each x-ray. What he received, instead, were dozens of images. In the AP folder alone, there appeared to be a possible original, several copies of that image, and many other copies that varied in size, exposure, and even content. Each x-ray had a page number and was inserted in a see-through plastic cover.

One of the first images Tom looked at was marked "AP #1" and appeared very similar to his own copy, except that it had much more detail. This x-ray was very clear, especially in the area of the right side of the head, which contained a great deal of information (unlike the published versions that showed almost nothing).

Because he was not allowed to make copies or take pictures, Tom had created generic skull models on his computer back home for each x-ray viewed in the National Archives, and then added key information based on his notes and observations. For this first-viewed AP #1 image, Tom documented the following: a white half-moon bullet fragment in the area of the right eye, a heavily fractured right orbit (bone just above eye), and a significant burn mark in the right temple area, which showed ripples at the surface and exposed the silver content of the film. Tom measured this burn mark as being exactly 6.5 centimeters from the centerline of the skull.

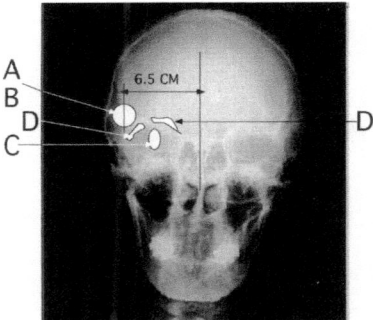

Generic schematic of an AP x-ray image in National Archives. A: burn mark (1.2 cm in diameter); B: silver exposed (on burn mark); C: bullet fragment; D: fractured right orbit.

In his notes for this image, Tom also stated there was no indication of a brain in the skull, and that the exit hole in the back of the head was visible and quite pronounced. Additionally, Tom could see a cylindrical device in the center of the skull that he interpreted to be the device he had seen in one of the autopsy photos.

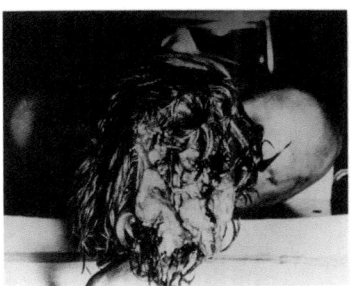

JFK Autopsy Photo, top of head.

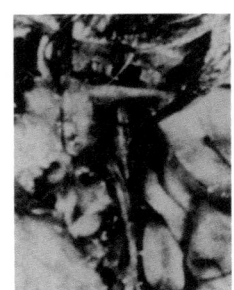

Close-up of cylindrical device.

Another image of the AP x-ray had even more detail. Obvious were the bullet fragment, the fractured right orbit, the burn mark, and the cylindrical device. However, when Tom looked at the image through his magnified stereo glasses, he was shocked to see that the bullet fragment appeared as a raised area on the outside of the x-ray. Further, he could not only see small bubbles in the area of the burn mark, but an additional, smaller burn mark just below the original burn mark. Also obvious to Tom in this image were metal flecks near the top of the skull, a beveling throughout the head in a direction toward the rear, and the very pronounced rectangular hole in the back of the head (which Tom measured as 2.5 cm by 6.0 cm).

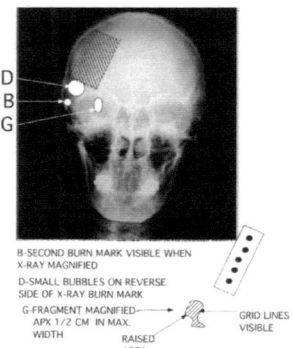

Generic schematic of an AP x-ray image in National Archives.

Opening another folder, Tom found a series of enhanced copies of the AP x-ray that were mixed in terms of observable detail. In the first image viewed, the rectangular hole in the rear of the skull was very pronounced – and the larger burn mark was located at the base and in the center of that rectangle. Tom could also easily see the second burn mark, the fractured right orbit, and the half moon bullet fragment. Additionally, the metallic fragments at the top of the head were much more clear and detailed.

There were a total of six enhancements contained in the folder. One was a mirror image (where the x-ray had simply been flipped). On this copy, the surface beveling of the skull was very pronounced. There was also an image where the skull was black. On some of the enhancements, there were indications of alteration. For instance, some of the holes in Jerrol Custer's personal marker were elliptical rather than circular. On another image, the number "1" appeared backwards in the lower right corner (this was not on the mirror image). And one x-ray had the words "US Naval Hospital" backwards.

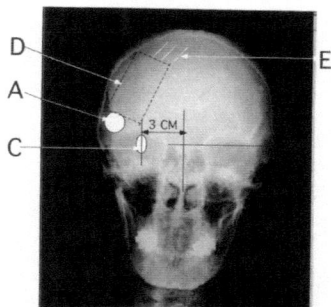

Generic schematic of an enhanced AP x-ray in National Archives.
A: burn mark (1.2 cm in diameter); C: bullet fragment; D: area missing from rear of skull (2.5 cm x 6 cm); E: metal bullet tracks visible.

The final AP folder Tom viewed contained several obviously altered images. One was on white stock that was wider and longer than the original x-ray. The bullet fragment near the right eye was obviously taped onto the x-ray before this copy was made, because the tape itself was visible. Tom measured the tape as being 2 centimeters by 3 centimeters and noted a serrated edge on one edge of the tape. In addition, the bullet fragment appeared black rather than white. A black triangle could also be seen touching the bullet fragment. "How can a taped bullet fragment appear on an 'original' and in official exhibits?" Tom wrote in his notebook.

This altered image further showed a hole in the top rear portion of the skull, but the rectangular opening was not visible. Neither was the large burn mark visible and, as further evidence of distortion and/or manipulation, the large circle in Jerrol Custer's metal ruler was overly elliptical. On a large black stripe across the top of the image were the signed initials of Dr. John H. Ebersole – JHE. There were also two duplicates of this image in the folder, each with the same signed initials.

A second altered image in the folder was printed on photographic film-like material. The back was plain paper, but the front consisted of a kind of shiny emulsion that Tom speculated might have been Polaroid film. On this image the bullet fragment was white and no tape was visible. In addition the rectangular exit hole in the back of the head was gone as were all evidence of a fractured right orbit, any burn marks, and all the metal tracks in the back of the head.

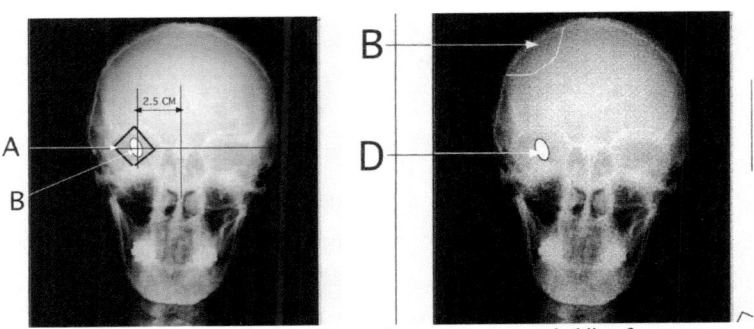

Generic schematic of an altered AP x-ray image (L). A: tape holding fragment on x-ray (tape measures 2 cm x 3 cm); B: bullet fragment. Generic schematic of altered AP image (R). B: rear portion of skull missing; D: bullet fragment.

After returning from the National Archives, Tom spoke with Jerry Custer about some of his observations. Custer stated that he had not seen such a large bullet fragment in the area of the right eye on the

AP x-ray he developed. But he had previously used Polaroid development paper in making copies. "I remember Bethesda was always the proving ground for new techniques and new apparatus," Custer recalled. "What you describe sounds like Polaroid and I specifically remember using it. The paper is a cellular base. One side is very smooth and the black strip where you saw Ebersole's initials is where the Polaroid stops."

Custer also told Tom that people could play games with x-rays. "You can take a Polaroid reproduction into a darkroom," he said, "place a non-exposed film on top, project a light source behind it, and then make a contact print." It was easy to add information on top of an existing x-ray in this manner, he pointed out. Custer also told Tom about another method of faking x-rays. "It's also possible to take an x-ray, place a fragment on top of the film, and then re-x-ray it," he said. "You'd come out with an image that shows a fragment appearing within the head. Then, if you enlarged it, you probably wouldn't be able to tell the difference."

The x-rays published in the HSCA Report in 1978 were darkened, enlarged and, as a result, hid all necessary detail needed to make an intelligent evaluation of damage to the skull. Moreover, it was clear to Tom that JFK Exhibit F-56, which was purported to be a "computer assisted image enhancement" was nothing of the kind. It was exactly the same as the image Tom had received, and from which he had performed all his image processing. This image, he believed, was the faked composite (made using one of the methods that Custer had described) that was enlarged, purposely darkened, and then released to the public.

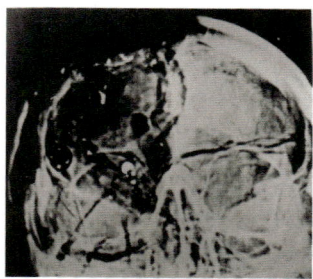
JFK Exhibit F-56.

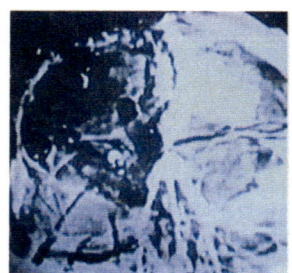
Tom's copy of the AP x-ray.

After spending four and one-half hours in the National Archives looking at all the copies of the AP #1 x-ray, Tom was convinced that the Deed of Gift contained hard evidence of faked copies that were made sometime after November 22, 1963. He further concluded that

Dr. John H. Ebersole had seen and reviewed these altered copies. In comparing these so-called "original" images with his own computer image processed versions, he felt that there was simply no other reasonable explanation.

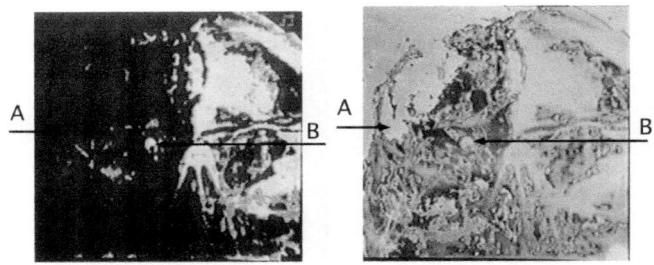

Enlargement of JFK Exhibit F-55 (L) and Tom's image processing of AP x-ray (R). Location of burn mark bottom of rectangular hole in back of head (A) and bullet fragment (B). HSCA's published version effectively hides all evidence detail.

Why was the AP x-ray altered? It was Tom Wilson's opinion that one possible motive was to mislead the government committees investigating the assassination of President Kennedy. Was it possible that some key members of the HSCA forensics panel were aware of the manipulation? Tom simply did not know.

> *"The Committee decided to display the autopsy x-rays to the public in a cropped fashion. In the hearings, the committee used the original x-rays only to verify the authenticity and accuracy of the cropped counterparts. . . ."*
>
> House Select Committee on Assassinations
> March 1979

* * * * *

Shortly after Dr. Ebersole burned the original AP x-ray during the autopsy at Bethesda Naval Medical Center, Dr. Pierre A. Finck, a third pathologist, arrived in the morgue to participate in the proceedings. Jerry Custer noted that when Finck (a lieutenant colonel in the Army) arrived, the demeanor of the room abruptly changed. "He came in and just took over," recalled Custer. "He barked out orders to Humes and Boswell. 'Stop that. Don't do that anymore. You take notes. You do this. You do that.'" Custer also noted that phone calls started coming in from Dallas and downtown Washington, and that Dr. Finck would confer with the same two men in the gallery who had been giving directions. *"There were more cohesive directions from the gallery after he arrived,"* noted Custer.

JFK autopsy pathologists Boswell, Humes, and Finck.

The next x-ray put up on the light board by Dr. Ebersole was the right lateral view. Almost immediately, Jerrol Custer blurted out a comment. *"This shows fragmenting from the front to the back of the head,"* he said. *"You actually have a conish effect there – where the bullet seems like it went through, started to disintegrate, and then went out."*

"Shut up, Custer!" Ebersole responded. *"It's none of your business."*

Once again, Jerry had been quieted. But he had enough experience to know that a bullet had entered at the right temporal area, fragmented into pieces, spread out as it passed through the skull, and then blew out the back of the head. *"There was tremendous trauma,"* Custer noted. *"There were metal flecks above the right eye socket (which was heavily fractured), and the farther back you went, the more destruction you had. The right lateral x-ray was the key to the whole situation. But nobody in the autopsy room would listen to me."*

After another lengthy conference with the pathologists and several people in the gallery, Dr. Ebersole went back to the film on the viewing box. He took a ruler and penciled in two lines on the image that converged at a point low on the back of the head. *"That's the entrance wound,"* Custer heard Ebersole say.

"Ebersole was clearly defining a trajectory," recalled Custer, *"but it was just the opposite of what had really happened. And then, all of a sudden, someone from the gallery yelled, 'Don't do that.' And Ebersole stopped his drawing on the x-ray."*

> "Sometime within a month of the assassination, I received a call from the White House medical staff [asking] me if I could review the skull x-rays for the purpose of getting some measurements for a sculpture. . . . . Those were the lines that I drew at the White House. . . . I don't know what happened to those measurements, whether they were used by the sculptor or not, but that is how [the lines] got on that lateral skull [x-ray]. . . . Those were not any attempt by any ballistics expert to show path of bullets."
>
> Dr. John H. Ebersole
> Testimony before the HSCA, p. 5, 67
> March 11, 1978

There was much less discussion when the left lateral x-ray went up on the light board – partly because Custer had finally given up talking, but mostly because it really didn't show very much. The first thing noticeable was that the bottom portion of the skull was cutoff, just as Jerry had thought it would be. The instability of the head, the flexibility of the canvas tabletop, and the bar that had to be shot over all combined to limit the back view.

Because it was a view of the left side of the head, the back portion of the skull could be seen still intact and the right eye's fractured orbital ridge was not clearly visible. However, as Custer observed, "You could still see metal flecks in the top of the head expanding from front to back. They were resting on the bone itself and they were clearly visible."

The two oblique view x-rays were also placed on the viewing box, but as with the left lateral, they drew limited discussion from the pathologists and the gallery. In general, Custer remembered seeing extensive fracturing of the skull with outward beveling toward the back of the head, a right eye area that was almost completely obliterated, and the same metal flecks that had been observed in each of the other head x-rays.

One specific thing Custer did remember was that someone in the gallery asked what the rectangular object was at the lower right of each of the images. After explaining that it was his personal measuring tool, Custer was told not to use it on any of the future x-rays.

Finally, Dr. Ebersole turned to Custer and reminded him that they were on a time limit, that they needed to make sure there were no *more bullets in the body, and that he was to hurry it up with the rest of the x-rays. "Okay, take the next set," Ebersole ordered.*

* * * * *

At the National Archives, Tom Wilson turned his attention to the lateral x-rays. Set out on his worktable, he had placed a transparency of his own copy of the lateral x-ray, and copies of HSCA Exhibits F-52 and F-53. Reviewing his notes, Tom recalled that the HSCA Report had not specifically mentioned whether these x-rays were right or left lateral, although they were both inferred to be right lateral. JFK Exhibit F-52 was described as "an enlarged copy . . . showing a side view of the skull of the President with the back of the head to your left." JFK Exhibit F-53 was described as "a lateral view of the president's head" and a "computerized enhancement," created because it brought "out some of the details of the x-ray more clearly." After what Tom had just seen in the AP x-ray folders, he was now extremely leery of the phrase "computerized enhancement" used to describe the x-rays. He was also most curious to see what the so-called "originals" showed in regard to right versus left lateral.

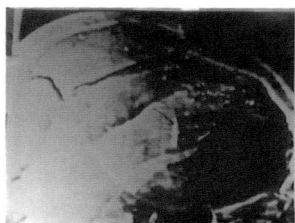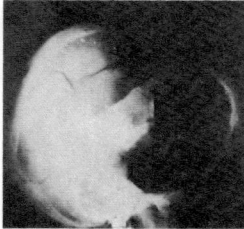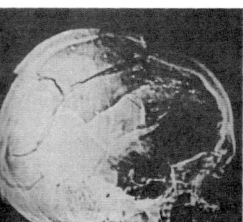

Tom's copy of the lateral x-ray (L); JFK Exhibit F-52 (C); JFK Exhibit F-53 (R).

The first image Tom looked at was labeled "#2 Right Lateral." It looked fairly similar to his copy of the lateral x-ray, but was much clearer and contained significantly more detail. The metallic fragment flow was obvious. Beginning at a point above the right eye socket, it expanded outward and upward toward the top rear of the head. Tom could also see a dense white mark above, behind, and to the left (looking at the photograph) of the right eye) that was flat on the posterior side, but oval on the anterior side. He guessed that this might be the cylindrical device (used to shore up the head) he'd seen in both the AP x-ray and in one of the autopsy photographs. In this same area, there was a marked disruption of the smooth contour of the skull – with an L-shape and a visible serrated edge. Tom interpreted this to be the flap in the skull located at the right temple entrance wound.

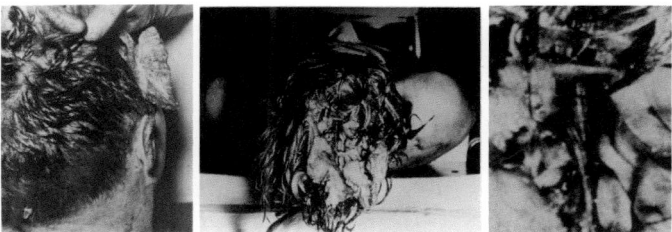

Right lateral x-ray in Archives suggests presence of skull flap and cylindrical device.

One of the most obvious items to be observed on this x-ray was a solid white mark located at the very front of the forehead. Was this another bullet fragment taped on the film to coincide with the half-moon fragment on the AP x-ray?" Tom wondered. If so, it was certainly located in the right place. Also visible on the image was the sella turcica bone, which had a 10-degree tilt to it (indicating the head was tilted slightly forward) – and a fractured lower right orbit bone.

Of particular interest to Tom was a white area at the very back of the head. In part, he could see that this area was heavily fractured, probably due to one bone riding over another and causing some double density on the x-ray response readings. More importantly, however, the white area, itself, (which measured 7.2 centimeters by 4 centimeters), appeared to have been altered. Tom's evidence for this was the fact that, while he observed grid lines in the holes of Jerry Custer's measuring tool, there were none in the white area on either side of the x-ray, which resulted in no visible depth. Because this was the exact area where there should have been a hole in the skull, it looked as if this was a copy of the original x-ray with the hole in the head filled in.

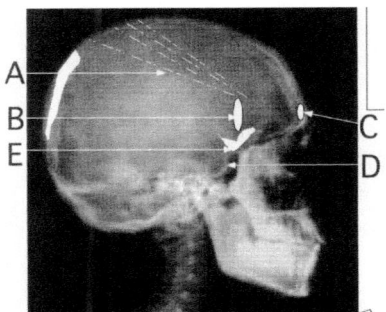

Schematic of a right lateral x-ray in Archives. A: metallic fragments (flow from front to top rear); B: dense white mark (oval on anterior side, flat on posterior side); C: solid white mark; D: sella turcica; E: fractured lower right orbit. White area at top back of skull is blasted out hole filled in (altered).

Contained in the same folder were three copies of the very same image. One of those copies included a picture that was upside down and facing left. "Why in the world would someone print an image in this manner?" Tom wondered. "For what purpose was it done?"

The next image viewed was an enhanced copy of the right lateral x-ray. Similar to the previous film, it showed the metallic fragments in the same area (flowing from front-to-back and down-to-up). Also present was the white area in the back of the skull, except on this film, grid lines *were* visible. And that made Tom wonder if this particular enhanced copy was made before the previous image (which had the white region filled in).

The most glaring addition on the enhanced x-ray, however, was the presence of two pencil lines that converged at a point in the occipital region of the skull. "Are these similar to the lines drawn by Dr. John Ebersole during the autopsy?" Tom wrote in his notebook. "If so, why are they on this enhanced copy? And where is the original that he drew them on?" At this point, Tom also began to speculate. "These lines could give the impression of an entrance wound at the back of the head and dispersal of bullet fragments from back to front. Were they [the lines] used as a guide to alter the x-ray?"

There were additional copies of the enhanced right lateral x-ray contained in the same folder in the Archives. Most were identical to the one with the pencil lines drawn on. But one had the skull white and another had the skull black.

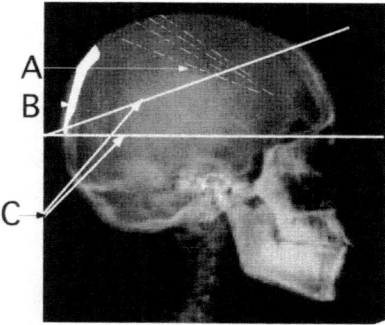

Generic schematic of an enhanced right lateral x-ray image in National Archives. A: metallic fragments (flow from front to top rear); B: no skull in this area; C: converging pencil lines.

In looking at an x-ray marked "#3 Left Lateral," Tom noted the same small white object at the front of the head, the metallic fragment tracks with a flow from front-to-back and down-to-up (approximately 35 degrees from horizontal), and smaller teeth, which denoted an x-ray source at an angle to the skull. In this image, the back of the head was not visible, which made Tom conclude that it may very well have been derived from the original left lateral x-ray taken by Jerry Custer. Recall that Custer had stated that the back part had been cut off due to a problem with the flexible canvas table top, the instability of the skull, and shooting over a raised bar on the end of the dissecting table.

In his notebook, Tom also jotted down his observations that there was a white circular mark near the eye (probably the same cylindrical device seen in the right lateral x-ray), that the back top of the skull was offset .4 centimeters (probably due to overriding fractured bones), and that the fractured right orbit was not visible "although the left lateral orbit appears normal." Furthermore, one enhanced copy of the "#3 Left Lateral" clearly showed that the white fragment at the forehead was, as Tom wrote, "on the surface of the skull, not in the skull." Several duplicate copies of the enhanced and unenhanced left lateral image were varied in what they revealed, including a mirror image that actually had the left lateral facing right (making it appear to be a right lateral). Tom also noted that a number of these copies contained visible fingerprints on them.

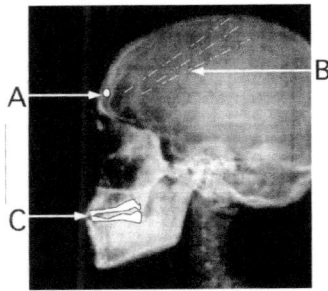

Schematic of a left lateral x-ray image in Archives. A: small white object; B: metallic fragment tracks (flow front-to-back, down-to-up); C: smaller teeth = x-ray source at angle to skull.

After Tom completed his analysis of the AP and lateral head x-rays, he began searching for the other views that Jerry Custer said he took. As he sifted through the other folders, he saw only the titles "Neck and Chest," "Shoulder," "Spine," "Pelvis and Hips," "Lower Extremities," and "Bone Fragments."

"I don't see the other head x-rays," Tom said, turning to Mr. Tilley's assistant (who was in the room with him). "There were two others taken; an oblique view looking down into the hole in the skull and a Towne view."

Steven D. Tilley showed up a few minutes after the assistant called for him, and Tom repeated his concern. "I'm sorry, Mr. Wilson, but you have all the x-rays," replied Tilley.

"But I know there were two additional head x-rays taken," Tom replied.

"Well, sir, this is all we have in the Deed of Gift. If they're not in these folders, we don't have them."

While Tom was quite disturbed with the revelation that the originals of these two critical head x-rays were not in the National Archives, he knew there was still enough evidence in the films present to show that both the Warren Commission and the House Select Committee on Assassinations were wrong in their conclusions about the Kennedy assassination. First, Tom felt the head x-rays proved that a bullet entered in the area of the right temple, exploded, and exited out the top back of the head. "In every head x-ray," he wrote, "there was total destruction of the right orbit (which occurred on impact of the entering bullet)." Furthermore, he also noted that the metallic fragment flow "is present in each head x-ray and never deviates in showing a conish effect" that proves the missile entered in the right temple and that "the path was front-to-back and down-to-up."

Second, Tom believed that, based on the myriad of copies, enhancements, and variations in the films contained in the National Archives, the head x-rays of President Kennedy were definitely faked. For example, on the AP x-ray, a bullet fragment was taped on the film and then re-developed to create a new, false composite image. This fragment was placed in the exact position of the bullet entry in the back of the head proposed by the HSCA – and its presence was then used as evidence for the Committee's conclusion.

> "There are extensive fracture lines radiating from the point of entrance marked by this relatively large metal fragment and the x-ray lines extending from it. This corresponds precisely to the point of entrance beneath the cowlick area...."
>
> House Select Committee on Assassinations
> March 1979

However, as Tom Wilson wrote in his notebook, there was no observable "defect in the cowlick area on either the right or left lateral-x-rays."

Another example of fakery involved the lateral x-rays. The massive hole in the right top of President Kennedy's skull was not visible in Archives copies of either the right or left lateral views. On one copy of the right lateral, the exit hole in the back of the head was filled in. Overall, Tom speculated that the "lateral" x-ray published in the HSCA report was probably a faked composite of both the right and left lateral views. The original right lateral, which may have shown part of the hole in the top of the head, was used as a base. A mirror image of the left lateral (showing the top and back of the head) may have been superimposed on top of the right lateral and then re-developed. The new image was then darkened sufficiently to hide any substantive detail. However, when subjected to Tom's computer processing, the darkened image in the area of the right temple clearly revealed the bullet entrance wound.

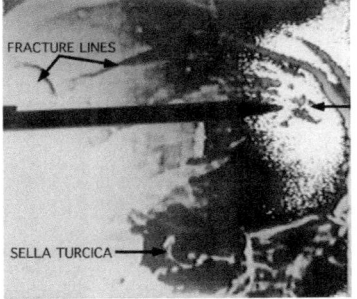

Tom's processed image of lateral x-ray showing entrance wound in right temporal area.

The original right lateral x-ray, as taken and viewed by Jerrol Custer on the night of the autopsy, could not be revealed because, as Custer stated to Tom, "[It] was the key to the whole situation." Nor could the two oblique views be shown, because they did not jive with the lateral x-ray.

After inspecting the head x-rays, Tom concluded that there were no originals present in the National Archives, and that "they have probably been destroyed." Moreover, those copies present in the Deed of Gift show verifiable evidence of manipulation, darkening, enhancement, and fakery.

> *"No evidence of fakery was discerned. The X-ray images have not been altered in any fashion except for: 1. Two small areas of thermal damage resulting from a light source that was once held too close to the "anterior/posterior" image; 2. . . . minor 'staining' on the coloration . . . due to incomplete processing of the film in the developing process."*
>
> House Select Committee on Assassinations
> March 1979

After the crowd in the autopsy room at Bethesda Naval Medical Center completed their preliminary viewing of the head x-rays, Jerrol Custer was ordered by Dr. John Ebersole to "take the next set." So Custer and his assistant, Ed Reed, carefully placed film cassettes under the president's neck and throat and took two AP (anterior/posterior) views. Then they began positioning the body for several x-rays of the shoulders and chest.

Custer had already taken x-rays of the head without the brain present, and now he was told to take x-rays without most of the organs present in the chest cavity. The lungs, for example, had already been removed. "I could hear the doctors as they worked at the dissecting table," Custer recalled. "They described scarring and a hemothorax [blood accumulation] in the left lung, which was caused by the trauma of a bullet hitting there. That finding was repeated by someone in the gallery. There was also mention of blood in the right lung."

When Custer and Reed lifted President Kennedy's body to place cassettes under the torso for the chest x-rays, a bullet "fell out of the body" onto the floor. "Dr. Finck quickly came over, picked it up with a pair of forceps, and dropped it into a little bottle," recalled Custer. "It was a king-sized fragment; about an inch and a half; the size of the first joint in my small finger." To say the least, having such a large bullet fall out of the body at this point in the autopsy was unusual. It had not fallen out when the body was first lifted out of the casket or when the body was transferred from the moveable table to the dissecting table. Now it had "appeared" when the body was very carefully lifted up to place an x-ray cassette underneath. In thinking about it later, it crossed Custer's mind that the bullet may have been found during the dissection process and then placed underneath the body. It also seemed suspicious that Dr. Finck was at the quick and ready with forceps and a little bottle, as if he was waiting for the bullet to drop.

As before, after taking this round of x-rays, Custer and Reed carried the cassettes up to the fourth floor (again escorted by a federal agent), developed the films, and then brought them back down to the morgue, where they were quickly put up on the light board by Dr. Ebersole. Forgetting himself, Custer immediately pointed to the AP neck x-ray. "Look here," he said, "bullet fragments in the C3, C4 area [lower neck vertebrae]."

"Mind your own business," Ebersole replied curtly.

Custer recalled later that there were "very, very apparent bullet fragments in and around the neck wound." As for the chest x-rays, he explained that "there was really nothing to look at, because the lungs had already been taken out." Ebersole then spoke with the autopsy doctors and subsequently went into another conference with key people in the gallery.

Custer ran through the same drill with the next set of x-rays, which was of the lower chest, the back, and the hips. He took them, ran them upstairs for development, and then brought them back down for review. The last series taken was of the lower portion of the body, including the abdomen, pelvis, and lower extremities. At this point, Custer turned to Ebersole and suggested they stop. "It's ridiculous to go any further," he said. "The president obviously wasn't shot in the legs." Ebersole agreed and no more x-rays were taken.

The conferences with the doctors and people in the gallery dragged the proceedings long into the night. "With each set, there was more interference," recalled Custer. "'We should take some more here,' or 'we should take some more there,' they said. I was just an E-4 and I did what I was told. The proceedings stretched out and I was there for a good while." Custer estimated that, in the end, there were "anywhere from 14 to 20 total original films taken that night." Finally, they were all gathered up and given to Secret Service Agent Roy Kellerman for safekeeping. "I never saw them again," said Custer.

Fifteen years later, during hearings and testimony before the House Select Committee on Assassinations, numerous references were made that x-rays had been taken during the autopsy of President Kennedy both before and after the Y incision had been made and, therefore, some images showed organs removed from the body. However, Jerrol Custer (who was not called to testify before the HSCA) was adamant that all x-rays were taken after the Y incision was made and the organs removed. "There was no second set of x-rays," he told Tom Wilson.

> "We were asked by the Secret Service agents present to repeat the films and did so. . . . The second group of x-rays were taken either before the incision was made or very shortly thereafter."
>
> Dr. John H. Ebersole
> Testimony before the HSCA
> March 11, 1978

* * * * *

After analyzing the head x-rays at the National Archives, Tom would not spend as much time viewing the remaining films largely because he had not previously obtained copies and, therefore, hadn't performed any image processing. However, Tom did prepare extensively by studying notes of his interviews with Jerry Custer, and by bringing along photos of additional x-rays published in 1978 by the HSCA. Unfortunately, Tom could not make heads or tails of these images, because the Committee had made it impossible to see any kind of detail.

While mentioning that members of the medical panel had reviewed JFK Exhibits F-28 and F-29, which were "two of the original 14 autopsy x-rays kept at the National Archives," the HSCA did not publish them. Rather, the Committee printed "enlargements of portions of the x-rays" in two different places and labeled them, "photograph of the anterior x-ray of the neck and chest."

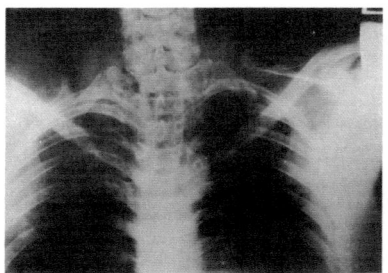

JFK Exhibit F-30 and Figure 11: "Photograph of the anterior x-ray of the neck and chest," (L); JFK Exhibit F-31 and Figure 10 "Photograph of an anterior x-ray of the neck and chest," (R).

As Tom pulled out the additional x-ray folders, he was hoping to see images with significantly more details than those contained in the HSCA exhibits. And based on Jerry Custer's description of observable bullet fragments, he was especially interested in seeing the original AP views of the neck. Unfortunately, there was not a single such neck x-ray contained in the National Archives – not in any folder, not even a cropped version. Nor could Tom find the two original "neck and chest" x-rays from which the HSCA medical panel said it had made the two published enlargements. The only images present were various copies of the chest x-rays that were nothing more than cropped enhancements. The original x-rays of the chest that Jerrol Custer had described taking at the autopsy were simply not present in the Deed of Gift.

Of the enhanced chest x-rays present, there was one black and white copy of each. And although they contained somewhat more detail than the HSCA published exhibits, Tom wrote in his notebook that he "could see no evidence of lung shadows." Therefore, he concluded that the evidence in the Archives supported Custer's claim that no bullet fragments could be seen in the chest x-rays due to the simple fact that the lungs and other key organs (which would hold such fragments) had been removed prior to the x-rays being taken.

> "The [chest] x-rays show that there is no missile present in the body at the time the x-rays were taken."
>
> House Select Committee on Assassinations
> March 1979

The next folder Tom opened was labeled "bone fragments." Recounting his taking x-rays of several skull fragments, Jerrol Custer had told an interesting story that differed from the HSCA account. The Committee, meanwhile, had published only one "photograph of an x-ray" of three fragments that, in keeping with other exhibits, was also woefully lacking in detail. In fact, in this particular image, most of the exhibit was black space, which made it even more difficult to see anything at all. These "three fragments of bone," read the HSCA Report, were "received by Dr. Humes and Dr. Boswell in the autopsy room while they were performing the autopsy" and supposedly came from "the limousine in which the president had been riding."

Interestingly, in the explanation for JFK Exhibit F-64, the HSCA described metal fragments "at one edge" of the larger triangular fragment, which "the panel concluded . . . was part of the gunshot wound of exit of the right side of the head of the president." Then, in describing Figure 26 (published in a different volume), the Committee stated: "On the triangular fragment are radiopaque shadows which have the appearance of tiny missile fragments."

 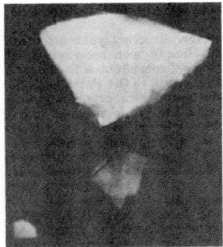

HSCA image of skull fragments; JFK Exhibit F-64 and Figure 26; [Right image enlarged].

According to the HSCA, these bone fragments were "displaced" from the right side of President Kennedy's skull by a bullet that was fired from above and behind the limousine. This explanation was illustrated in a "scale drawing of the frontal and right side of a human skull," which was printed twice and labeled JFK Exhibit F-66 (in Volume I) and Figure 29 (in Volume VII).

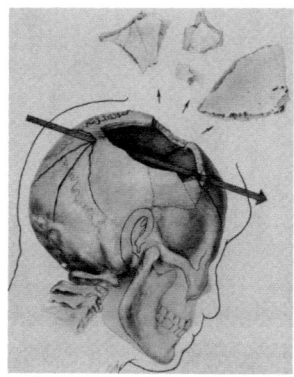

JFK Exhibit F-66 and Figure 29.

Within the folder marked "bone fragments," Tom found only three x-rays. All of them were obvious copies of originals (which were not present), all had Dr. John H. Ebersole's initials (JHE) on them, and none were the same as the image published in the HSCA Report. The first image was printed on white stock that was glossy on one side and dull on the other. It was an x-ray of only the large bone fragment – and both metallic fragments and scotch tape were visible on it. The second image was an identical copy of the first and no apparent differences could be detected.

The third x-ray contained all three bone fragments and revealed enough detailed information that Tom decided to make a sketch complete with measurements. Metallic fragments were contained on three areas of the large bone – on the upper part of which Tom could see tape. In addition, the mid-sized skull bone (at the lower left part of the image) had a smaller piece of bone taped to it. Tom could distinguish the smaller bone and the tape that was holding it on. In reality, then, there were actually four total bone fragments of the skull.

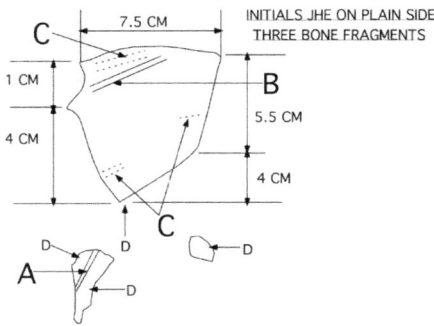

Tom's sketch (w/ measurements) of bone fragments x-ray in National Archives. A: Small piece taped to larger piece; B: tape observed on large fragment; C: metallic fragments on three areas of large bone fragment; four total bone fragments in all.

After Tom made his sketch of the three bone fragments, he pulled out the detailed notes of his interview with Jerrol Custer. Once again, Custer's version of the events surrounding the taking of this x-ray seemed to have more credibility than the story presented in the HSCA Report.

* * * * *

During the early afternoon on November 23, 1963 (the day after the autopsy was performed), Dr. John Ebersole arrived at Bethesda Medical Center with four bone fragments from President Kennedy's skull and three or four small bullet fragments. "*He said he had just come back from a briefing at the White House,*" *recalled Jerrol Custer,* "*and he told me that he had spoken with the head of the Secret Service.*"

"*I want these bones x-rayed with the metal fragments on them,*" *Ebersole told Custer.* "*They are going to be used to make measurements for a bust of President Kennedy.*"

At first, Custer remained silent. But he knew Ebersole was not making a simple request. He was issuing a direct order.

"*I want you to take these x-rays with the portable machine you used yesterday,*" *continued Ebersole.* "*And don't use your metal marker. I better not see it on these films.*"

Ebersole then ordered Custer to tape the metal fragments on specific portions of the large bone fragment. He also issued an instruction to tape the smallest bone fragment onto one of the other bones, effectively making four bones into three for the purpose of showing them on the x-rays.

"*I did as I was ordered,*" *Custer recalled.* "*Ebersole was my superior officer and I was just an E-4. I followed the chain of command.*"

Custer then carried the bones and the bullet fragments up to the X-Ray Department on the fourth floor. He used scotch tape to adhere the fragments onto the bones and then placed the bones onto film cassettes. Then he went into a side room where the portable x-ray machine was located and took several different exposures at different distances. Each bone was x-rayed separately and then all three were placed on one cassette and taken together. "I took a total of four x-rays," Custer remembered. "Then I developed the films and took them back downstairs to Dr. Ebersole. I was alone when I took and developed the x-rays. No one else was in the room."

> "Later in the evening . . . , perhaps about twelve thirty . . . , at Dr. Finck's request, I x-rayed these [bone fragments]. These were the last x-rays I took . . . . The autopsy was still going on . . . . At the time the fragments were x-rayed, Dr. Finck was present."
>
> Dr. John H. Ebersole
> Testimony before the HSCA
> March 11, 1978

Upon receiving the x-rays from Jerrol Custer, Dr. Ebersole issued a stern warning. "Everything you have seen, you should forget," he told Custer. "You are not to say anything – *anything*. If you do, high-level people are going to make sure you will be quite sorry."

* * * * *

As Tom Wilson closed out the last of the folders in the Deed of Gift that were supposed to contain originals of x-rays taken at the autopsy of President Kennedy, he asked to see Special Access Chief Steven D. Tilley again. "Mr. Tilley, there are no AP x-rays of the neck present in these folders," said Tom. "I am certain some were taken and, according to my source, they revealed the presence of bullet fragments. I believe numerous original x-rays are also missing from these files. Could there possibly be folders somewhere else in the Archives that contain them?"

"No, sir," responded Tilley. "This is all we have."

Shocked and disappointed, Tom could not believe the state of the x-ray evidence that existed in the Deed of Gift. After all, it was the President of the United States who had been murdered.

"Well, if that's all the x-rays there are," said Tom, "then I'd like to see the autopsy photographs now."

The time was 3:41 p.m. on September 25, 1995.

11 / <u>Autopsy Photographs in the National Archives</u>

Tom Wilson prepared for his inspection of the autopsy photographs by reviewing the published images and noting the timing of their release over a period of twenty-five years. Just as with the autopsy x-rays, the photos were not presented in the Warren Report or the accompanying 26 volumes released by the Warren Commission. More than fifteen years after the assassination (in 1978), the HSCA published only sketches of some of the photographs along with a few cropped enlargements of the real photos. [Several shown below with HSCA exhibit reference.]

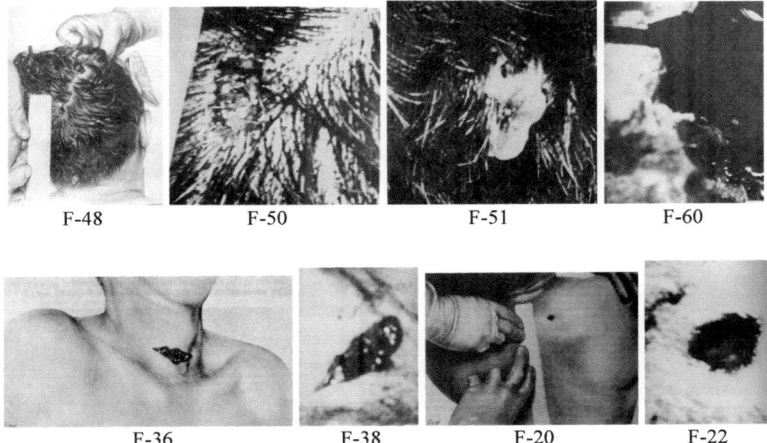

F-48   F-50   F-51   F-60

F-36   F-38   F-20   F-22

Finally, in 1988, ten years after the HSCA Report, and a full quarter century after the assassination, itself, the so-called "Fox" set of autopsy photographs made their way into the public sector. [Key photos shown below]. Tom set out all these copies on his worktable, along with transparencies of his own computer processed images.

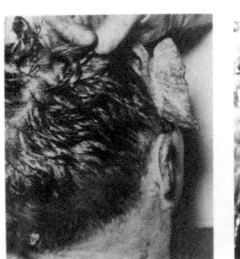  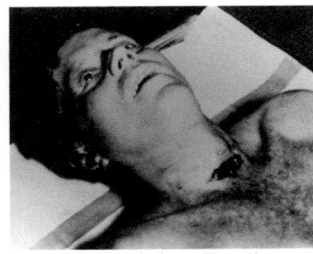

Back of head (Fox 3)   Top of head (Fox 8)   Head and chest (Fox 1)

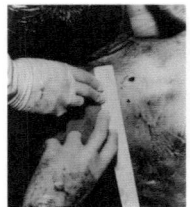 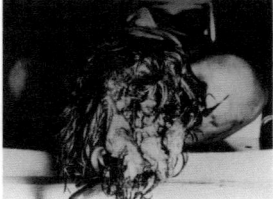 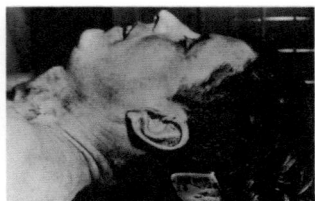

Back (Fox 5)   Top of head (Fox 7)   Left profile (Fox 4)

As the original autopsy photographs contained in the Deed of Gift were being retrieved by Archives personnel, Tom reviewed Jerry Custer's related comments about autopsy photos on the evening of November 22, 1963 at Bethesda Naval Hospital.

* * * * *

"Photographs were being taken all the time," recalled Custer. "When I'd finish a set of x-rays, Floyd Riebe would come over and take pictures. Then, when I would take another set, he'd back off and pick up again after I was done. It was a constant thing."

Floyd Riebe, an assistant medical photographer, was one of two photographers mentioned by Jerrol Custer as being present at the autopsy. [Other witnesses have mentioned John Stringer (Riebe's boss) as having also been there.] Custer explained that Riebe would take a roll of film, empty his camera, place the film in a container, re-load and then take another roll. Each roll of film, however, was forcibly taken from Riebe by Secret Service agents in the room. "They were ripped right out of his hand," explained Custer. "Floyd got to the point where he was upset about it."

The second person mentioned by Custer as having taking pictures at the autopsy was Lieutenant Commander William Pitzer, who was in charge of video at Bethesda. "Pitzer was taking movies," Custer recalled. "And there were quite a few upset people from the gallery that didn't like that. But he kept right on going. 'I'm doing my job,' Pitzer said."

> Lieutenant Commander William Bruce Pitzer was found dead in his office at Bethesda Naval Medical Center on October 29, 1966. According to an FBI teletype released the same day, Pitzer was found dead "in TV production studio . . . with gunshot wound in head. Body laying face down on floor, and a pool of blood with a thirty eight caliber revolver laying close to body."
> Three separate government investigations ruled the death a suicide. Controversy still exists, however. Some investigators speculate that Pitzer was murdered to prevent release of autopsy videos upon his upcoming retirement. No video film of President Kennedy's autopsy has ever surfaced.

When Jerrol Custer finished his work in the early morning hours of November 23, 1963, he replaced the metal "C" headrest on the autopsy table, and then he and his assistant, Ed Reed, took the portable x-ray machine and all materials back up to the fourth floor. *[The x-rays remained with Secret Service Agent Roy Kellerman.]* "The last time I saw the president's body, it was literally butchered. There was body fluid everywhere. It was a mess."

As Custer was leaving the morgue, the mortician and his assistants were just arriving. "I never saw the body after restorative work was done," he said. "As I was leaving, I saw the gray ambulance that came with the Mrs. Kennedy's entourage. It was parked off to the side of the loading dock."

After working most of the night, an exhausted Jerrol Custer went to temporary quarters at the medical center, laid down on his bunk, and fell fast asleep.

* * * * *

Steven D. Tilley and his assistant brought in a series of folders containing autopsy photographs. All the folders were numbered, but few gave any kind of clue as to what would be found inside. There was also one rather large Archives package containing 43 8" x 10" prints (both black & white and color) of a variety of views.

Two of the folders Tom opened contained color photographs of the brain and a couple of black and white copies (and one color) of the back. The brain pictures were of a whole brain and looked nothing like the sketch published in the HSCA volumes. Because he knew the brain, itself, had been missing from the Deed of Gift for years, Tom took a few measurements and recorded them in his notebook. The photos of the back seemed to be exact copies of the photo he already had (Fox 5). On the reverse of the color image, however,

Tom was surprised to see the initials "JB" handwritten in ink. "JB?" he thought. "That must be J. Thorton Boswell, one of the pathologists. Makes sense that he would review the photos. After all, he was present at the autopsy when they were taken."

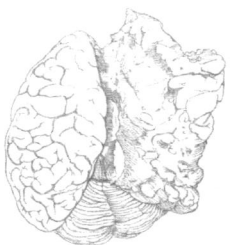 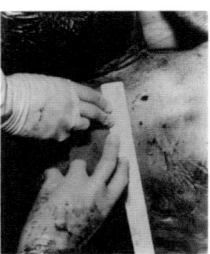

Sketch of brain; HSCA,Figure 32, (L);Autopsy photo of back; Same image in Archives.

Another folder contained five black & white and two color prints of a view equivalent to the front head and chest autopsy photo (Fox 1). The initials "JB" were on the back of each print. Two copies were identical to the photo Tom had, but the others were varied in content. The tracheotomy neck wound, for instance, was in focus on one image and out of focus on the other. When viewed in stereo, the in-focus photographs clearly showed the depth of the wound.

In a separate print, there was clear evidence of photographic retouching in the area of the right temple and back of the head. A black triangle was superimposed on the temple area. However, it was poorly done, because the bullet entry hole was still visible. Also visible was beveling in a portion of the skull near the back of the head. This photograph appeared to Tom as a partial step in the process of getting to the end result, which would be an image that showed no original entry and exit wounds at all.

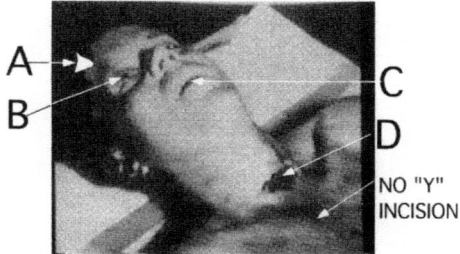

Front head and chest autopsy photo in National Archives (Fox F1 used for comparison base).
A: area retouched; beveled skull visible under one portion; B: both eyes clear; C: teeth normal;
D: neck wound out of focus on one image, in focus on another; shows depth of wound.

Although shocked at the obvious forgery of this crucial evidence, Tom was gratified that his computer image processing had been proven accurate.

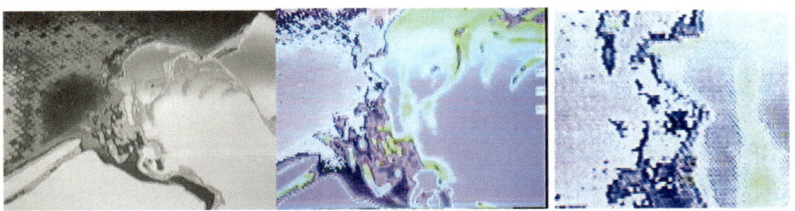
Photos in Archives verified image processing findings of bullet hole in right temporal area.

After Tom finished with the head and chest autopsy photos, he began analyzing a new image. It was similar to Fox 7, which showed the back of the president's head with a cylindrical device inside the skull and brain material hanging down. However, this photo was taken at a higher angle so that the chest was visible, and Tom could see that the Y incision had not yet been made. There were a total of nine copies in the envelope – five color and four black & white. The initials "JB" were on the back of each.

Similar to what Tom had seen in his copy of Fox 7, these color images showed wet hair, brain and scalp material, and the cylindrical device used to shore up the head. Also visible was non-human white material inside the skull, possibly the plaster of paris Jerry Custer had described. The color images also contained some information that was not seen on Fox 7. Because the camera angle was high, there was a clear view of the eyes. Tom wrote in his notebook that while the left eye appeared normal, the right eye lens was white and cloudy, and the right eyelid was sunken. Also, smooth edges of the skull were visible in the right temporal area – possibly associated with the skull flap. Seeing this smooth edge was noteworthy, because in other photos the same edge appears serrated. Finally, Tom documented the presence of non-human white material in the right temporal region.

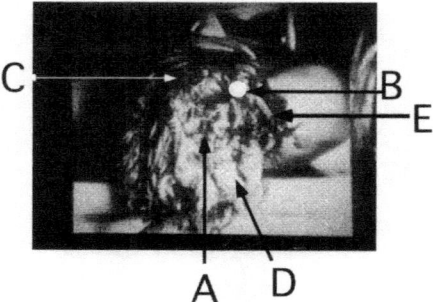

Back head photo (color) in Archives (Fox 7 comparison). A: cylindrical device to prevent head collapse; B: non-human white material; C: wet hair; D: brain material; E: smooth skull edge.

On one of the black and white photographs, rather than white material, the right temporal area was *blackened* in. This was evidence of photographic retouching, which appeared in the form of a sideways black "V" over the bullet entrance hole. In looking at these photos in total, it seemed to Tom as if somebody was experimenting with different ways to cover the wound.

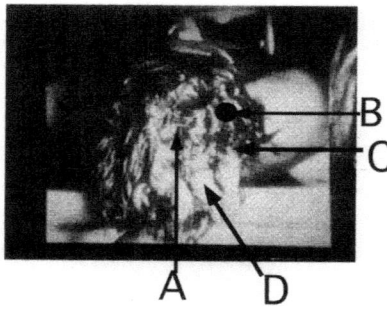

Back head photo (B&W) in Archives (Fox 7 comparison base). A: cylindrical device to prevent head collapse; B: area in right temple blackened in; C: no cut in skull; D: brain material.

The next folder Tom opened contained six color and two black & white copies of the massive cavity in the top of President Kennedy's head (equivalent to Fox 8). Some of the photographs were in sharp focus and some were blurry, which led Tom to write in his notebook: "What photo did the forensics panel see?" On the back of every copy were the initials "JB."

Similar to his copy of Fox 8, Tom could see that the hole was an empty cavity and that the brain had already been removed. He also confirmed that beveling of the skull was visible to the naked eye, and that the bullet flow that created it was from inside-to-out and down-to-up. But due to the clarity of the sharply focused photographs,

Tom was able to record additional observations that were not visible in the Fox 8 image. For example, non-human white material (possibly plastic) was pushed down into the cavity against the inside of the skull, and up into the wound created by the bullet that entered the right temporal area. Also, Tom could see that the area he had originally believed might be the entrance wound was, in fact, only head material. Rather, he could clearly see the real bullet entrance hole in the right front of the skull. So clear was this hole that it could be measured as being .5 centimeters in diameter. Now Tom had a second autopsy photograph that clearly showed the bullet entrance hole in the right temporal region.

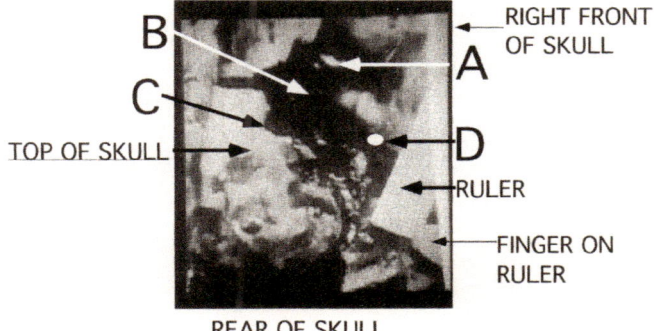

Photo in Archives (Fox 8 for comparison). A: head material, not a hole; B: no brain in skull; C: beveling of skull is inside-to-out; D: entrance wound at front right temple area; hole .5 cm.

When Tom pulled out the next set of photographs, he was excited to see the so-called "official autopsy photograph" that he had first seen in 1989 in the video *The Men Who Killed Kennedy*. Back then, his image processing proved photographic alteration.

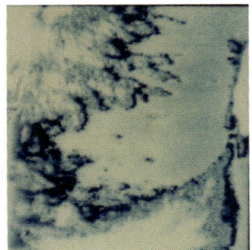

Image processing of "official autopsy photograph" (Fox 3) proved alteration.

This photograph showed the back of President Kennedy's head. But unlike the sketch in the HSCA Report, which inferred that the body was upright, the head was actually lying on the table and tilted slightly back. Also obvious to Tom was that the person's right hand in the photo was pulling the scalp toward himself.

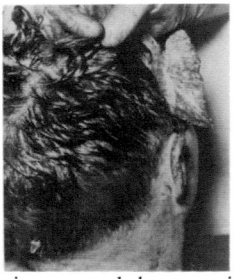 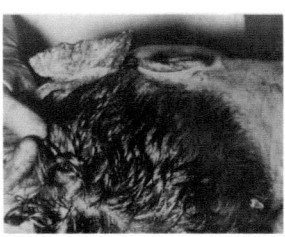

Archives image revealed proper orientation of JFK lying on side with hand pulling scalp.

In the folder, there were two color copies of this image, and three black & white. "JB" was initialed on the back of each. While the black & white images showed some variations from copy to copy, Tom observed several things in common. First, the hair did not appear normal or consistent. In fact, it appeared both wet and dry. Second, there was a white plastic retainer present behind the right ear. Third, the skull flap in the right temporal region went all the way to the upper tip of the ear. And finally, there were two small holes in the back of the head that, according to Tom's notes, "were clearly added to the photograph." One was high, in the cowlick area, and corresponded to HSCA Exhibit F-50.

HSCA JFK Exhibit F-50   HSCA JFK Exhibit F-51

The other was low, just above the hairline, and appeared to be a 22-gauge hole. It looked like a small triangle and was equivalent to HSCA Exhibit F-51. The HSCA Report had labeled this "extraneous dried brain tissue on top of the scalp hair."

> "When questioned by panel members, the autopsy pathologists stated that the piece of brain tissue on the lower rear of the head just above the hairline covered the entrance wound they described in their report. The majority of the panel concludes, however, that the brain tissue actually lies on top of the hair and does not obscure a wound of any kind."
>
> House Select Committee on Assassinations
> March 1979

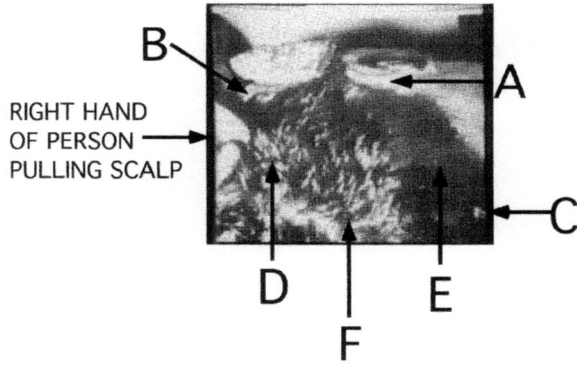

Rear view of head photo (B&W) in National Archives (Fox 3 used for comparison base).
A: ear retainer, white plastic; B: skull cut in this area; C: small hole under white area;
D: wet hair; E: Dry hair; F: small hole in area of cowlick, .2 cm in diameter.

Tom also noted that the two color copies of this photo revealed several points of new information. The ear was colored red (possibly indicating the presence of blood) and the retainer behind it appeared pinkish white plastic. There was white tape visible in an area near the top of the head where a portion of the skull was exposed. And finally, an obvious photographic alteration was present behind the skull flap and looked like it had been painted in.

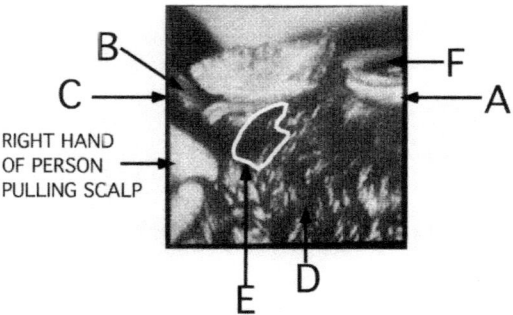

Rear view of head photo (color) in National Archives (Fox 3 for comparison). A: ear retainer shows pink, white plastic; B: skull exposed; C: white tape visible near exposed skull; D: wet hair; E: photographic retouching, area painted in; F: ear colored red.

The next folder Tom opened contained four black & white and three color photos of the left profile of President Kennedy (equivalent to the Fox 4 image). Some images were overexposed, some underexposed. But once again, Dr. J. Thornton Boswell's initials (JB) were scrawled on the back of each print.

Tom made very few observations about this set of photographs. He only noted that the tracheotomy wound was visible, that the head was held by the metal "C" Custer had removed prior to taking the x-rays (and put back on when he left the morgue), and that a Navy towel was on the table. Most importantly, perhaps, Tom reported that the left eye lens of the president could not be seen. This was important, he wrote, because in the Fox 4 and Fox 1 autopsy photographs, both eyes were wide open and the lenses clearly visible.

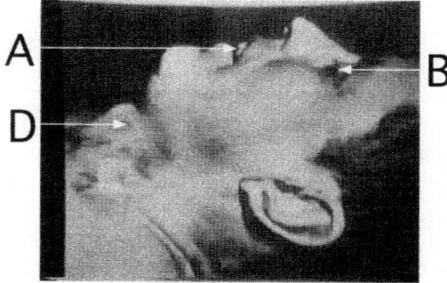

Left profile photo in National Archives (Fox F4 used for comparison base).
A: teeth normal; B: left eye lens not visible; D: tracheotomy neck wound visible.

Although Tom had spent a day and a half looking at all kinds of new evidence related to the autopsy x-rays and photographs, he was absolutely shocked at what he saw in a folder containing a series right profile pictures. No one in the public sector had ever seen a right profile photograph taken at President Kennedy's autopsy and, after reviewing the images, Tom understood why.

There were four black & white and three color copies in the folder. But no one photo was exactly like the others. Each seemed to reveal something new and different. One thing they all had in common, however, were the initials "JB" on the back. And because Tom had no right profile photograph, he used a mirror image transparency of the Fox 4 (left profile) image upon which to mark observations.

Tom noted that in the background of all photos, he could see the bar fence in front of the gallery, the metal "C" clamp holding the head, and that no Y incision had yet been made. In a departure from the left profile photo (Fox 4), the back of the head was not darkened, but clearly visible – and it wasn't a pretty sight. Bloody hair, brain, and scalp matter was hanging down similar to what was seen on the Fox 7 photo (back top of head). Two drops of blood had dripped onto a white towel with the lettering "US Navy" on it. Part of the skull was visible and Tom noted that outward beveling was clearly evident. He also documented that there was no plastic white retainer behind the right ear as he had seen in the rear head view (Fox 3). There was swelling above the right eye, which, unlike Jerrol Custer's description, was *not* protruded. The eye lens, itself, was convex and cloudy.

The area around the right temporal region varied considerably from photo to photo. In one copy, white non-human material, probably plastic, was obviously used to cover the bullet entrance hole. In another copy, it was not visible. In still another image, there was a black triangle over everything. When Tom looked through his stereo glasses, it appeared as though the white material was raised and the black triangle had no depth (as if painted on). In another photograph, Tom noted that "the entrance hole of the incoming missile was visible to the human eye. "Why did the HSCA panel not notice this?" he wrote in his notebook.

> "We [members of the forensics panel] believe that another missile did not enter the right front of the head within the area of the large defect. We find no evidence supporting this speculation in the photographs of the head. . . ."
>
> HSCA; March 1979

While most of the black & white photographs were similar in nature to the color prints, there were a number of items that Tom reported could only be seen on the color images. For example, there was a dark bruise in the area of swelling above the right eye. The president's skin, rather than appearing placid and gray as Jerrol Custer had described, was orange on the color photographs, which led Tom to believe that it may have been taken after the mortician had performed restorative work. And finally, Tom documented that, on one of the color photographs, there were three drops of blood (rather than only two) on the white US Navy towel.

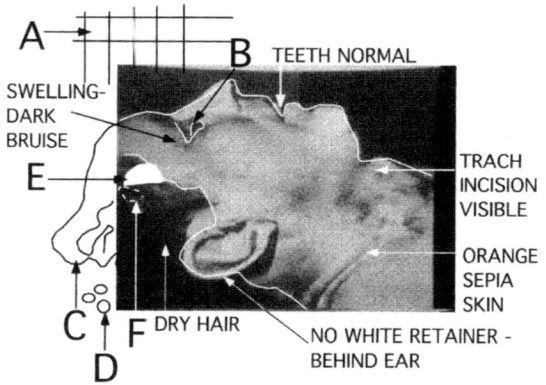

Right profile photo in Archives (Fox F4 mirror image for comparison).
A: bar fence in front of gallery; B: convex eye lens, cloudy, not protruding; C: brain matter; D: two drops of blood on USN towel; E: non-human material partially hiding entrance wound, bullet hole visible ; F: skull exposed.

After carefully scrutinizing all the right profile photographs in the Deed of Gift, Tom wrote in his notebook that "these photos are unique, because they show real wounds." He also pointed out that he believed the varying information in the photos demonstrated an obvious "step process" in the forging of the photographs that were released to the public and, perhaps, shown to the HSCA forensics panel. After all, in one photograph, the bullet entrance hole in the right temporal region was clearly visible. In another, there was white material in the hole. And in still another, a black triangle was covering the entire wound.

At this point in time, Tom had completed his viewing of all the autopsy x-rays and photographs. That left him with only one more thing to do, which was to quickly look at the other artifacts contained in the Deed of Gift (President Kennedy's clothing). Then Tom would leave the National Archives, go home to Pittsburgh, and meet with Jerry Custer about what he had seen.

* * * * *

At 5 o'clock in the morning on November 23, 1963, Jerrol Custer was awakened from a sound sleep by Dr. John H. Ebersole and Captain Loy Brown who commended Custer on his performance the night before. Dr. Brown was the chief of the Bethesda Radiology Department and had apparently driven all night from Chicago where he had been attending a conference. "I really was asleep for only a few hours," recalled Custer. "So I just looked at them, said thank you, and then rolled over and went back to sleep."

By early afternoon, Custer had awakened and gone down to the cafeteria to get something to eat. Upon his return to the fourth floor, he was walking down the hall behind Ebersole and Brown, who were discussing something. As Custer came up behind him, he heard Ebersole tell Brown that "certain pertinent things were taken care of." But then Custer was noticed and the conversation stopped.

Right after that incident, Dr. Ebersole asked Custer to come down to the room where the duty log book was kept. The previous day, Custer had written in the book (as procedure required) that he had been dispatched to the morgue to take x-rays of President Kennedy. He wrote down the date, time, what he was asked to do, and that he was taking along his assistant Ed Reed.

"I want you to tear the entry page out and hand it to me," said Ebersole.

Custer paused a moment, but then realized that Ebersole was not joking. So he tore the page out of the duty log book and handed it over. Ebersole then lit it on fire. "Wait! Wait!" cried an alarmed Jerry Custer. "Why are you burning that up? It's government property!"

"It's none of your business," replied Ebersole.

A few days later, Custer was called up to the office of the Commanding Officer of the Bethesda Medical Center, Admiral Calvin B. Galloway. With armed guards standing behind him, Custer was ordered by the admiral to sign a document stating that he would not discuss anything that happened on November 22 or 23, 1963. If he did, he would be subject to court martial. "It was made quite clear to me I would not get out of that room without signing the gag order," recalled Custer. "And then after I signed, I was told if anything, no matter what, got out, it would be the sorriest day of my life. I'd spend most of my time behind prison walls.

"That was the most traumatic thing that happened to me over those two days," said Custer. "It was terrible."

* * * * *

The last thing Tom Wilson did at the National Archives was to look at the clothes President Kennedy was wearing on November 22, 1963. He later described it as a "very, very moving experience" to see the president's blood-stained shirt, his suit jacket, his shoes, his black socks, his necktie, and even his back brace. Although he took measurements of the back brace and the bullet "nick" in the tie, it was the shirt and jacket he found particularly interesting – although he was disappointed that they did not yield significant new information.

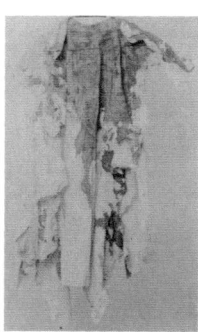

HSCA Exhibits of President's suit coat and shirt showing front left parts cut away.

The House Select Committee on Assassinations had published photographs of the front and back of the suit jacket and the front of the heavily blood-stained shirt. The written discussions of these exhibits took particular care to note that the bullet holes in the back of each were visible. It did not, however, call similar attention to the fact that the left side of both the shirt and jacket were cut off and missing. The HSCA's only explanation was that the "suit jacket, shirt, and tie were cut during emergency procedures at Parkland Memorial Hospital, Dallas, Tex to afford easy removal."

The Committee did, however, document the fact that additional holes were present in the back of both the president's jacket and the shirt. But the HSCA Report stated that they were not bullet holes, but were made by the government in order to gather material for additional analysis. Were they really the bullet entrance holes that Tom had delineated in his image processing of the autopsy photo of the back (Fox 5)?

Regarding the suit jacket, the HSCA wrote that "two defects are noted." The first, it attributed as being an entrance bullet hole that measured 1.5 by 1.0 centimeters. "The second defect was artificially created in the FBI laboratory to obtain a sample of material for subsequent studies" and measured 0.9 by 0.8 centimeters. With respect to the defects in the shirt, the HSCA described the "bullet hole" as measuring 1.2 centimeters by 0.8 centimeters. "A second defect was created in the shirt in order to obtain control cloth for FBI spectrographic analysis," read the Report. The dimensions of this "defect" were listed as 1.7 by 0.3 centimeters.

The dimensions of the second "defect" in the shirt indicated that it was more of a slit than a hole. Was this a cut made purposely to obscure the other bullet holes Tom had seen in his image processing? Did the slit connect two bullet entrance holes? And was the second "defect" in the suit jacket similarly created to obscure additional bullet holes?

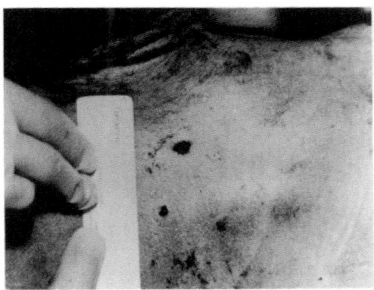

Photo of JFK's back showing Tom's interpretation of three bullet holes [12 o'clock (exit hole), 9 o'clock (entrance hole), and 6 o'clock (entrance hole)]. See Chapter 4 for detail.

Tom's image processing work showed that there was an exit wound in the back (the larger hole at 12 o'clock). That bullet may have been fired from the front of the limousine, penetrated the windshield, and hit the president in the center left front of the chest – going through the jacket, shirt, left lung, and exiting the back. This would account for comments from the autopsy doctors about blood in the left lung. Of course, if evidence existed that bullet holes were in the front left of the suit jacket and shirt, no one will ever know, because they were cut off and apparently discarded.

Additionally, if two bullets entered the president's back and lodged in the right lung, it would explain Custer's statement that the autopsy doctors mentioned the presence of blood there. Unfortunately, both lungs were removed before chest x-rays were taken, and any possible bullet trajectories through the chest cavity were not traced with probes.

Overall, with regard to President Kennedy's suit jacket and bloody shirt, a case can be made that significant evidence has been altered or completely lost. Whatever the explanation, it is a fact that additional holes and slits were made by the government in the back of the jacket and shirt in the same area where Tom Wilson's image processing had delineated three bullet holes (two entry and one exit).

* * * * *

Tom visited the National Archives to verify that the autopsy x-rays and photographs upon which he had conducted computer image processing were copies of the originals. Basically, that was confirmed. But in the process of inspecting these crucial pieces of evidence in the assassination of President Kennedy, Tom got more than he bargained for. The Deed of Gift contained evidence that had never before been released to the public. Some key evidence was missing. And perhaps most unbelievable, there was evidence of a step-by-step forgery process of some autopsy photographs.

Evidence never before released to the public includes:
- A conical path of metallic bullet fragments that originate in the right front temporal region and expand outward to the top back of the head.
- Beveling of the skull from inside-to-out and down-to-up.
- X-rays that show almost total destruction of the right orbit, while photographs depict the right eye as normal (indicating that the photos have been altered).
- A visible bullet entry wound in the right front temporal region.
- A large exit wound in the top back of the head visible on key x-rays and altered on both x-rays and photographs.

Key missing evidence includes:
- Two oblique x-rays of the head.
- AP x-rays of the neck.
- Most, if not all, of the original x-rays taken by Jerrol Custer at the autopsy.
- Most, if not all, of the original photographs taken at the autopsy. [If photographs were constantly being taken as Custer reported, then the vast majority of those photos are missing.]

Forged and/or obscured evidence includes:
- Planted bullet fragments on the x-rays.
- Composite x-rays.
- Non-human material added to the inside of the head.
- Small "entrance" holes added to photos of the back of the head.
- Photographic retouching.
- Sketches and cropped enlargements printed in the HSCA Report and accompanying volumes that hide details found in the National Archives.
- Cropped enlargements in various stages of manipulation.

- Various folders or "professional job envelopes" containing a step-by-step process of photographic alteration.

As Tom considered all the new information he had discovered in the National Archives, he wondered why the Warren Commission and HSCA experts had not reported the truth. Were they shown only forged and enhanced copies of the autopsy x-rays and photographs? Or were they part of a massive cover up? Tom didn't know. He only knew what he had seen. And the evidence contained in the National Archives indicated a deeper, darker truth regarding the assassination of President John F. Kennedy.

* * * * *

Back home in Pittsburgh, Tom Wilson met with Jerry Custer to review what he had seen in the Deed of Gift. He went through his detailed workbook, which included sketches, measurements, observations, and notes. Both agreed that the Tom's findings verified Jerry's story and proved that the Warren Commission and the House Select Committee on Assassinations were wrong. And both men were amazed that the proof had been in the National Archives all this time – ever since the assassination in 1963 – for 32 years.

"Jerry, this is the end of the line for me," Tom said to Custer. "My only ambition now is to submit this hard evidence to the government. I hope they do something with it. The American people have a right to know the truth."

Epilogue: *<u>The Darker Truth</u>*

At 12:30 PM CST on Friday November 22, 1963, John F. Kennedy, 35th President of the United States, was assassinated in Dallas, Texas. He had been on a two-day trip to the state, having stopped the day before in San Antonio and Fort Worth. After speaking at a Fort Worth breakfast gathering in the morning, Kennedy boarded Air Force One for a short flight to Love Field in Dallas where he was scheduled to attend a luncheon at the Trade Mart. Afterwards, the itinerary called for him to fly to Austin for a Democratic Party fundraiser. First, however, he would ride in an open limousine during a 10-mile motorcade through downtown. It would be the last sixty minutes of his life.

President and Mrs. Kennedy's arrival at Dallas Love Field.

The presidential limo, second in the procession, was driven by Secret Service Agent William Greer with Agent Roy Kellerman sitting on the passenger side of the front seat. Texas Governor John Connally and his wife, Nellie, sat in the middle seat, while the President and Jacqueline Kennedy rode in the back seat. Riding in the lead car just in front of the President were Dallas Police Chief Jesse Curry (driver), Dallas County Sheriff Bill Decker, and Secret Service Agents Winston G. Lawson and Forrest Sorrels. Behind Kennedy was his "follow-up" car, which included most of the President's security guard. The rest of the procession included the Vice President's car and "follow-up" vehicle, five cars for local officials, three press cars, and three buses for White House staff and other members of the press. Finally, a number of Dallas Police motorcycle officers, acting as escorts and providing security, were scattered throughout the procession and along the route.

Presidential limousine shortly after leaving Love Field.

The motorcade left Love Field at 11:30 AM CST. At the end of Main Street, the procession turned right onto Houston Street, proceeded north for one block, and then took a 120-degree left turn onto Elm Street for the slow downhill glide into Dealey Plaza. At this intersection, there were three structures on the corner: the Dal-Tex building, the Dallas County Records building, and the Texas School Book Depository. Now the motorcade had only one block to go before its planned exit onto Stemmons Freeway and the five-minute drive to the Trade Mart.

In the presidential motorcade route.

Dealey Plaza was a 3-acre, triangle-shaped bowl where three main east-west Dallas arteries (Main, Commerce, and Elm Streets) converged under a railroad bridge called the triple underpass. On the north and south sides of the plaza were two small white pergolas situated on grass knolls. The north side of Elm Street also featured a line of trees and shrubs along a five-foot high wooden picket fence that ran west up to the triple underpass. Behind the fence was a parking lot and, beyond that, the Dallas rail yards.

Dealey Plaza from the air (L). Looking down Elm Street toward the triple underpass (R).

It was here in Dealey Plaza that a professional team had assembled to assassinate President John F. Kennedy. The motorcade was running about five minutes late, because the president had twice stopped his car to shake hands with people along the way. That caused anxiousness among the shooters, who were spread out and strategically positioned to catch the president in a crossfire. Two were behind the picket fence on the knoll; both armed with rifles and dressed in police uniforms. One man had brown eyes, coarse dark hair, and a mole or pox mark just below the left eye. Another shooter, armed with a rifle and dressed in civilian clothes, was located about fifteen feet farther west along the picket fence. Several gunmen were positioned behind the presidential limousine. At least one was in the westernmost 6th floor window of the Texas School Book Depository. Another may have been on the roof of the Dal-Tex building (as some researchers believe). And a third, sporting a goatee and armed with a high-powered telescopic weapon, was located on the second floor of the Dal-Tex building. There may also have been up to three shooters located in front of the motorcade. One was at the intersection of the triple underpass and the picket fence on the north side of Elm Street. A second was in the storm sewer drain at the base of the steps coming down the grassy knoll. And another shooter may have in the back of a pickup truck stopped on the south end of Commerce Street near the triple underpass.

All the individuals on the assassination team were equipped with communication devices in order to coordinate gunfire, which was to be conducted in at least three volleys. The shooters had electronic transmitting devices in their ears. Their assigned cohorts monitored the progress of the motorcade with hand-held two-way radios. And one, perhaps two individuals were specifically assigned to coordinate the firing of the volleys. One may have been a man named Jim Hicks, who was located in the grass area between Elm and Main streets. The primary coordinator, however, was positioned in the eastern-most window (sniper's window) on the sixth floor of the Texas School Book Depository. He had on a communications headset that included an earphone made out of plastic and rubber, a microphone, and a connecting wire going up into the headset's headband. This individual had long eyelashes, a bulb-type nose, and a tattoo (or sticker) on his left cheek that read "F9s." He was also wearing a military-type beret with a large spread eagle sewn on the front.

 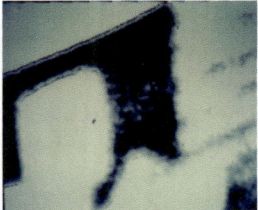 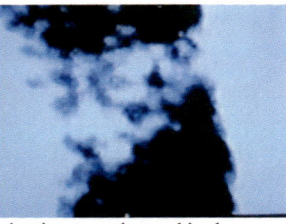

Primary communications coordinator for the assassination team located in the Western-most window (sniper's window) on the sixth floor of the Texas School Book Depository. This man was obviously not Lee Harvey Oswald.

Other members of the assassination team present in Dealey Plaza included a number of people dressed in suits and identifying themselves as federal agents. There were two others standing at the base of the Stemmons Freeway exit sign on Elm Street – a Caucasian holding an umbrella and a Hispanic-looking man with a camera and a two-way radio. And there was also an individual behind the picket fence holding a sophisticated large format camera with viewfinder and bellows – ready to take pictures of President Kennedy being cut down.

At this point in the motorcade route, the crowds of onlookers had significantly thinned. However, there were still several hundred people scattered about as the first few cars in the procession descended into Dealey plaza. Moving slowly, the presidential limousine stayed in the center of three lanes. President Kennedy was waving to his right, Mrs. Kennedy to her left.

Limo turns onto Houston St. (L); on Elm St. (R), moments before the first shot

Suddenly, as the limousine neared the Stemmons Freeway exit sign, the first volley of shots rang out. Four gunmen (all with high-powered, telescopic rifles) fired simultaneously – two from the front, and two from the back. Witnesses described the shots as sounding like "a firecracker", "a motorcycle backfiring," or a "burst of gunfire." One bullet hit President Kennedy near the base of his Adam's apple, nicked his necktie as it went in, and exited at the back of his neck. The President immediately stiffened and his hands jerked upward to his throat.

Volley #1: President Kennedy struck in the neck by a frontal shot, he stiffens, and his hands jerk upward to his throat. Zapruder frames #225 (left) and #230 (right).

The angle of this shot (as determined by a straight line connecting the small entrance hole in the front of the neck to the larger exit hole in the back) came from the right front. It was probably fired by a gunman behind the picket fence on the grassy knoll (about 15 feet down from the corner).

> "I saw a stocky man wearing a dark blue business suit and black hat standing near the stockade fence about 15 feet down from the corner. He looked over the fence, there was a puff of smoke, and then he ran east along the fence line. Near the metal switch box, I saw him toss the rifle he was carrying to a tall, thin railroad worker who quickly dismantled the weapon, stashed it in a tool box, and then started running north along the railroad tracks. The gunman in the blue suit and black hat then turned around, pulled down on his coat, ran his hands along the sides of his head and, now composed, walked back along the picket fence in the direction of the Texas School Book Depository."
>
> Ed Hoffman
> Eyewitness, overlooking the scene from
> northbound lane of the Stemmons Freeway.

> "Shots were fired from behind the wooden stockade fence on the grassy knoll. . . . Equally good locations can be found up to 25 feet along the fence either north or west of its corner."
>
> HSCA Acoustical analysis
> March 1979

A second frontal shot (perhaps fired from the north end of the triple underpass where it meets the picket fence) penetrated the limo's windshield, struck President Kennedy in the left upper center of his chest, and exited at the upper part of his back.

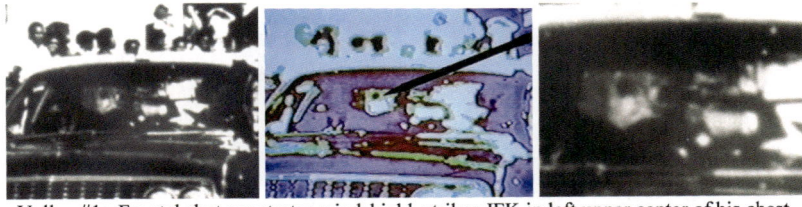

Volley #1: Frontal shot penetrates windshield, strikes JFK in left upper center of his chest.

Another shot entered the President's back at a 45-degree downward angle. Its trajectory indicated an origination point near the westernmost sixth floor window of the Texas School Book Depository.

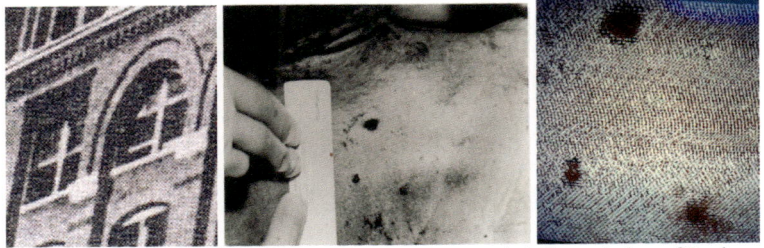

Volley #1: One shot in back came from westernmost sixth floor window of Book Depository (L). Autopsy photo of JFK's back wounds (C); exit wound (12 o'clock), 45-degree and entrance wound (6 o'clock), and horizontal entrance wound (9 o'clock). Image processing of back three wounds (R).

The fourth shot in this first volley was fired more on the horizontal and also struck Kennedy in the back. It appears to have been fired by the man with the goatee on the second floor of the Dal-Tex building. This shot startled a bystander who was sitting on the fire escape above the shooter's window. It is not known whether the two bullets that hit President Kennedy in the back exited his chest cavity.

However, both lungs were most likely penetrated by three of the four shots from the first volley.

  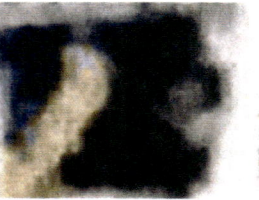 

<u>Volley #1</u>: Shot from second floor of Dal-Tex building hits JFK in the back. Bystander on fire escape startled. Shooter is man sporting goatee armed with high-powered telescopic weapon.

As the limousine proceeded slowly forward, the Caucasian man near the Stemmons Freeway exit sign opened his umbrella and frantically pumped it up and down several times – a possible signal to other assassination team members that the target had been hit. At the same time, the Hispanic-looking man standing next to him raised his fist high into the air, in what may have been a gesture of defiance or revenge.

Frame #332 of the Zapruder film. Notice umbrella on left and man raising fist on right.

Governor John Connally then turned around in his seat to see that President Kennedy had been shot and was slumping to the left toward his wife. At precisely this moment, a second volley rang out. At least five shots were fired simultaneously – four from behind the presidential limousine, one from the front. Two bullets struck Governor Connally wounding him in the back, wrist, and thigh. [Note: Some researchers present a good case that Connally was hit by three separate missiles.] These shots were most likely aimed at President Kennedy, but missed perhaps because he had started to slump to the left toward his wife. Their precise origin is unclear, but they may have come from an upper floor in the Texas School Book Depository and/or the roof of the Dallas County Records Building.

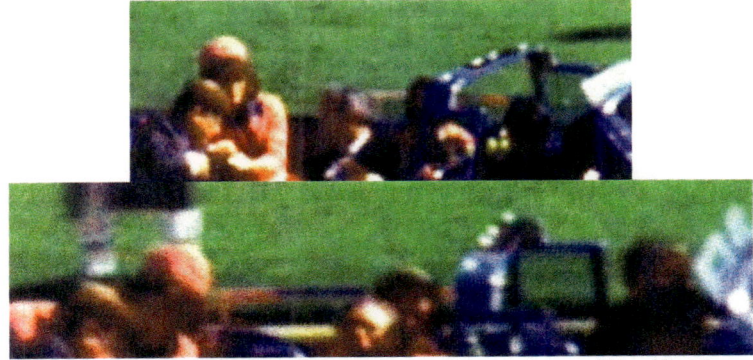

Volley #2: Zapruder frame #274 (top) shows JFK slumping to left toward his wife. Moments later, Connally struck by two shots and is pulled down by Mrs. Connolly (frame #300, bottom).

Another bullet fired from the same general area missed the limousine completely, struck a curb on the south side of Main Street, and sent a shower of concrete debris into the face of bystander James Tague, cutting him on the cheek. A fourth bullet, which may have been fired by the shooter sporting a goatee on the second floor of the Dal-Tex building, traveled more on the horizontal and struck the windshield's metal trim. In the Mary Moorman Polaroid, a bullet fragment and dent can very definitely be observed.

Volley #2: Moorman image processing reveals dent and bullet fragment in trim of windshield.

A fifth shot was fired from the left front of the limousine, passed through the windshield, and missed President Kennedy. It is unknown where this bullet ended up.

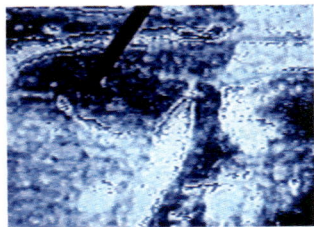

Volley #2: Moorman Polaroid processing reveals bullet hole in left side of windshield.

This shot may have been fired from the bed of a pickup truck stopped on the south end of Commerce Street near the triple underpass. Less than thirty seconds after the presidential limousine sped away, UPI photographer Frank Cancellare took several pictures – one of which showed this pickup truck with a man in the back. However, frame #408 of the altered Zapruder film has the man removed and a flat cover placed over the bed of the pickup. This alteration may have been made, because the Zapruder film (exposed less than thirty seconds earlier) may have shown the individual holding a rifle.

UPI photographer Cancellare's photo (L); Zapruder frame #408 (R). [Jack White insert; in Fetzer; *Murder in Dealey Plaza*, p. 14-15.]

Enlargements of Cancellare photo (left) and Zapruder frame #408 (right) reveal that the Zapruder film has been altered to remove the man in the bed of the pickup and replaced with a flat cover. [Jack White insert; in Fetzer; *Murder in Dealey Plaza*, p. 14-15.]

Before the third volley of shots was fired, Secret Service Agent Roy Kellerman, who had looked into the back of the limousine to see a wounded President Kennedy, quickly slid over in the front seat closer to the driver, William Greer. Kellerman also held a notebook up to the left side of his face as if to shield himself from something. Secret Service Agent Greer then looked into the back seat directly at President Kennedy. At this point, the presidential limousine may have come to a complete stop (as many witnesses later stated). Did Kellerman and Greer know the third volley was about to be fired?

Zapruder frame #275 (top) shows Agent Kellerman in front seat looking back at Kennedy. By frame #308 (bottom), Kellerman has moved over close to the driver, Agent Greer, who now is looking back.

In Altgens #5 (L), Agent Kellerman is seated next to door. Six seconds later, in Moorman Polaroid (R), he is in middle of front seat shielding his face with a notebook.

The second and third bursts of gunfire were much closer together than the first and second. So close were they, in fact, that there had to have been separate communications coordinators. At the point where this final volley was fired, the presidential limousine was far enough down Elm Street to be to the right of Abraham Zapruder's pedestal, to the left of Mary Moorman (who was about to take her famous Polaroid picture), and only about 50 feet in front of the corner of the picket fence on the grassy knoll. "Ready. Aim. Fire!" (or something to that effect) spoke the coordinator into his microphone. And then at least three shots were fired simultaneously at President Kennedy.

Zapruder frame #305 (L) just before third volley.   Nix film (R) shows location on Elm Street.

There were two shooters behind the picket fence. Both were armed with rifles, both were wearing electronic ear transmitters, and both were dressed in police uniforms complete with badges and nameplates. [There may also have been a third man dressed in a police uniform behind the fence.] The left shooter (looking at the fence) had brown eyes, coarse dark hair parted on his left side, and a mole or pox mark near his left eye. He fired 1/5 of a second before the gunman next to him. Together, their rifles produced a large puff of smoke that bellowed out in front of the fence and the trees. A 23-year-old soldier (Gordon Arnold), who was standing in front of the fence filming the motorcade with a movie camera, immediately dropped to the ground as the bullets whizzed past his left ear.

<u>Volley #3</u>: Moorman image processing reveals two shooters firing. Left gunman (looking at fence) and two puffs of smoke (center). 3-D image of badge worn by gunman on left.

The bullet fired by the shooter on the left struck President Kennedy in the right side of his neck, making a small entrance wound. The shot from the right shooter whizzed past the president's head and ripped into the grass on the south side of Elm Street (a few feet down from Mary Moorman). This second shot missed, because it came a split second after the shot in the volley that hit President Kennedy in the head and propelled him backwards.

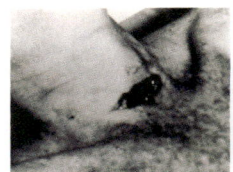 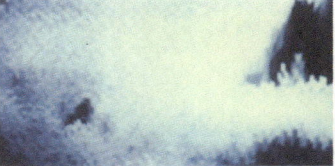 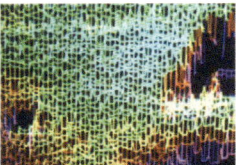

<u>Volley #3</u>: Autopsy photo image processing reveals small bullet hole in the right side of President Kennedy's neck, inflicted during third burst of gunfire.

The head shot was fired from a man crouched in the storm sewer drain on Elm Street near the base of the steps leading down from the grassy knoll. Possibly using a high-caliber handgun, the shooter's bullet struck President Kennedy in the right temple. It shattered the bones of the right orbit, ripped the surrounding muscles, and dislodged the right eyeball from its socket. The bullet immediately split into two larger fragments and began to disintegrate as it traveled through the head in a down-to-up, front-to-back direction. Both fragments exited the top right back of President Kennedy's head creating a hole about the size of a baseball, the upper part of which was shaped like a rectangle.

<u>Volley #3</u>: Shot fired from storm sewer on Elm Street (L, C), struck Kennedy in right temple. Bullet split into two fragments and exited top back of head as shown in Moorman Polaroid (R).

 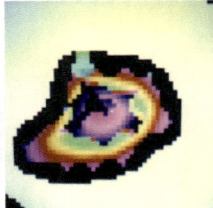 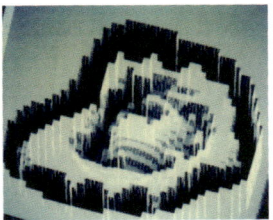

<u>Volley #3</u>: Close up of head wound from Moorman (L). Zapruder #313 image processing reveals exit wound (about the size of a baseball) with bullet or bone fragment exiting (C, R).

When the bullet fragments exited, the President's head exploded with pieces of bone, brain, scalp, and blood flying into the air. Two Dallas motorcycle officers (Bobby Hargis and B. J. Martin) riding to the left rear of the presidential limousine had their uniforms, helmets, and windshields splattered with this material.

 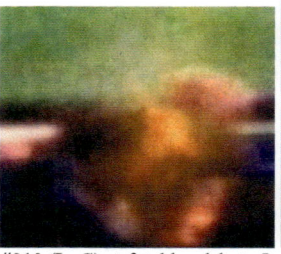 

Volley #3: Zapruder frame #313 (L, C) at fatal headshot. Image processing (R) reveals film altered to hide airborne bone, brain, scalp, and blood exploding from JFK's head.

At the moment the shots were fired from the third volley, the operator of the large format camera snapped a picture. And KBOX Radio news reporter, Sam Pate, driving his red Pontiac Catalina in the front of the motorcade, looked in his rearview mirror and saw a puff of smoke rise from the storm sewer drain.

  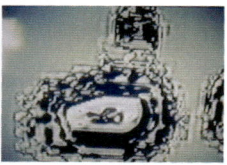

Processing of Moorman Polaroid reveals camera behind picket fence next to left shooter. Enlargement (L); camera and gunsmoke (C); possible large format or movie camera detail (R).

As her husband slumped down, Jacqueline Kennedy instinctively crawled out onto the trunk of the limousine to retrieve a piece of his skull. Secret Service Agent Clint Hill, who had sprung from the follow-up car immediately after the first volley, now jumped onto the presidential limo and pushed Mrs. Kennedy back into her seat. Seeing the right rear portion of the President's head missing, Agent Hill slammed his fist onto the trunk several times in anger and anguish. The limousine then accelerated and sped off through the triple underpass. The entire shooting sequence lasted less than ten seconds.

Clint Hill jumps on limo (top); car heads through triple underpass (L); speeds to Parkland (R).

In the lead car, Dallas Police Chief issued an order on his radio: "Get a man on top of that triple underpass and see what happened up there," he said. "It looks like the President has been hit. Have Parkland stand by." County Sheriff Bill Decker issued similar instructions: "Move all available men out of my office into the railroad yard to try to determine what happened in there," he ordered. Listening to Channel 2 (the radio frequency used by the Dallas Police), KBOX Radio news reporter Sam Pate picked up his microphone and made a live broadcast.

> *"There is trouble in the motorcade. I repeat, there is trouble in the motorcade. Parkland has been notified to stand by."*
>
> Sam Pate, KBOX Radio
> November 22, 1963
> 12:30 PM CST

The presidential limo then sped up the ramp onto Stemmons Freeway and raced toward Parkland Memorial Hospital, which was just a few miles away.

KBOX Radio Newsman Sam Pate (L), riding in front of the presidential motorcade in a 1963 Pontiac Catalina (R) made the first news announcement of the assassination at 12:30 PM CST.

In Dealey Plaza, hundreds of onlookers were stunned. Many froze in their places while others had fallen to the ground to avoid the gunfire. Within moments of the final volley, Gordon Arnold (who hit the dirt in front of the picket fence) had two police officers standing over him. One, with dirty hands and no hat, kicked Arnold and demanded his film. The other officer was holding a rifle – his face streaked with tears and shaking as if very upset. After Arnold handed over his movie film, the two men walked off.

Down on Elm Street, several motorcycle officers leaped off their bikes and drew weapons. Up near the intersection of Elm and Houston, a passerby told patrolman Joe Marshall Smith that someone was shooting at the president from the bushes on the grassy knoll. Officer Smith quickly ran into the parking lot behind the picket fence. When he saw a man in a suit coming toward him, he drew his weapon. "He saw me coming with my pistol and right away showed me . . . that he was a Secret Service agent," recalled Smith. The officer then holstered his gun and continued looking around the parking lot. The man with the Secret Service credentials simply walked away.

> "A police officer came around the north end of the fence. He saw and confronted the [shooter in the blue business suit and black hat who was walking back up along the picket fence]. The policeman held his service revolver in both hands, arms extended forward, legs spread and slightly squat. The man in the suit first held both arms out to his side, as if to gesture, 'It wasn't me. See, I have nothing.' Then he reached inside his suit coat and pulled out something (presumably identification) and showed it to the police officer. The officer relaxed, and both men mingled with the crowd coming around the fence."
>
> Ed Hoffman
> Eyewitness, overlooking the
> scene from the northbound lane
> of the Stemmons Freeway.

As reality began to set in among the rest of the bystanders in Dealey Plaza, the stunned silence turned into screaming and confusion. Dozens of people rushed up the hill toward the picket fence and triple underpass. Others streamed into the parking lot and the rail yards.

Onlookers drop to ground, rush up grassy knoll where picket fence and underpass merge.

Jean Hill (Mary Moorman's friend) ran across Elm Street and up the grassy knoll to the picket fence. Behind it, she saw a uniformed policeman holding a rifle. Seventeen-year-old Beverly Oliver (who had been standing behind Moorman and Hill on the south side of Elm Street) reported seeing two Dallas police officers hurriedly walk across the steps in front of the grassy knoll. She later identified the two men as Roscoe White (the husband of her friend Geneva White) and Sergeant Patrick Dean.

After a few minutes, other members of the assassination, like Jim Hicks (who had a two-way communications radio in his back left pocket), simply walked away from the scene. The Caucasian man (who had pumped an umbrella up and down just after the first volley) and the Hispanic-looking man (who had raised his fist in a gesture of revenge or defiance) stood up from their sitting positions on the Elm Street curb and casually walked off in opposite directions.

Three possible members of the assassination team casually walk away minutes after the shooting. Possible communications coordinator Jim Hicks (L). Caucasian man and Hispanic-looking man sit on curb (C) and then get up and walk off in opposite directions. One walking south on Elm Street (R).

> *"We interrupt this program to bring you this special report from ABC Radio. Here is a special bulletin from Dallas, Texas. Three shots were fired at President Kennedy's motorcade today in downtown Dallas, Texas. This is ABC Radio . . . . We're going to stand by for more details on the incident in Dallas. Stay tuned to your ABC station for further details. Now we return you to your regular program."*
>
> Don Gardner, ABC Radio
November 22, 1963
12:36 PM CST

Ten minutes or so after the shots were fired, Deputy Sheriff Buddy Walthers spoke with James Tague and inspected the curb where a bullet had hit and sprayed concrete up into Tague's face. Then he walked over to the positions of Mary Moorman and Jean Hill on the south side of Elm Street where he noticed something had torn the grass. Walthers then leaned over and picked up what he later said was a bullet, which he gave to the FBI agent standing next to him.

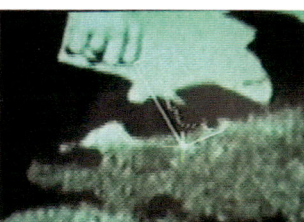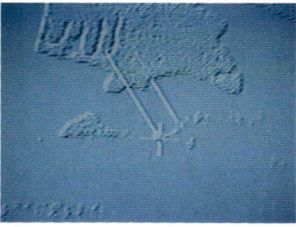

Deputy Sheriff Buddy Walthers picks up bullet from grass on south side of Elm Street (L, C). Processing confirms bullet presence (R).

Approximately ninety minutes after President Kennedy was shot, a freight train leaving the rail yard behind was stopped by tower operator Lee Bowers so it could be inspected. Three men, often described as winos, derelicts, or tramps, were pulled off one of the boxcars and taken into custody. Many researchers believe these three men were part of the assassination team. While being escorted to the police station, a civilian in a business suit was observed to have a wire from an electronic device connected to his eyeglasses and extending down, along the bottom of his hairline, and into his shirt collar just below the right ear. This individual may have been part of the assassination team.

Civilian (passing three "tramps") wearing electronic device may have been part of assassination team.

The limousine carrying President Kennedy arrived at Parkland Hospital at 12:37 PM CST followed closely by Vice President Lyndon Johnson's car. As Johnson got out of the car, he was quickly surrounded by Secret Service agents and escorted into the building. Senator Ralph Yarborough, who had been riding next to LBJ, walked over to Kennedy's car and was shocked at what he saw. "Mrs. Kennedy was still there on the back seat with her head bowed over her husband's head," Yarborough later recalled. "His blood [was] on her clothes and running down her leg. 'They've murdered my husband. They've murdered my husband.' she was saying."

> *"CBS NEWS BULLETIN [Interrupting television program* As The World Turns*]: "Here is a bulletin from CBS News. In Dallas, Texas, three shots were fired at President Kennedy's motorcade in downtown Dallas. The first reports say that President Kennedy has been seriously wounded by this shooting."*
>
> Walter Cronkite, CBS News
> November 22, 1963
> 12:40 CST

President Kennedy was placed on a gurney and wheeled into Emergency Trauma Room One. The doctors and nurses observed massive amounts of blood and noted that, even though there was a faint, intermittent pulse, he was barely breathing and had no blood pressure. They also observed two frontal entry bullet wounds. One was in the neck at the base of the Adam's apple. "It was just a little hole in the middle of his neck . . . about as big around as the end of my little finger," remembered attending Nurse Margaret Henchliffe. They also saw the small bullet hole in the right temple and concluded that it passed through the cranium and exited out the back top right of the head, leaving a sizeable hole. "The wound was about the size of a baseball," Dr. Charles Crenshaw recalled. The doctors present further noted that it was obvious that a lot of brain material had been blasted out, and some of what remained was spilling onto the floor.

It was clear to those present in the room that President Kennedy's wounds were fatal and that he could not possibly recover. Still the doctors and nurses took numerous actions to try to save him. They cut away his clothes, put an endotrachial tube down his throat for air, and inserted fluid tubes into his arms, legs, and chest. In hopes of increasing air flow, a small incision was made in the neck for a tracheostomy, and closed chest cardiac massage was performed. Finally, all hope was lost and the resuscitative efforts stopped. President Kennedy was officially pronounced dead at 1:00 PM CST.

Shortly thereafter, Deputy Press Secretary Malcolm Kilduff announced that Kennedy "died of a gunshot wound in the brain." Pointing to his right temple, Kilduff explained: "Dr. Burkely [Kennedy's personal physician] told me it was a simple matter of a bullet right through the head. . . . It is my understanding that [the bullet] entered in the right temple." Some early newspaper articles also reported that the President had been hit in the right temple and in the front of the throat.

Parkland Hospital shortly after arrival of Presidential limousine (IL). Kilduff points to right temple (R). "It was a simple matter of a bullet right through the head," he explained.

The President's body was subsequently wrapped in sheets and placed in a bronze ceremonial casket. However, as it was wheeled out of the emergency room and into the main hall, an argument ensued between Dr. Earl F. Rose, Dallas County Coroner, and Secret Service Agent Roy Kellerman. Dr. Rose stated that Texas law required an autopsy be performed in Dallas so as not to break the chain of evidence. But Kellerman, backed up by other armed agents, stated that the President's body was going to be taken to Washington, D.C. It was obvious that Kellerman was going to use force, if necessary, to have his way, so Dr. Rose stepped aside. The casket was then taken to Love Field and loaded onto Air Force One, where at 2:38 PM CST, Lyndon Baines Johnson was sworn in as the 36th President of the United States. The airplane took off less than ten minutes later.

Vice President Lyndon Baines Johnson was sworn in at 2:39 PM CST on Air Force One. President Kennedy's bronze ceremonial casket was in the back compartment.

Back in Dallas, less than 45 minutes after the assassination (between 1:00 and 1:15 PM CST), Dallas Police Officer J. D. Tippit was shot and killed near the intersection of 10th Street and Patton Avenue in the suburb of Oak Park. Half an hour later, 24-year old Lee Harvey Oswald was arrested at the Texas Theater about a mile from the scene of the Tippit shooting. He was brought to Dallas Police Headquarters at approximately 2:00 PM CST, interrogated, and held in isolation. Later that night, Oswald was formally charged with the murders of both Officer Tippit and President Kennedy. While in custody, however, Oswald never confessed to either crime. In fact, he consistently maintained his innocence. "I'm just a patsy!" he professed.

  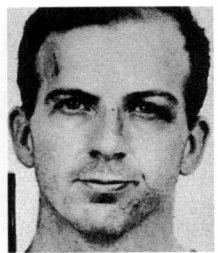

Officer J. D. Tippit (L); Oswald arrested at Texas Theater (C); Oswald mug shot (R).

Several researchers suggest that J. D. Tippit was not killed by Lee Harvey Oswald. Rather, they believe that Tippit was part of the assassination team, and that one of his tasks (along with fellow Dallas police officer Roscoe White) was to eliminate Oswald before the "patsy" could be brought to trial. However, it is believed that Tippit was shaken by the murder of President Kennedy and refused to kill Oswald, which then necessitated his own murder by the conspirators.

It may be that J. D. Tippit was one of the two shooters behind the picket fence, just as has been suggested by various researchers. Recall that Gordon Arnold stated that one of the officers who confronted him and demanded his movie film was holding a rifle – his face streaked with tears and shaking as if very upset. That policeman, who was described as not wearing a hat, may very well have been Tippit. Furthermore, J. D. Tippit fit the description of the left shooter on the grassy knoll behind the picket fence (as seen through image processing of Mary Moorman's Polaroid photograph). He had brown eyes, coarse dark hair parted on the left side, and would obviously have been wearing a police uniform complete with badge. And finally, a photograph of Tippit reveals he had a pox mark below his left eye in the same location as the shooter behind the picket fence.

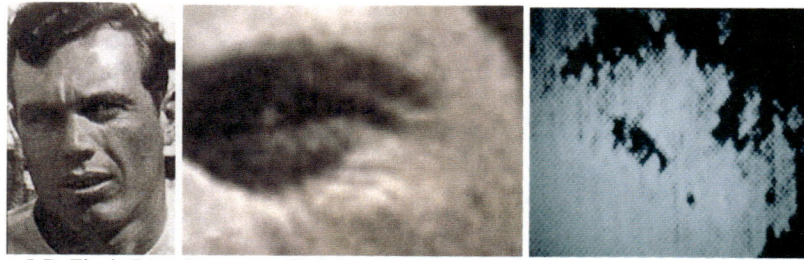

J. D. Tippit (L); enlargement of left eye showing pox mark (C); shooter behind fence (R).

Two days after Tippit and President Kennedy were murdered (on Sunday, November 24th at 11:21 AM CST), Lee Harvey Oswald was shot by nightclub owner Jack Ruby in the basement of Dallas Police Headquarters while being transferred to the county jail. Oswald was pronounced dead an hour and forty-five minutes later at Parkland Memorial Hospital.

Nightclub owner Jack Ruby shoots Oswald on November 24, 1963.

On November 22, 1963, Air Force One arrived at Andrews Air Force Base at 6:08 PM EST, slightly less than three hours after it took off from Dallas. By 6:15 PM EST, the bronze ceremonial casket had been loaded into a gray hearse and was on its way to Bethesda Naval Medical Center where the official autopsy was to be conducted. Riding along with the casket was Jacqueline Kennedy and Robert F. Kennedy, the President's brother. The drive would take some 45 minutes.

Mrs. Kennedy and Robert F. Kennedy at Andrews Air Force Base. The bronze ceremonial casket is loaded into a gray hearse for the 45-minute drive to Bethesda Naval Medical Center.

President Kennedy's body, however, was not in the bronze ceremonial casket. It had been removed at some point between the Parkland Hospital emergency room and the time Air Force One took off from Dallas. Exact details of the removal are unknown. But the body was most likely flown to Washington, D. C. via a separate plane and may have been taken to Walter Reed Army Medical Center where it was altered.

Most of the alterations were made to the head. The scalp was sheared and folded back. A huge hole was then made in the top right portion of the skull, essentially extending the exit wound in the upper right back of the head. Several skull fragments removed to create this wound were later taken to the morgue at Bethesda and represented as having come from the presidential limousine in Dallas. The brain was surgically cut and removed from the cranial vault. It was then destroyed.

Exit wound in top right back of head from Morman Polaroid (L). Autopsy photo (R) showing extended hole in top of head; original exit wound at lower right; no brain in cranial cavity.

The skull was smashed with a hammer of some type until it was fractured to the point of being like hard boiled egg that had been rolled around on a rigid surface. This left the skull so full of tiny cracks and breaks, that it became completely unstable. An artificial cylindrical shaft, along with some plaster of paris (or white plastic substance), was placed in the area of the right eye to shore up the head. This created artificial swelling of the face in that area. Also, the skull was surgically sawed, and a flap created, over the bullet entrance wound in the right temporal region. And finally, a different human brain was placed in the cranial vault.

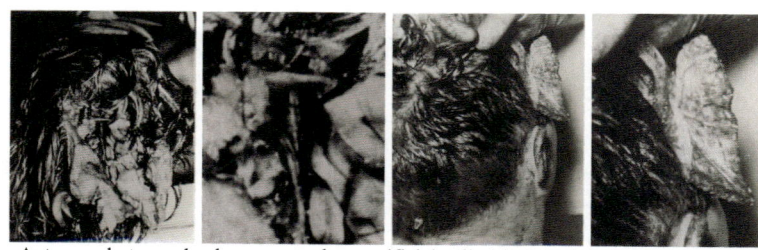

Autopsy photos and enlargements show artificial cylindrical device placed in head for stability (L), and flap created over bullet entrance wound in right temporal region (R).

A major incision was made in the front of the President's neck to make it appear as a wound of exit. This had the effect of obscuring both the small bullet entrance wound and the tracheotomy incision made by the doctors at Parkland Memorial Hospital.

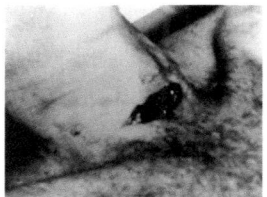 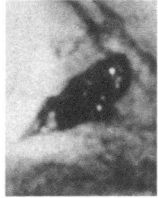

Autopsy photo and enlargement showing major incision in neck to obscure both small bullet entrance hole and small tracheostomy slit made by the doctors at Parkland Memorial Hospital.

All of these alterations to President Kennedy's body were purposely done to obscure and completely obliterate the real wounds that had been inflicted only hours earlier in Dallas. The brain was taken out and replaced to hide its real damage and to prevent the path of the bullet from being traced, which would have been normal procedure at the upcoming autopsy. And the skull was so severely fractured that no one could visually determine that a bullet had entered in the front and exited out the back. The alteration process may have been supervised by Dr. Pierre Finck (a lieutenant colonel in the Army), who then had to clean up and get over to Bethesda, where he would arrive late, but still participate in the official autopsy.

According to Jerrol Custer, the x-ray technician, President Kennedy's altered body was then flown by helicopter to Bethesda Naval Medical Center, where it arrived at 6:15 PM EST. It was then driven from the helicopter to the morgue in a black ambulance. If all this is true, then it occurred at the exact time that the Kennedy entourage left Andrews Air Force Base with the bronze ceremonial casket. In that case, the President's body could not possibly have been on Air Force One for the flight from Dallas.

Air Force One arrived at Andrews Air Force Base at 6:08 p.m. At approximately 6:15 p.m., a gray ambulance left Andrews with Jacqueline Kennedy, Robert Kennedy, and the bronze ceremonial casket for the 45-minute drive to Bethesda Naval Hospital. This was the same time that the helicopter landed at Bethesda with JFK's body, which may have been flown over from Walter Reed Army Medical Center. If true, the President's body couldn't have been on Air Force One for the flight from Dallas.

President Kennedy's body arrived at the Bethesda morgue in a plain metal shipping casket, light gray in color. When lifted out and placed on a table, the head was wrapped in a plastic bag and a bloody sheet. At this point, the autopsy was being supervised by Doctors James J. Humes and J. Thornton Boswell. The material covering the head was removed, and the brain was taken out of the cranial vault and put in a bucket of formaldehyde. After a series of photographs were taken, Humes and Boswell cut the autopsy Y incision in the body and began removing various internal organs for analysis.

A series of head x-rays were then taken using an old portable GE machine. The x-ray technician, Jerrol Custer, was told that the portable unit would be used rather than taking the body all the way up to the fourth floor to use equipment that produced higher quality images. The doctors were only interested in looking for bullet fragments remaining in the body, they told him, so the portable unit would be sufficient.

After taking five x-rays of the head (including the AP, right lateral, left lateral, and two oblique exposures), Custer and his assistant were escorted by a federal agent to the fourth floor darkroom where the films were to be developed. On the way up, they paused as Jacqueline Kennedy and Robert Kennedy came through main lobby, boarded the elevators, and went up to a higher floor in the towers. Their entourage had just arrived with the bronze ceremonial casket. The time was approximately 7:15 PM EST.

After developing the head x-rays, Custer took them back down to the morgue, where he saw the bronze ceremonial casket on the floor next to the metal gray casket in the cooler room. Custer then handed the developed images to Dr. John H. Ebersole (the resident radiologist on call) who put them up on the viewing light board one by one.

Upon his return with developed head x-rays, Custer saw a gray shipping casket (L) and a more formal bronze casket (R) on the floor of the "cooler" room next to the morgue.

The frontal (AP) x-ray showed what appeared to be a bullet entrance hole in the right temporal region. After a small conference with the Humes, Boswell, and several others, Dr. Ebersole held the x-ray next to a portable light bulb and actually burned the film in the area of the right temple – breaking down the chemical base, exposing the silver, and crinkling the film. Also clearly visible on the AP x-ray were: the fractured right orbit, the partially rectangular-shaped hole in the back right of the head, and metallic bullet tracks that had adhered to the inside of the skull.

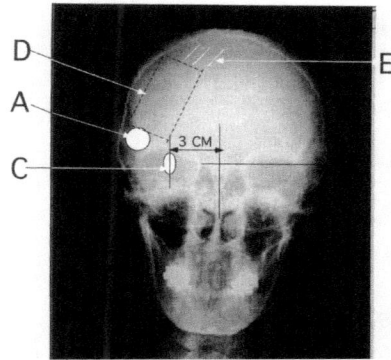

Generic schematic of an enhanced AP x-ray image in National Archives.
A: burn mark; D: area missing from rear of skull; E: metal bullet tracks visible

The left lateral x-ray also showed a trail of small metallic bullet fragments in the head. However, in this side view, they produced a cone-shape that converged at a point in the right temporal area. Obviously, these tracks were the remains of the path from front to back of the bullet that entered President Kennedy's head and then fragmented. The right lateral x-ray was even more revealing. Not only was the cone-shaped metallic trail there (going front-to-back and down-to-up), but so was the opening in the right back of the head. Also visible in this view was the top of the artificial cylindrical device providing stability to the head, and a very obvious shattered right orbit. More than any other x-ray, it was the right lateral that showed the magnitude of head wound suffered by President Kennedy. And strangely, when this film was on the light board, Dr. Ebersole drew two pencil lines on it that converged at a point in the back of the skull. Some researchers have speculated that these lines were drawn in to provide a guide for a reversed bullet trajectory (from back-to-front).

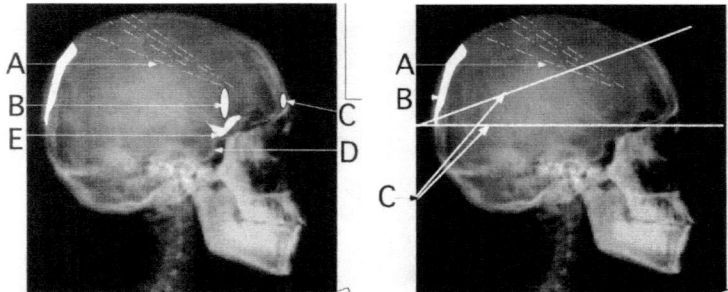

Generic schematic of right lateral x-ray image in Archives. A: metallic fragments (flow from front to top rear); B: exit hole; C: converging pencil lines (R); E: fractured right orbit (L).

By all accounts, the morgue was crowded with people taking notes, making comments, and shouting orders. Several key individuals in the gallery seemed to be directing almost every aspect of the autopsy. In particular, one four-star general and a man dressed in civilian clothes (who may have been Dr. George G. Burkeley, President Kennedy's personal physician) engaged in frequent small conferences with the doctors. And when Dr. Pierre Finck arrived (shortly after Ebersole burned the AP x-ray), he not only conferred with the same two individuals, but also began issuing orders to Humes and Boswell. Clearly, there were more cohesive directions from the gallery after Finck arrived.

JFK autopsy pathologists Boswell, Humes, and Finck.

Several additional sets of x-rays were taken at the Bethesda autopsy. One in particular, the neck images, revealed the presence of a significant amount of bullet fragments. In fact, those fragments may have derived from two shots: one from the front (in the first volley) and one from the side (in the third volley). On the other hand, the set of chest x-rays showed absolutely no bullet fragments, largely because they had been taken after the autopsy Y incision had been made and the lungs removed. Of particular note was the fact that during positioning of the body for these x-rays, a large bullet fragment seemed to have fallen out of the back onto the floor. Dr. Finck then quickly came over, picked it up with a pair of forceps, and dropped it into a small bottle. Some researchers believe this bullet may have been planted (when the body alterations were made) in order to demonstrate one shot to the back.

The total number of original x-rays taken at the Bethesda autopsy was between 14 and 20. At the end of the evening, they were all gathered together and handed over to Secret Service Agent Roy Kellerman for safekeeping. Interestingly enough, the Secret Service also assumed control of still photographic film taken that night. Both color and black and white pictures were being taken all through the autopsy. And just as soon as a roll of film was removed from a camera, a federal agent seized possession of it. Some video film was taken that night of by the Navy officer in charge of video at Bethesda. That film, however, was not seized, because the camera was hooked into a recorder on a different floor. A series of photographs were also shot after a team of morticians had worked on the body.

The morticians came in after the formal autopsy was completed and performed restorative artwork on the head. Among other things, they filled the bullet wound in the right temple with mortician's wax (or some other non-human material) and covered it and the rest of the face with makeup. Essentially, they masked the original frontal head entrance wound fired from the storm sewer drain during the third volley of shots.

Image processing of autopsy photo reveals restorative work performed on the head, including right temporal bullet entrance wound.

A few days after the autopsy, several key technicians who had participated in the process were called into the office of the Commanding Officer at Bethesda Medical Center and required to sign formal gag orders. They were also threatened with court martial and prison time if they ever spoke about the events associated with President Kennedy's autopsy.

Over the ensuing months, the international news media portrayed Lee Harvey Oswald as the lone assassin of President Kennedy. Of particular note was a February 21, 1964 cover story by *Life* magazine, which published backyard photographs linking him to both alleged murder weapons used in the killing of Kennedy and Officer Tippit. However, there is considerable evidence that the two backyard photographs in question were faked to incriminate Oswald.

Backyard photographs (L, C). February 21, 1964 cover of *Life* (R).

Detailed analysis showed that both were composites (of the individual and the background), that the face of Oswald was superimposed on another body, and that they were taken by an individual 5 feet 11 inches tall, rather than by Oswald's wife, Marina (as stated by the Warren Commission), whose height was only 5 feet 3 inches. Moreover, image processing of both photos revealed that areas of alteration included most of the face, the shadow under the nose, part of the mouth, portions of the ears, the entire chin, part of the neck, the newspaper (in its entirety), part of the rifle (stock, end, and strap), part of the right arm, all of the right hand, the fingers of the left hand. And finally, a photographic "mask" was superimposed on the person posing for the photograph. Areas altered included most of the face, the chin, part of the mouth, and portions of the ears.

 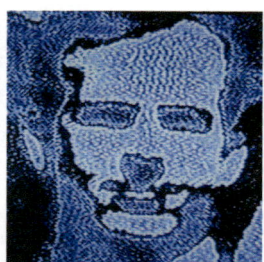 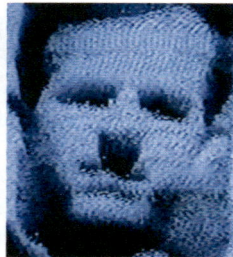

Image processing of face (L) reveals the mask that was photographically superimposed (C), and a closer representation of the real face of the individual in the backyard photograph (R).

On November 29, 1963 (one week after the assassination), President Johnson issued Executive Order 11130, which "appointed a Commission" to "examine the evidence developed by the FBI and any additional evidence that may come to light" and to "evaluate all the facts and circumstances surrounding" the assassination. Appointed to serve on this Commission were: Senator Richard Russell (D-Georgia), Senator John Sherman Cooper (R-Kentucky), Representative Hale Boggs (D-Louisiana), Representative Gerald R. Ford (R-Michigan), John J. McCloy, former assistant secretary of war during World War II and former US high commissioner in occupied Germany, and Allen Dulles, who had formerly served for nine years as Director of the Central Intelligence Agency. The Chairman would be the sitting United States Supreme Court Chief Justice, Earl A. Warren, which is why the popular name given to the investigative body was the "Warren Commission."

After a ten-month investigation, an 888-page "Warren Report" was released to the American public (on September 27, 1964). Two months later (November 1964), and almost exactly one year after the assassination, the Commission published 26 volumes consisting of more than 16,000 pages of testimony and exhibits to support its findings.

Warren Commission members give final report to President Johnson.

Almost immediately, many researchers and experts questioned the methods and conclusions of the Warren Commission. Among other things, they pointed out that no autopsy x-rays or photographs were studied or properly utilized. Overall it was charged that the Commission did not really conduct a proper investigation and, instead, gathered information to ensure a preexisting scenario; that it failed to take testimony from key witnesses, especially those whose observations differed from that scenario; that it did not explore lines of evidence indicating conspiracy; that it accepted brazen misrepresentations and testimony from questionable witnesses; and that it rejected key evidence in its possession.

Generally, the Commission reversed the direction of the key shots fired at President Kennedy with a scenario that placed Lee Harvey Oswald in the "sniper's window" on the sixth floor of the Texas School Book Depository. Three shots, and three shots only, it stated, were fired by one lone nut.

Specifically, the Warren Commission concluded that Lee Harvey Oswald, "using a Mannlicher-Carcano 6.5-millimeter Italian rifle . . . owned by and in [his] possession," fired three shots from the southeast window on the sixth floor of the Texas School Book Depository. One bullet "entered the base of the back of President Kennedy's neck slightly to the right of the spine and exited from the front of the neck." This same bullet, the Commission stated, continued onward and struck Governor Connally in the extreme right side of his back, traveled through his chest, exited, passed through his right wrist, and caused a wound to his left thigh. Another bullet struck President Kennedy in the "rear portion of his head, causing a massive and fatal wound." A third bullet missed the presidential limousine entirely.

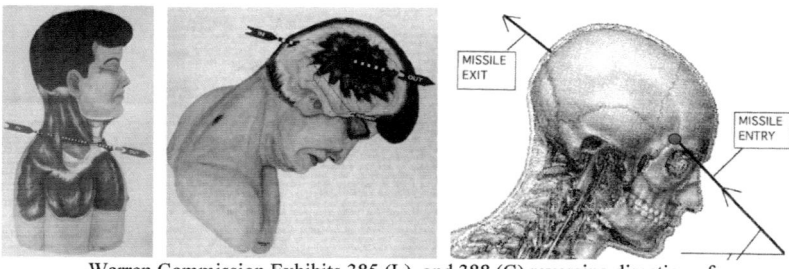

Warren Commission Exhibits 385 (L), and 388 (C) reversing direction of shots; Tom Wilson's diagram of the real shot to the head (R).

The Commission further concluded that Lee Harvey Oswald killed Dallas Police Officer J. D. Tippit, and that the bullets that killed him were fired from a revolver owned by Oswald and in his possession. Finally, the Warren Commission wrote that it "found no evidence that Lee Harvey Oswald was part of any conspiracy, domestic, or foreign, to assassinate President Kennedy." It concluded that he acted alone and that his motives included a" deep-rooted resentment of all authority," an "inability to enter into meaningful relationships with people," an "urge to try to find a place in history," a "capacity for violence," and an "avowed commitment to Marxism and communism."

The main reason that autopsy photographs and x-rays were not used by the Warren Commission was the fact that most of them were at odds with the "Lee Harvey Oswald-three-shot" scenario. They simply could not be used. Over time, however, some of this crucial evidence was altered to hide the real wounds inflicted on President Kennedy and, in some instances, to manufacture new evidence that conformed to the conclusions reached by the Warren Commission.

For instance, the "official" autopsy photo of the back of the head showed a bullet hole entrance in the cowlick area and a piece of flesh in the area of the lower hairline. Neither were present in the original photograph. What was visible in the original were two exit wounds – one in the top right back of the head and another in the back of the neck. Photographic alteration to this image was performed using three specially prepared mattes. The first matte wiped out the area to be altered. The second added imagery that looked like normal hair. And the third matte added the fake missile entry hole and the piece of flesh. Then the new bullet hole and dried tissue were photographed in two stages to provide an illusion of depth.

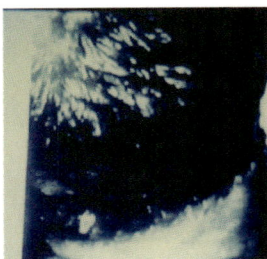 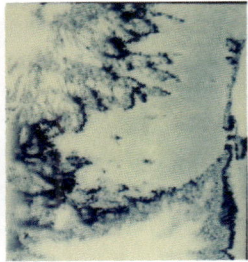 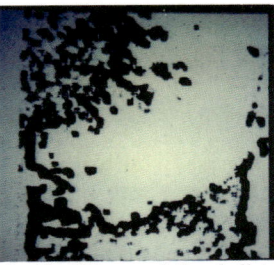

Processing of back of head photograph reveals exit hole in back of head removed, then bullet entrance hole in cowlick area and piece of flesh at lower hairline photographically added.

Image processing also reveals that the exit hole in back of neck was photographically removed.

Another "official" autopsy photograph (of the frontal head and chest) was similarly altered in three areas. The bullet entrance hole in the right temporal area and the massive exit wound in the top right back of the head were both blackened in. And the right eye (which had been seriously damaged from the frontal shot to the head) was painted on to make it appear normal.

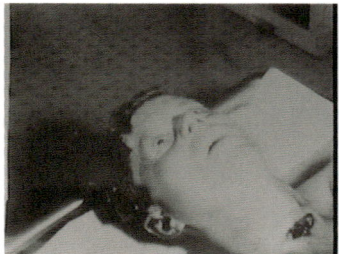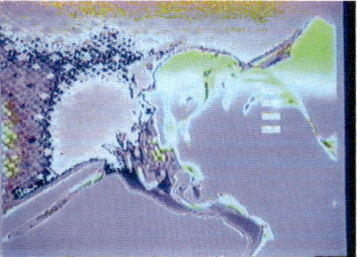

Image processing of frontal head and chest autopsy photograph reveals right temporal entrance wound and exit hole in back of head were photographically blackened.

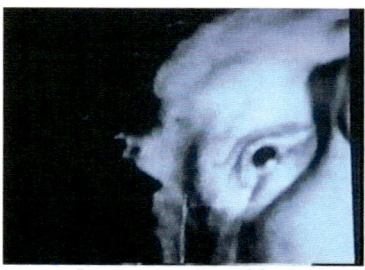

Image processing of frontal head and chest autopsy photograph reveals that the right eye was painted on the photograph.

Nearly every copy of every altered photograph (both color and black & white) had the initials "JB" signed on the back. It can obviously be inferred that this individual reviewed and approved each image – and that that individual was Dr. J. Thornton Boswell, one of the autopsy pathologists.

Some of the x-rays taken at the autopsy were also altered, and even forged to hide the real wounds inflicted on President Kennedy. For example, a bullet fragment was taped to the outside of the anterior/posterior (AP) x-ray near the right eye. It was then re-exposed to make it appear as though the bullet was inside the head. In essence, it was a faked composite. Copies of this x-ray were then darkened, which eliminated crucial detail – such as the entrance wound in the right temporal area, damage to the right orbital bones, and the rectangular exit hole in the back of the head.

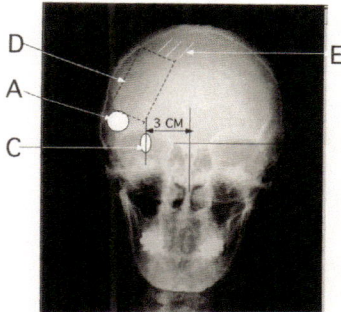

AP x-ray was altered and darkened to hide true wounds. Tom Wilson's sketch of AP x-ray in National Archives (left); A: burn mark, C: planted bullet fragment, D: rectangular exit hole, E: trail of metallic bullet fragments.

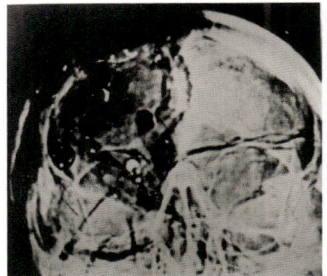 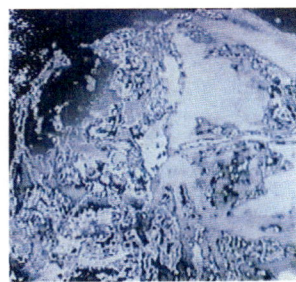

AP image shown to government panel (L); Tom's image processing (R).

On the backs of copies of the altered x-rays were the initials "JHE." It obviously can be inferred that this individual reviewed and approved each image – and that he was Dr. John H. Ebersole, the resident radiologist on call the night of the autopsy (who caused the burn mark on the AP x-ray and drew the pencil lines on the right lateral). Furthermore, because Navy doctors Ebersole and Boswell initialed copies of the x-rays and photographs, respectively, there is a high probability that at least some of the alterations were made at Bethesda Naval Medical Center.

The right lateral and left lateral x-rays were also turned into one composite image, presumably to show to future government investigators and, eventually, the American public. In this case, the original right lateral image was used as a base. A mirror image of the left lateral (showing the top and back of the head intact) was superimposed on the right lateral, and then redeveloped. Additionally, a bullet fragment was taped to the outside of the film at the front of the head near the right eye, and then reexposed to make it appear that the bullet was present inside the head. The resulting new image was then sufficiently darkened to hide any substantive detail, including the cone-shaped trail of metallic bullet fragments and the bullet entrance wound in the right temporal region.

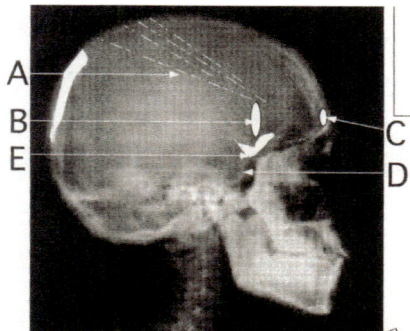

Tom's sketch of right lateral in Archives. A: trail of metallic bullet fragments, B: artificial stabilization device, C: planted bullet fragment, E: fractured right orbit; composite image.

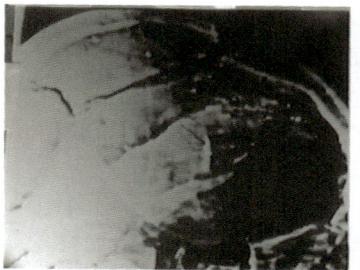 

Right lateral x-ray combined to create composite "lateral" image in order to hide true wounds to head. Wilson's image processing reveals bullet entrance hole in right temporal area.

On the night of the autopsy, four head fragments (created from the large altered head wound) were brought into the morgue and portrayed as having come from the presidential limousine in Dallas. The next day, after a meeting at the White House, Dr. Ebersole brought the head pieces to Bethesda and ordered Jerrol Custer to tape metallic fragments on them, place the smallest piece on top of a larger one, and then take x-rays. Custer followed orders. Although not published by the Warren Commission, the resulting image was darkened and the later used to portray the skull fragments as having come from a large wound in the top right of the head caused by a bullet that entered in the cowlick area.

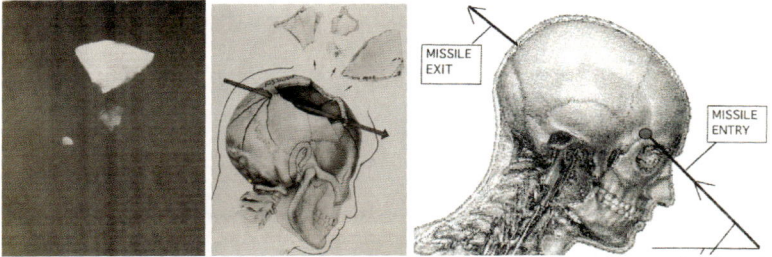

Skull fragments x-ray, JFK Exhibit F-64 (L) was darkened and portrayed as coming from top of head wound caused by a bullet fired from behind and having entered in the cowlick area, JFK Exhibit F-66 (C). Tom Wilson's diagram of the real shot to the head (R).

In addition to the forgeries of the autopsy photographs and x-rays, other images taken on November 22, 1963 were altered, including two of the most important pieces of evidence in the assassination case – the Mary Moorman Polaroid photograph and the Zapruder film.

Even though the Moorman Polaroid was taken at the moment of the fatal headshot, it was not used by the Warren Commission, nor was it even present in the Warren Report's accompanying 26 volumes of hearings and exhibits. Furthermore, there is clear evidence that the photograph was altered. Shortly after the assassination, the image appeared in countless newspapers and magazine articles. But in almost all these published versions, the obvious hole in the back of President Kennedy's head was not visible. When full-frame images were printed, the exit wound was obviously too small to see clearly. However, when cropped enlargements were printed, the back of President Kennedy's head was blackened in so the hole could not be seen.

Early printed versions of Moorman photo show back of head blackened in (L,C). Cropped and enlarged image of original (R) clearly shows exit hole in back of President Kennedy's head.

Shortly after the assassination, Mary Moorman handed over her photograph to federal agents, who kept it for a brief time. Upon its return, there was a huge thumb- or fingerprint in the area of one of the motorcycle officers riding at the back of the limousine. [Recall that both officers stated shortly after the assassination that they had been splattered with bits of bloody bone, brain, and scalp material.] There was also an apparent alteration in the area of the pedestal that Abraham Zapruder was supposed to be standing on when he filmed the assassination. An elongated (up and down) oval area seems to have been added to the photograph in that area. Moreover, the individual represented as Zapruder looks like a startled young man wearing some sort of beanie. [A taller woman, presumably secretary Marilyn Sitzman, was standing behind.] Also, the movie camera is not up to his face. Rather, it is in his right hand, a foot or so below his eyes.

Apparent alteration of Moorman Polaroid; thumbprint (C); elongated (up and down) oval area may have been added to area of Zapruder pedestal. Note: figure appears as startled young man with camera held in right hand a foot or so below his eyes.

Some researchers believe that such factual observances point to a possibility that Abraham Zapruder actually may not have taken the famous film named for him. Rather, it may be a composite of more than one film. Certainly, it has been well established that the Zapruder film was altered in order to hide the real wounds inflicted on President Kennedy.

Other researchers have documented splices in the film at key intervals. Three such notable cuts occur 1) when the presidential limousine turns onto Elm Street from Houston Street, 2) just before the first volley of shots when the limousine is behind the Stemmons Freeway exit sign, and 3) at a key point between the second and third volleys.

Key areas of the Zapruder film show clear evidence of splicing. One example is in frame #212 when the presidential limousine is behind the Stemmons Freeway exit sign.

As a matter of fact, enough splicing was done so as to actually alter the position of the presidential limousine at the precise moment of the fatal headshot. Detailed on-site calculations show that frame #313 actually occurred 7 feet, 6 inches farther down Elm Street than indicated in the Zapruder film. This alteration took President Kennedy out of range of the storm sewer drain at the base of the steps on the grassy knoll, and made it appear that the fatal headshot could not possibly have come from that position. The reality is, however, that the limousine was much closer to the storm sewer drain, and in perfect position for the gunman to have hit the president in the right temple with a high-powered handgun.

Fatal shot to JFK's head occurred 7' 6" farther down Elm Street than Zapruder film indicates.

Additional alterations were made to the Zapruder film using sophisticated, 1963 state-of-the-art equipment that performed half-tone and insert matte photography. For example, grass in the background was altered to eliminate the presence of airborne head debris. Additionally, the orange-reddish blob at the front of President Kennedy's head (in frame #313 and several succeeding frames) was artificially added to the film. Also altered by these processes were the President's front face, right hand, back neck, back head, and front chest (possibly to mask damage from a frontal shot).

Image processing of Zapruder frame #313 (original, L) reveals alteration of grass in background to hide presence of airborne head debris. First layer removed (C); second layer removed (R).

Image processing of frame #316 (original left) reveals orange-reddish blob at the front of President Kennedy's head artificially added to the film. First layer removed (R) shows areas of alteration in white.

Another major alteration of the Zapruder home movie was the gradual cutting off of the bottom portion of the film leading up to the fatal headshot in frame #313, and its gradual addition in frames after the shot. This modification is barely perceptible when watching the Zapruder film at normal speed, especially because the viewer's attention is drawn to the events actually taking place. Recall that KBOX radio newsman Sam Pate reported seeing smoke rise from the storm sewer at the time of the headshot. This key alteration of the Zapruder film eliminated any visible rising gunsmoke, and further obscured other evidence of a shot from that location.

Representative Zapruder frames show how lower portion of film was removed to eliminate all evidence (such as smoke) of fatal headshot from storm sewer drain. [From left to right, Zapruder frames #'s 228, 244, 265, 313 (headshot), 331, 333, 382] Note gradual elimination of bottom part of film leading up to #313 and gradual increase thereafter.

Within a week of President Kennedy's assassination, *Life* magazine purchased the original Zapruder film (for $150,000) and maintained strict control of its visibility to the American public. Over the first few years of ownership, *Life* published select individual frames in several of its issues. It also allowed the Warren Commission to reproduce 158 frames of extremely poor quality. Five years later, in 1969, New Orleans District Attorney Jim Garrison subpoenaed a copy of the film and it was shown for the first time at the trial of suspected conspirator Clay Shaw. And it was not until 1975 that it was widely seen by a national television audience (when broadcast by the ABC program *Good Night America*).

Alterations to the Zapruder film were most likely performed within the first few years after the assassination, but probably not all at once. Some individual frames contained in the Warren Commission's exhibits clearly showed evidence of splicing. But the film, as a whole, may or may not have been altered while the official investigation was under way. It appears clear, however, that the Zapruder film's alterations were coordinated with those of both the autopsy x-rays and photographs and with the Warren Commission's published account. The purpose of all this altered evidence was obviously done to hide the real wounds inflicted on President Kennedy, to give the impression that all the shots were fired from behind the presidential limousine, and to conform with the government's pre-existing scenario.

As of 2008, there is no confirmed original of the Zapruder film in existence. Most likely, it was destroyed soon after final alterations were completed. All Zapruder film copies in the public domain and in the National Archives are reproductions of the altered original.

On the other hand, autopsy x-rays and photographs contained in the National Archives (as of 1995) represent hard evidence in the truth of President Kennedy's assassination. These images include both originals and copies in various stages of alteration. Some show the real wounds (such as the entrance hole in the right temporal area and the exit hole in the back right top of the head) and traces of metal fragments on the inside of the skull. Evidence of conspiracy also exists by what is *not present* in the National Archives. For instance, most of the photographs taken at the Bethesda autopsy are gone. Also the two oblique head x-rays and the AP neck x-ray have disappeared. Most of these images were probably thrown out, because they were inconsistent with the Warren Commission's conclusion. For example, the neck x-ray was discarded due to the fact that it revealed significant amounts of bullet fragments and, therefore, negated the single (or "magic") bullet theory.

Over the years, increased public discontent with the government's findings resulted in several more formal investigations. The Ramsey Clark Panel (1968) and the Rockefeller Commission (1975) both affirmed the conclusions reached by the Warren Commission, although neither explained the basis of their findings in public hearings. Finally, more than fifteen years after John F. Kennedy's death (in March 1979), the 13-member House Select Committee on Assassinations (HSCA) published a report and twelve accompanying volumes on its three-year investigation into the assassination. The HSCA's conclusions were as follows:

Lee Harvey Oswald fired three shots at President John F. Kennedy from the sixth floor window of the southeast corner of the Texas School Book Depository building.

The second and third shots struck the president. The third shot killed the president.

There is a high probability that two gunmen fired shots at the president [and therefore,] John F. Kennedy was probably assassinated as a result of a conspiracy.

That's what the history books say.

But it's not the truth.

Although the Committee interviewed many new witnesses and uncovered a significant amount of new information that indicated a conspiracy, it also relied on much of the same forged evidence, methodology, and improper conclusions reached by the Warren Commission. Among other things, the HSCA Report utilized tightly cropped photographs and drawings of autopsy images to hide evidence, darkened already altered x-rays to further obscure evidence, and presented the same false scenario of the assassination.

The truth is that a team of assassins was waiting in Dealey Plaza for President Kennedy's motorcade to arrive. Dozens of people, including multiple gunmen, were involved. Three volleys of gunfire were fired at the president. At least six shots missed him (from the front, back, and sides). Two, possibly three of those bullets wounded Governor John Connally. Others hit the trim of the windshield, a street curb, and perhaps the Stemmons Freeway exit sign.

At least six bullets struck John F. Kennedy. Two in the neck, two in the back, one in the chest, and one in the head. The final headshot killed him instantly.

That's what really happened on November 22, 1963 in Dallas, Texas.

. . . and that's what the history books *should* say.

Author's Note

On November 24, 2001, almost exactly 38 years after the assassination, Tom Wilson passed away from complications of a prolonged heart condition. He was 69 years old.

In the last years of his life, Tom continued, as best he could, to bring his findings to the attention of the American public. Among other things, he appeared in the sixth installment of Nigel Turner's documentary *The Men Who Killed Kennedy*, wrote letters to every member of the United States Congress, and made a formal presentation to the Assassination Records Review Board (ARRB).

Largely due to public reaction of Oliver Stone's movie, *JFK*, the US Congress passed the John F. Kennedy Assassination Records Collection Act of 1992, which ordered the gathering of government records and information related to the death of the President. The ARRB was created to oversee the job and, as part of its collection process, conducted interviews with many assassination researchers. Tom's presentation took place in Washington, DC on September 11, 1998, lasted two hours, and included a 40-minute videotape. Three weeks later, the ARRB ceased operations, and no follow up occurred by any government official, government agency, or media outlet.

In retirement, Tom supplemented his income by serving as a consulting technical expert in criminal law cases where his image processing work was accepted as hard evidence in American courts of law. Similarly, the results of Tom's work in the JFK assassination can be viewed as hard evidence. As he told the ARRB: "Nothing is conjecture. The final image is clear and processed without any alteration of the original image regardless of its condition. The data is repeatable and verifiable at any stage of the process. It's all basic computing and can be reproduced by anybody at any time. Nothing is theory. Nothing is speculation."

For years after his death, Tom's work sat stored away in a safe place. With the approval of his family, I spent years pulling together his story. I thank them for their encouragement, support, and trust. And I hope they find this book worthy of Tom's integrity and his personal commitment to the truth.

The last time I spoke with Tom Wilson, he asked me to get involved. "Don," he said, "we need young people like you to pick up torch and carry it forward after we are gone." Likewise, I hope people of good will take the information, techniques, and evidence discovered by Tom Wilson – and run with them.

There have been a great many technological advances since Tom performed his work. For those of you who may be experts in computers, image processing, or photography, go get a copy of the Zapruder film and pick it apart. Obtain copies of other key films and photos taken on November 22, 1963 in Dallas. Analyze, discover, enlighten. Help us find out more details about President John F. Kennedy's assassination.

Carl Sandburg once wrote: "Life is like an onion. You peel it off one layer at a time, and sometimes you weep." When I peeled away layers of the assassination images and saw what really happened to President Kennedy on November 22, 1963, I cried.

The American people can handle the truth. Let's put it to rest.

Tom Wilson

Reference Notes & Credits

Prologue:
"a firecracker," Warren Report [WR], United States Government Printing Office, Washington, DC, 1964, p. 65; "a motorcycle backfire," Warren Commission Hearing and Exhibits, 26 volumes [WC], United States Government Printing Office, Washington, DC, 1964, Vol. XVIII, p. 723; "a burst of gunfire," UPI Teletype, November 22, 1963; Curry's order, from Curry, Jesse, *JFK Assassination File*, American Poster and Printing Company, Inc., Dallas, p. 30-31; Decker's order, WC, Vol. 23, p. 913; Kilduff statement, Press Conference, 11-22-63; Secret Service Report #154-10002-10194, transcript also in LBJ Library (1327B); "I'm just a patsy," made at 7:55 PM CST at Police headquarters, WC, Vol. XX, p. 366; "examine the evidence," US Government document, Executive Order 11130, 11-29-63; "using a Mannlicher-Carcano," WR, p. 19; "entered the base of the back of President Kennedy's neck," WR, p. 3; "rear portion of his head," WR, p. 3; "found no evidence," WR, p. 21; Oswald's motives, WR, p. 18-23; HSCA's conclusions, Report of the Select Committee On Assassinations, U.S. House of Representatives [HSCA], United States Government Printing Office, 1979, p. 41, 47, 65, 95. Photographs: (Repeat images not cited) P. 5: Cecil Stoughton, JFK Library; Clint Grant, *Dallas Morning News*. P. 6: AP; Library of Congress; Clint Grant, *Dallas Morning News*. P. 7: Dallas Municipal Archive and Records Center; Dallas Municipal Archive and Records Center; Richard O. Bothun; AP. P. 8: Abraham Zapruder, AssassinationScience.com, John P. Costella edit; Abraham Zapruder, AssassinationScience.com, John P. Costella edit; Abraham Zapruder, AssassinationScience.com, John P. Costella edit; James W. Altgens, AP; FBI. P. 9: Wilma J. Bond; Jim Towner; Frank Cancellare, UPI. P. 10: George Smith, *Fort Worth Star-Telegram*; Thomas Atkins, JFK Library; Cecil Stoughton, JFK Library. P. 11: Dallas Municipal Archive and Records Center; *US News and World Report*; Dallas Municipal Archive and Records Center; WC, Vol. XXI P. 19: Cecil Stoughton, LBJ Library.

1 / Metal Badge: Manchester, William, *The Death of a President*, Harper & Row, New York, 1967; Lifton, David S., *Best Evidence*, MacMillan, New York, NY, 1980; Scheim, David E., *Contract On America: The Mafia Murder of President John F. Kennedy*, Shapolsky Publishers, New York, NY, 1988; Garrison, Jim, *On the Trail of the Assassins*, Sheridan Square Press, New York, NY, 1988. Photographs: (Repeat images not cited) P. 16: Mary Ann Moorman. P. 18: Tom Wilson. P. 19: *The Men Who Killed Kennedy*. P. 20: *The Men Who Killed Kennedy*. P. 21: Tom Wilson (all). P. 22: Tom Wilson (all). P. 23: Tom Wilson. P. 24: Tom Wilson (all). P. 26: Tom Wilson (all).

2 / The Zapruder Film:
Photographs: (Repeat images not cited) P. 28: WFAA-TV, Dallas; Library of Congress. P. 29-30: Abraham Zapruder, AssassinationScience.com, John P. Costella edit (32 total frames used in all). P. 32: Tom Wilson (all). P. 33: Tom Wilson. P. 34: Tom Wilson (all). P. 36: Tom Wilson (all). P. 39: Tom Wilson. P. 40: Tom Wilson (all). P. 41: Tom Wilson. P. 42: Tom Wilson (all). P. 43: Tom Wilson (all). P. 44: Tom Wilson (all).

3 / Somebody Has to do Something:
"a very small injury," WC, Vol. VI, p. 32-33; *Herald Tribune*, 11-23-64; "The right posterior portion of the skull had been extremely blasted," WC, Vol. VI, p. 33; "It was just a little hole," WC, Vol. VI, p. 141; "In the process of positioning and stabilizing," Lattimer, Dr. John K, *Kennedy and Lincoln: Medical & Ballistic Comparisons of Their Assassinations*, Harcourt Brace Jovanovich, New York, NY, 1980; "As the car got directly in front of us," Interview with WFAA-TV, 11-22-63; "the size of a baseball," Crenshaw testimony before the Assassination Records Review Board, 3-19-97; "His head exploded," WC, Vol. VI, p. 294. Photographs: (Repeat images not cited) P. 47: Tom Wilson (all). P. 48: Tom Wilson. P. 49: Tom Wilson (all). P. 50: Tom Wilson. P. 51: Tom Wilson (all). P. 52: Tom Wilson (all). P. 53: Tom Wilson (all). P. 54: Tom Wilson (all). P. 55: Tom Wilson (all). P. 57: Tom Wilson (all). P. 58: Tom Wilson. P. 59: Tom Wilson.

4 / Five Autopsy Photographs:
JFK Exhibit F-48, HSCA, Vol. I, p. 235; JFK Exhibit F-50, HSCA, Vol. I, p. 236; JFK Exhibit F-51; HSCA, Vol. I, p. 237; "In deciding to release the autopsy photographs," HSCA, Vol. I, p. 235; "a typical type of tracheostomy incision," HSCA, Vol. I, p. 217; "near the base of President Kennedy's neck," WR, p. 87; "by projecting from a point of entry," WR, p. 88; JFK Exhibit F-36, HSCA, Vol. I, p. 214; JFK Exhibit F-38, HSCA, Vol. I, p. 216; HSCA Exhibit F-123, HSCA, Vol. I, p. 104; JFK Exhibit F-20, HSCA, Vol. I, p. 186; JFK Exhibit F-22, HSCA, Vol. I, p. 186; JFK Exhibit F-46; HSCA, Vol. I, p. 231. Photographs: (Repeat images not cited) P. 69: Cyril Wecht. P. 71: House Select Committee on Assassinations (HSCA). P. 72: HSCA (all). P. 74: National Archives; Tom Wilson. P. 75: National Archives; Tom Wilson. P. 76: National Archives (all). P. 77: National Archives. P. 78: National Archives (all). P. 79: Tom Wilson (all). P. 81: Tom Wilson (all). P. 82: HSCA (all). P. 83: National Archives; Tom Wilson. P. 84: National Archives; Tom Wilson. P. 85: National Archives. P. 86: Tom Wilson (all). P. 87: James W. Altgens, AP. P. 88: HSCA; National Archives. P. 89: National Archives; Tom Wilson; HSCA. P. 90: HSCA. P. 91: HSCA. P. 92: Tom Wilson.

5 / On the Ground in Dallas:
Photographs: (Repeat images not cited) P. 94: Tom Wilson. P. 96: Tom Wilson (all). P. 98: Tom Wilson (all). P. 99: Tom Wilson; Oliver Stone. P. 101: *The Men Who Killed Kennedy* (all). P. 103: Tom Wilson (all). P. 104: Tom Wilson; Orville Nix. P. 105: Tom Wilson (all). P. 106: Tom Wilson.

6 / Suspicious Images in Dealey Plaza:
"The shots which killed President Kennedy," WR, p. 18; "Lee Harvey Oswald fired three shots," HSCA Report, p. 41, 47; Willis Exhibit #1, "sniper window," HSCA, Vol. XXI, p. 773; Powell photo, Exhibit F-123, HSCA, Vol. I, p. 104. Photographs: (Repeat images not cited) P. 110: George Smith, *Fort Worth Star-Telegram*. P. 113: William Allen, *Dallas Times Herald*. P. 114: Tom Wilson (all). P. 115: Phil Willis; Tom Wilson. P. 116: Tom Wilson; Clint Grant, *Dallas Morning News*. P. 118: Tom Wilson (all). P. 119: Jim Towner; Tom Wilson. P. 120: Tom Wilson. P. 121: Tom Wilson. P. 122: Tom Wilson (all). P. 123: Tom Wilson. P. 124: Tom Wilson (all). P. 125: Tom Wilson (all). P. 126: Tom Wilson (all). P. 127: Tom Wilson; ABC. P. 129: James W. Altgens; Tom Wilson. P. 130: FBI. P. 131: Warren Commission; HSCA; FBI. P. 132: Tom Wilson. P. 133: Tom Wilson (all). P. 134: Tom Wilson.

7 / The Oswald Backyard Photographs:
Marina took two pictures, WR, p. 125-126; "obtained a search warrant," WR, p. 181; "photographs were shown to Oswald," WR, p. 181; "at the proper time," WR, p. 181; *Life* magazine, 2-21-64; "The Commission has concluded," WR, p. 125; "The rifle used to assassinate," WR, p. 129; Commission Exhibit No. 134, WR, p. 126; "authenticity of these pictures," WR, p. 127; Figure IV-37; HSCA, Vol. VI, p. 173; "no evidence of fakery," HSCA Report, p. 56; "dates surrounding the taking of this picture," WR, p. 127; "10 days prior to the attempt," WR, p. 128; "Oswald had undoubtedly received the rifle," WR, p. 128; "Given the view shown," HSCA, Vol. VI, p. 171; Exhibit 133-A, WC, Vol. XVI, p. 510; Exhibit 133-B, WC, Vol. XVI, p. 510; *Dallas Times Herald*, 11-16-91. Photographs: (Repeat images not cited) P. 136: Dallas Municipal Archive and Records Center (all). P. 138: *Life*; Warren Commission. P. 139: HSCA. P. 142: Tom Wilson (all). P. 143: Tom Wilson. P. 144: Tom Wilson (all). P. 145: Tom Wilson (all). P. 146: Tom Wilson (all). P. 147: Tom Wilson (all).

8 / X-Rays and More:
WC Exhibit 388, Vol. XVI, p. 984; JFK Exhibit F-68, HSCA, Vol. I, p. 255; JFK Exhibit F-65, HSCA, Vol. I, p. 251; JFK Exhibit F-66, HSCA, Vol. I, p. 252; JFK Exhibit F-59, HSCA, Vol. I, p. 247; Figure 25, HSCA, Vol. VII, p. 119; JFK Exhibit F-60, Vol. I, p. 247; "four of the original 14 x-rays," HSCA, Vol. I, p. 246; "The committee wished to permit public examination," HSCA, Vol. I, p. 246; JFK Exhibit F-55; HSCA, Vol. I, p. 243; JFK Exhibit F-56; HSCA, Vol. I, p. 244; "a missile fragment," HSCA, Vol. VII, p. 109; JFK Exhibit F-52, HSCA, Vol. I, p. 239; JFK Exhibit F-53; HSCA, Vol. I, p. 240; "an enlarged copy of that specific x-ray," HSCA, Vol. I, p. 239; "a lateral view of the president's head," HSCA, Vol. I, p. 241; "a computerized enhancement," HSCA, Vol. I, p. 241; "Many small white areas in the

x-ray," HSCA, Vol. I, p. 241. Photographs: (Repeat images not cited) P. 152: National Archives; Tom Wilson. P. 153: Tom Wilson (all). P. 154: Tom Wilson (all). P. 155: Tom Wilson (all). P. 156: Tom Wilson (all). P. 157: To Wilson (all); National Archives. P. 159: Warren Commission; HSCA. P. 160: National Archives (all). P. 161: HSCA (all). P. 162: Tom Wilson (all). P. 163: Tom Wilson (all). P. 164: HSCA (all). P. 165: Tom Wilson (all). P. 166: Tom Wilson (all).

9 / The Fatal Headshot:
"I was in such a position," WC, Vol. VI, p. 22; Pate observed a puff of smoke, Pate Statement, HSCA, JFK Document 014913, 1-28-78; "Have Parkland stand by," Curry, p. 30-31; "it seemed to have some type of echo," WC, Vol. II, p. 138; "the majority of his portion of the tape is not an authentic one," HSCA, JFK Document 014513, 3-10-64; Hoover to Rankin, HSCA JFK Document 014512, 6-10-64. Photographs: (Repeat images not cited) P. 169: Tom Wilson (all). P. 170: Tom Wilson (all). P. 172: Tom Wilson (all). P. 174: Tom Wilson (all). P. 175: Tom Wilson. P. 176: Tom Wilson (all). P. 177: KBOX Dallas (all). P. 180: Mary Ann Moorman.

10 / Autopsy X-Rays in the National Archives:
"The skull films were definitely taken before the autopsy," Ebersole HSCA testimony, p. 8, 18, 32, 3-11-78; "I personally carried," Ebersole testimony, p. 3-4; "It may have happened that night," Ebersole HSCA testimony, p. 18, 3-11-78; JFK Exhibit F-55, HSCA, Vol. I, p. 243; JFK Exhibit F-56, HSCA, Vol. I, p. 244; "The Committee decided to display the autopsy x-rays," HSCA, Vol. I, p. 246; "Sometime within a month of the assassination," Ebersole HSCA testimony, p. 5, 67, 3-11-78; JFK Exhibit F-52, "an enlarged copy," HSCA, Vol. I, p. 239; JFK Exhibit F-52, "a computerized enhancement," HSCA, Vol. I, p. 241; "There are extensive fracture lines," HSCA, Vol. I, p. 246; "No evidence of fakery was discovered," HSCA, Vol. VI, p. 227-228; "We were asked by the Secret Service," Ebersole HSCA testimony, p. 4, 8, 3-11-78; JFK Exhibits F-28, F-29, "two of the original 14," HSCA, Vol. I, p. 196; JFK Exhibits F-28, F-29, "enlargements of portions of the x-rays," HSCA, Vol. I, p. 199; JFK Exhibit F-30, HSCA, Vol. I, p. 197; JFK Figure 11, HSCA, Vol. VII, p. 98; JFK Exhibit F-31, HSCA, Vol. I, p. 198; JFK Figure 10, HSCA, Vol. VII, p. 97; "no missile present in the body at the time the x-rays were taken," HSCA, Vol. I, p. 199; JFK Exhibit F-64, "three fragments of bone," HSCA, Vol. I, p. 249; "the panel concluded," HSCA, Vol. I, p. 250; Figure 26, "On the triangular fragment," HSCA, Vol. VII, p. 121; JFK Exhibit F-66, "a scale drawing," HSCA, Vol. I, p. 252; Figure 29, HSCA, Vol. VII, p. 125; "Later in the evening," Ebersole HSCA testimony, p. 5, 20, 3-11-78. Photographs: (Repeat images not cited) P. 183: Bethesda Naval Medical Center; Walter Reed Medical Center. P. 184: AP. P. 185: Bob Phillips, *Life*. P. 189: Tom Wilson. P. 190: Tom Wilson. P. 191: Tom Wilson. P. 192: AP (all). P. 193: JFK Lancer (all). P. 196: Tom Wilson. P. 197: Tom Wilson. P. 198: Tom Wilson. P. 199: Tom Wilson (all). P. 201: Tom Wilson (all). P. 202: Bethesda Naval Medical Center. P. 207: Tom Wilson. P. 208: Tom Wilson. P. 209: Tom Wilson. P. 215: National Archives (all). P. 217: HSCA (all). P. 218: Tom Wilson.

11 / Autopsy Photographs in the National Archives:
Pitzer found dead, FBI teletype, 10-29-66; Figure 32, HSCA, Vol. I, p. 130; JFK Exhibit F-302; Vol. I, p. 328; JFK Exhibit F-50, HSCA, Vol. I, p. 236; JFK Exhibit F-51, HSCA, Vol. I, p. 237; "extraneous dried brain tissue," HSCA, Vol. I, p. 238; "When questioned by panel members," HSCA, Vol. VII, p. 177-179; "We believe that another missile did not enter," HSCA, Vol. VII, p. 178; Figure 1, HSCA, Vol. VII, p. 81; Figure 2, HSCA, Vol. VII, p. 83; Figure 3, HSCA, Vol. VII, p. 84; "were cut during emergency procedures," HSCA, Vol. VII, p. 82; "second defect was artificially created," HSCA, Vol. VII, p. 82; "second defect was created in the shirt," HSCA, Vol. VII, p. 83. Photographs: (Repeat images not cited) P. 224: HSCA. P. 225: Tom Wilson. P. 227: Tom Wilson (all). P. 228: Tom Wilson. P. 231: Tom Wilson (all). P. 232: Tom Wilson. P. 234: Tom Wilson. P. 237: HSCA (all).

Epilogue: The Darker Truth:
"a firecracker," Warren Report [WR], United States Government Printing Office, Washington, DC, 1964, p. 65; "a motorcycle backfire," Warren Commission Hearing and Exhibits, 26

volumes [WC], United States Government Printing Office, Washington, DC, 1964, Vol. XVIII, p. 723; "a burst of gunfire," UPI Teletype, November 22, 1963; "I saw a stocky man," Hoffman, Ed and Ron Friedrich, *Eye Witness,* JFK Lancer Productions and Publications, Grand Prairie, TX, 1997; p. 7-8; "Shots were fired from behind the wooden stockade fence," HSCA, Vol. VIII, p. 16; differences in pickup truck on Commerce Street, White, Jack, *The Great Zapruder Film Hoax,* p. 13-14, in Fetzer, James H, editor, *Murder in Dealey Plaza: What We Know Now that We Didn't Know Then about the Death of JFK,* Catfeet Press, Chicago, 2000; Curry's order, from Curry, Jesse, *JFK Assassination File,* American Poster and Printing Company, Inc., Dallas, p. 30-31; Decker's order, WC, Vol. 23, p. 913; "He saw me coming," WC, Vol. VII, p. 535; "A police officer came around the north end of the fence," Hoffman, p. 9; Jean Hill comments, Sloan, Bill with Jean Hill, *JFK: The Last Dissenting Witness,* Pelican Publishing, Gretna, Louisiana, 1992, p. 24; Beverly Oliver comments, Oliver, Beverly with Coke Buchanan, *Nightmare In Dallas,* Starburst, Publishers, Lancaster, Pennsylvania, 1994, p. 123; Senator Ralph Yarborough comments, in Turner, Nigel, *The Men Who Killed Kennedy*; "It was just a little hole in the middle of his neck," WC, Vol. VI, p. 141; "about the size of a baseball," Crenshaw testimony before the Assassination Records Review Board, 3-19-97; Kilduff statement, Press Conference, 11-22-63, Secret Service Report #154-10002-10194, transcript also in LBJ Library (1327B); "I'm just a patsy," made at 7:55 PM CST at Police headquarters, WC, Vol. XX, p. 366; *Life* magazine, 2-21-64; "examine the evidence," US Government document, Executive Order 11130, 11-29-63; "using a Mannlicher-Carcano," WR, p. 19; "entered the base of the back of President Kennedy's neck," WR, p. 3; "rear portion of his head," WR, p. 3; WC Exhibit 385, Vol. XVI, p. 977; WC Exhibit 388, Vol. XVI, p. 984; "found no evidence," WR, p. 21; Oswald's motives, WR, p. 23; JFK Exhibit F-64, HSCA, Vol. I, p. 249; JFK Exhibit F-66, "a scale drawing," HSCA, Vol. I, p. 252; Pate observed a puff of smoke, Pate Statement, HSCA, JFK Document 014913, 1-28-78; 158 frames, WC, Vol. 18, p. 1-80; HSCA's conclusions, Report of the Select Committee On Assassinations, U.S. House of Representatives [HSCA], United States Government Printing Office, 1979, p. 41, 47, 65, 95.

Photographs: (Repeat images not cited): P. 251: Jack White in Fetzer: *Murder in Dealey Plaza*; P. 252: Jack White in Fetzer: *Murder in Dealey Plaza.* P. 283: Tom Wilson. P. 289: AP. P. 290: Reuters.

Author's Note:
Photographs: (Repeat images not cited) P. 292: Marcie Wilson.